Scientific Literature in Sanskrit

PAPERS OF THE 13TH WORLD SANSKRIT CONFERENCE

Edinburg, Scotland (UK) [10-14 July 2006]

General Editors

PETER BISSCHOP

PAUL DUNDAS

ISBN: 978-81-208-3529-0(Set)

Vol. I. **Scientific Literature in Sanskrit :**
Ed. by S.R. SARMA, GYULA WOJTILLA

Vol. II. **Battle, Bards and Brahmins :**
Ed. By JOHN BROCKINGTON *(In the Press)*

Vol. III. **[Veda :**
Ed. by JOEL BRERETON, THEODORE PROFERES]

Vol. IV. **[Āgamas and Tantras :**
Ed. by BRUNO DAGENS, GAVIN FLOOD]

Vol. V. **[Linguistics :**
Ed. by JARED S. KLEIN, ELIZABETH TUCKER]

Vol. VI. **[Poetry, Drama and Aesthetics :**
Ed. by MANDAKRANTA BOSE, DAVID GITOMES, DAVID SMITH]

Vol. VII. **[Philosophy :**
Ed. by JONARDON GANERI]

PAPERS OF THE 13TH WORLD SANSKRIT CONFERENCE
Volume I

Scientific Literature in Sanskrit

Edited by
S. R. SARMA
GYULA WOJTILLA

MOTILAL BANARSIDASS PUBLISHERS
PRIVATE LIMITED • DELHI

First Edition : Delhi, 2011

ISBN: 978-81-208-3530-6 (Vol. I)
ISBN: 978-81-208-3529-0 (Set)

MOTILAL BANARSIDASS
41 U.A. Bungalow Road, Jawahar Nagar, Delhi 110 007
8 Mahalaxmi Chamber, 22 Bhulabhai Desai Road, Mumbai 400 026
203 Royapettah High Road, Mylapore, Chennai 600 004
236, 9th Main III Block, Jayanagar, Bangalore 560 011
Sanas Plaza, 1302 Baji Rao Road, Pune 411 002
8 Camac Street, Kolkata 700 017
Ashok Rajpath, Patna 800 004
Chowk, Varanasi 221 001

Printed in India

**By Jainendra Prakash Jain at Shri Jainendra Press,
A-45 Naraina, Phase-I, New Delhi 110 028
and Published by Narendra Prakash Jain for
Motilal Banarsidass Publishers Private Limited,
Bungalow Road, Delhi 110 007**

General Preface

The Thirteenth World Sanskrit Conference was held in Edinburgh, Scotland on the 10th-14th July 2006. To the delight of the organisers it was attended by a record number of participants from all parts of the world. At a time when the study of Sanskrit and related Indological subjects is becoming increasingly embattled in certain countries, such regular gatherings assume a particular importance in confirming scholarly solidarity as well as disseminating the most recent fruits of research.

The conference was divided into fourteen subject sections, each chaired by two scholars: 1. Veda; 2. Epics; 3. Purāṇas; 4. Āgamas and Tantra; 5. Vyākaraṇa; 6. Linguistics; 7. Poetry, Drama and Aesthetics; 8. Scientific Literature; 9. Buddhist Literature; 10. Jaina Studies; 11. Philosophy; 12. History, Epigraphy and the Arts; 13. Law and Society; and 14. Culture and Society.

As now customary, arrangements for the publication of the proceedings became the responsibility of the conference organisers. To this end, the various section chairs were requested to edit the proceedings volume of their subject after inviting the submission of papers from participants and then submit a manuscript to the general editors for inspection and final formatting. It should be noted that the chairs of two thematic subpanels of the Philosophy section (Śāstrārambha-Philosophical Introduction and New Directions in the Study of Yoga), of History, Epigraphy and the Arts, and of Law and Society, wished to make their own arrangements for publication elsewhere. In addition, it was decided that papers in the Culture and Tradition section which had been invited for publication should be placed in appropriate volumes of the proceedings.

It is hoped that these Proceedings of the Thirteenth World Sanskrit conference will reveal the impressive breadth and depth of Indological research at the present time and gain the appreciation of the interested scholarly world.

Peter Bisschop
Paul Dundas
General Editors, Proceedings of the Thirteenth World Sanskrit Conference.

Contents

Preface

David Pingree and G. Jan Meulenbeld have made us aware of the enormous volume and the astonishing diversity of Sanskrit literature on Jyotiḥśāstra and Āyurveda respectively through their monumental works, *Census of the Exact Sciences* and *History of Indian Medical Literature.* Literature on other scientific subjects, though not so stupendous, is still very large. This rich diversity of Sanskrit scientific literature is reflected in the papers presented in Section 8 on Scientific Literature of the 13th World Sanskrit Conference, held at Edinburgh on 10-14 July 2006, and collected in this volume. These ten papers cover a wide spectrum of areas like astronomy, mathematics, divination, alchemy, gemmology, musicology and perfumery.

The proceedings open with K. Ramasubramanian's paper on the 'Nature of Proof in Indian Science,' where he seeks to correct the wide-spread misconceptions in Western historiography regarding Indian astronomy and mathematics: that they are bereft of proofs, that no distinction is made between the rational and irrational quantities, and so on. He argues cogently that proof is not an alien concept to Indian tradition as is evident from the diverse discussions concerning proof in Indian philosophical texts. In the case of astronomy and mathematics, proof or rationale (*upapatti, vāsanā*) is provided in the commentaries and not in the primary texts. Citing copiously from the commentaries by Nṛsiṃha, Nīlakaṇṭha and others, he elaborates their views on proof, on the incommensurability of the circumference and diameter of a circle and similar matters. The major part of the paper is devoted to examples of different types of proof given in the commentaries: *upapatti* in the form of logical reasoning, *upapatti* by geometrical definition, and *upapatti* by mathematical analysis. Here the relevant texts are cited in accurate translation, followed by a well-structured explanation using modern notation.

In the next paper, S. Balachandra Rao argues that, though Nicolaus Copernicus ushered in the scientific revolution by his heliocentric theory, his method of computing the mean planetary positions is not as accurate as those of his Indian contemporaries Nīlakaṇṭha Somyājin and Gaṇeśa Daivajña. This he demonstrates by computing the planetary positions on 19 March 1520, the epoch of Gaṇeśa's *Grahalāghava*, according to the respective procedures adopted by these three astronomers: the planetary positions obtained by the methods of Gaṇeśa and Nīlakaṇṭha are appreciably closer to those derived by the modern procedures, than the values obtained by the method of Copernicus.

Kim Plofker, in her contribution 'Why did Sanskrit Mathematics ignore Asakṛt Methods?,' explores the boundaries between mathematical astronomy and mathematics proper to see how the mathematical techniques developed for astronomical computations were received in mathematical texts. The iterative approximation, an algorithm performed repeatedly until its successive results converge as closely as desired to the exact solution, was widely used in solving many astronomical problems, but it was never mentioned in strictly mathematical treatises. The paper discusses this striking omission and offers possible reasons for it.

Like scientific texts, scientific instruments also constitute important documents for reconstructing the scientific progress of an era. A Sanskrit astrolabe (*yantrarāja*) of 1644, which is preserved fortuitously in Edinburgh, the venue of the 13th World Sanskrit Conference, is the subject of the 'Yantrarāja at Edinburgh' by Sreeramula Rajeswara Sarma. After an overview of the Sanskrit literature on this instrument, he gives a detailed technical description of the Edinburgh astrolabe and discusses its importance for the history of the astrolabe in India.

The *Muhūrtalakṣaṇa*, an astrological text from Java is brought to light by Amrit Gomperts in his paper. This slender text, consisting of twenty *ślokas* in Javano-Sanskrit and their paraphrase in Old Javanese, fills an important gap in our understanding of Jyotiṣa in Java, because the Javanese calendar-makers made use of this text for determining the *muhūrta* hours mentioned in the inscriptions of the period AD 1000-1500. This text prescribes that the times of the *muhūrta* hours be determined with a solar gnomon, which is possible only during the sunlight hours. Gomperts is of the view that the *muhūrta*-s were actually computed, both in the day-time and at night, in combination with the cycle of *lagna* or the 'ascendant in the horoscope'. An analysis of twenty-one inscriptions also shows that *lagna* is a better estimator of diurnal time than *muhūrta*. An edition of the text of the *Muhūrtalakṣaṇa*, together with an English translation of the Old Javanese paraphrase, is provided in an Appendix.

Martin Gansten, in his contribution 'Nāḍī Divination and Indian Astrology,' introduces an interesting branch of astrology which is practiced in Tamilnadu. After a cogent elucidation of the fundamental principles of astrology, which are rarely stated but generally implied, Gansten explains the nature of the *nāḍī* divination and how it differs from classical astrology in its assumptions and practice. The Sanskrit texts related to the *nāḍī* divination, such as the *Gurunāḍī*, *Aṃśanāḍī*, and *Dhruvanāḍī*, contain individual horoscopes, organised according to the *nāḍī* (1/150th part of a zodiac sign) in which a person is born. Since the number of *nāḍī*-s are finite, so are the number of possible patterns of human life. Here the *nāḍī* divination makes a departure from the mainstream Hindu orthodoxy in as much as it views human life not as 'an infinitely variable flux, but rather in the nature of a flow chart in which movement, though voluntary, takes place from one pre-defined square to the next.'

The alchemist believed that all base metals could be transmuted to the pure state of gold and that likewise the perishable human body could be transmuted to an imperishable state. In his attempt to find the proper means for this transmutation, the alchemist acquired through the centuries great skills in handling a variety of chemical substances. In 'Beliefs, Aspirations and Accomplishments of the Medieval Indian Alchemist as depicted in the Rasopaniṣad,' Vijaya Deshpande shows how a vast database of substances and their interaction came into existence in the texts on Rasaśāstra, in particular the voluminous eleventh century text *Rasopaniṣad*, and explains some of the valuable chemical-metallurgical insights recorded in this text.

Kauṭilya's *Arthaśāstra* (Book II.11.28-41) contains the earliest discussion of gems, their properties and the places of occurrence. Therefore, this portion is rightly considered to be the earliest text on gemmology. However, the text is problematic at places and the contents intermingle scientific theory with commercial matters, leading to terminological inconsistencies. In his paper 'Ratnaśāstra in Kauṭilya's Arthaśāstra,' Gyula Wojtilla attempts to restore the text with the help of commentaries and to reinterpret it in the light of philology and modern gemmology.

In his contribution 'The Body of the Musician: Embryology and Anatomy in the Indian Musicological Literature,' Makoto Kitada touches upon several disciplines like musicology, embryology, anatomy, and Haṭhayoga. The musicological text *Saṅgītaratnākara* composed by Śārṅgadhara in the thirteenth century deals with Āyurvedic topics like embryology and anatomy, and Haṭhayogic matters like *cakra*-s and *nāḍī*-s. Kitada seeks to answer the questions as to why these topics are dealt with in a musicological text and what is the source of the Ayurvedic theory of embryology and anatomy presented in this text.

The last paper of these proceedings is 'The Art and Science of Perfumery in the Nāgarasarvasva by James McHugh. The chapter on perfumery in the erotic manual *Nāgarasarvasva* is unique in the sense that it places perfumery in the clear context of accessories to erotic pleasure. After an overview of aromatic preparations, the paper focuses on a type of incense, named evocatively *Ratināthakāntā*, and discusses some of the ingredients used for this incense, their origins, cultural and economic significance, and olfactory properties. McHugh did not just study the *śāstra* of perfumery, he also tried his hand at *prayoga*, and prepared the incense according to specifications. After presenting the paper, he made the audience smell the *Ratināthakāntā* incense, by burning it outside the venue of the conference, thus bringing the proceedings of the Section on Scientific Literature to a 'fragrant' conclusion.

It remains for us now to thank all those who have contributed to the success of the Section and to the production of this volume: first and foremost, the scholars who presented these highly interesting papers deserve our deep appreciation. Our sincere thanks to the Organizing Committee of the 13th World Sanskrit Conference for entrusting us with the responsibility of conducting the Section on Scientific Literature. It is a pleasure to record the help and advice extended by the Secretary General of the Conference, Professor John Brockington, in organizing the Section. We should like to thank Dr Paul Dundas and Dr Peter Bisschop, the General Editors of the Proceedings, for their support and advice in the preparation of the volume.

We are grateful to Professor Vempaty Kutumba Sastry, the then Vice-Chancellor of the Rashtriya Samskrit Samsthan, New Delhi, (and now President of the International Association of Sanskrit Studies) for readily acceding to our request and providing financial assistance to some of the participants so that they could attend the conference. The major burden of preparing the volume lay on the shoulders of Professor K. Ramasubramanian who prepared the press copy in LaTeX. We are greatly indebted to him.

In this decade the historiography of Indian Science suffered the loss of four eminent scholars. We recall here the memory of

Professors K. V. Sarma, David Pingree, Kripa Shankar Shukla and Priya Vrat Sharma for their rich and abiding contributions to the study of Jyotiḥśāstra and Āyurveda.

S. R. Sarma

Gyula Wojtilla

The Notion of Proof in Indian Science

K. RAMASUBRAMANIAN

1 Introduction

There seems to be a striking unanimity amongst the historians of mathematics in presenting the view that Hindu astronomy and mathematics are bereft of proofs, however laudable their contributions to the fields may be. Books on the history of mathematics—written as late as the twentieth century—are replete with statements to the effect that Hindus could not make a distinction between the rational and irrational quantities, curvilinear and rectilinear magnitudes, the discreteness of number and continuity of geometrical magnitude, and so on. Historians also assert that, while the geometrical and rational features of mathematics had a great appeal to the Hellenic mind, such a thing seemed to be superfluous to the Hindu mind. For instance, commenting upon mathematics as practised by the Hindus, the renowned historian C. B. Boyer observes:

> With the Hindus the view was different. They saw no essential unlikeliness between rectilinear and curvilinear figures, for each could be measured in terms of numbers; arithmetic and mensuration, rather than

> geometry and considerations of congruence, were fundamental. The strong Greek distinction between the discreteness of number and the continuity of geometrical magnitude was not recognized, for it was superfluous to men who were not bothered by the paradoxes of Zeno or his dialectic. Questions concerning incommensurability, the infinitesimal, infinity, the process of exhaustion, and the other inquiries leading toward the conceptions and methods of calculus were neglected.[1]

Boyer is also of the view that the whole trend of Arabic mathematics was, like that of Hindus, directed away from speculations on the incommensurable, continuity, the indivisible and the infinity.[2] This view has been presented not once, but on several occasions throughout the book. As an illustration, here we present just one quotation.

> The Hindus and the Arabs on the other hand, had not clearly distinguished between rational and irrational numbers. ...[3]

Another mathematician of more recent times, Morris Kline, who is credited with more than a dozen books on various aspects of mathematics such as history, philosophy, and pedagogy, while commenting on Hindu geometry and trigonometry, observes:

> Sometimes the Hindus were aware that a formula was only approximately correct and sometimes they were not. Their values of π were generally inaccurate; $\sqrt{10}$ was commonly used, though the better value of 3.1416 appears at times. For the area of any quadrilateral they gave the formula $\sqrt{(s-a)(s-b)(s-c)(s-d)}$,

[1] Boyer 1949: 62.
[2] Ibid, p. 63.
[3] Ibid, p. 97.

> where s is half the perimeter and a, b, c, and d are the sides, a formula which is correct only for quadrilaterals inscribed in circles. They offered no geometric proofs; on the whole they cared little for geometry. In trigonometry the Hindus made a few minor advances ... There is much good procedure and technical facility, but no evidence that they considered proof at all.[4]

A variety of sources presenting similar views on Indian mathematics have been cited by M. D. Srinivas in his recently published scholarly article.[5] In spite of the fact that these scholars have based their assessment on a network of references cited in their articles, ironically, it turns out that the picture presented by them is far removed from the truth.

What is more striking, such views are projected by some of the well established mathematicians and historians of the recent past,[6] notwithstanding the fact that an entire text known as *Yuktibhāṣā*—completely devoted to the rationale behind the procedures given in Indian astronomical and mathematical works—has been brought to light by C. M. Whish as early as 1834.[7] The burden of such projections has resulted in false ideas getting permeated that (a) Hindus neglected questions concerning incommensurability, infinitesimal, infinity and the like and that, (b) they were least concerned about proving a result and so on. The present article aims at correcting this situation in its own humble way.

---

[4]Kline 1972: 188–190.

[5]Srinivas 2005.

[6]Morris Kline (1908–1992) was Professor of Mathematics at New York University. Carl Benjamin Boyer (1906–1976) was made a 1954 John Simon Guggenheim Memorial Fellow for his contributions in History of Science.

[7]Whish 1834.

2 Gaṇita—not merely a Science of Calculation

The term *gaṇita* in Sanskrit stems from the verbal root '*gaṇa*' which means 'to count/calculate/compute'. Thus *gaṇita* refers to mathematics in general which includes algebra, arithmetic, computation of planetary positions, representation of planetary motion in the celestial sphere including the demonstration/explanation of the rationale behind the procedures prescribed and so on. This being the case, the famous historian Boyer, commenting upon the choice of the word *gaṇita*, while making general observations about Hindu mathematicians and their contributions, observes:

> The Hindus apparently were attracted by the arithmetical and computational aspects of mathematics, rather than the geometrical features of the subject, which had appealed so strongly to the Hellenic mind. Their name for mathematics, *gaṇita*, meaning literally the "science of calculation", well characterizes this preference.[8]

In contrast to the above interpretation, which presents the meaning of the term *gaṇita* in a very limited sense, the interpretations provided by astronomers and mathematicians in the Indian tradition are quite different. For instance, Nṛsiṃha Daivajña in AD 1621 gives an all-encompassing definition as follows:

> *Gaṇita* is [the science of] computation. The discipline of study (*śāstra*) which explains that (computation) is [also] called so. That [part] which deals with addition, [subtraction] etc., which is well known to the high and low (*uccāvaca* ≡ all members of the society), with

[8]Boyer 1949: 61.

> explicit values [of the numerals mentioned] is arithmetic (*vyakta*). That [part] which deals with the computation by representing the expected and the given (*yāvattāvat*) [measures] by the letters of the alphabet (*varṇa*) is algebra (*avyakta*). [The computations that are done] with the planetary motions [are called] planetary computations (*grahagaṇita*). The computations that are made by [making] observations (*vedhādinā*) on the celestial sphere, [supported] by demonstrations (*savāsana*) is [known as] celestial computations (*golagaṇitaṃ*), since they are based on the [co-ordinates obtained from the] celestial sphere. Thus the chapter on *gaṇita* consists of four parts dealing with [different types of] computations.[9]

It may be noted that the above defintion, among other things, also includes the notion of *upapatti/vāsanā*[10] which will be discussed in detail later in the article. A very similar explanation—in fact a much more detailed and comprehensive one, in about eight verses—has been provided by the ninth century Jaina mathematician Mahāvīrācārya:

> ... In relation to the movements of the sun and other heavenly bodies, in connection with eclipses and conjunction of the planets, in the [calculation] of direction, place and time (*tripraśna*) and in the lunar orbit, everywhere it (*gaṇita*) is utilized. The number, the diameter, and the perimeter of islands, oceans, and

[9]Nṛsiṃha Daivajña, *Vāsanāvārttika*, p. 9: *gaṇyate saṅkhyāyate tad gaṇitam; tatpratipādakatvena tatsaṃjñaṃ śāstram ucyate| tatra vyaktena, spaṣṭena, uccāvaca-prasiddhamārgeṇa saṅkalanādinā yad ucyate tad vyaktam| yavattavadadi-varṇakalpanapekṣabudhya gaṇitam avyaktam| grahakarmaṇā grahagaṇitam| golena vedhādinā savāsanaṃ gaṇyate iti golāśritatvāt golagaṇitam| gaṇitacatuṣṭayātmako gaṇitaskandhaḥ|*

[10]These words do not have an exact equivalent in English. However, they can be roughly translated as logical argument/proof/rationale/demonstration.

> mountains, ... are all known [only by] *gaṇita*. ... Why keep lamenting more? In all the three worlds made up of the stationary and moving objects, anything that you want [to know] about any entity, cannot be [known] without *gaṇita*.[11]

While the mathematicians and astronomers of the Indian tradition present this kind of definition/description for the term *gaṇita*, it is an irony that the western historians have to give a different shade to the word and present it merely as 'science of calculation' and thereby pass infelicitous remarks.

Before getting into detailed discussion of what constitutes a proof, whether the Indian astronomers/mathematicians had any notions of proof, etc., in the following section, by citing a passage from one of the works of the renowned Kerala astronomer Nīlakaṇṭha Somayājī (AD 1444–1545), we would like to demonstrate that Hindus did make a distinction between the rational and irrational quantities, the discreteness of number and continuity of geometrical magnitude, as against the allegation made by Boyer, Kline and others (see section 1).

[11] Mahāvīra, *Gaṇitasārasaṅgraha* 1.9–16.
laukike vaidike vāpi tathā sāmayike 'pi yaḥ |
vyāparas tatra sarvatra saṃkhyānam upayujyate ||
kāmatantre 'rthaśāstre ca gāndharve nāṭake 'pi vā |
sūpaśāstre tathā vaidye vāstuvidyādivastuṣu ||
chando'laṅkārakāvyeṣu tarkavyākaraṇādiṣu |
kalāguṇeṣu sarveṣu prastutaṃ gaṇitaṃ param ||
sūryadigrahacāreṣu grahaṇe grahasaṃyutau |
tripraśne candravṛttau ca sarvatrāṅgīkṛtaṃ hi tat ||
dvipasāgaraśailānaṃ saṃkhyāvyāsaparikṣipaḥ |
bhavanavyantarajyoti-lokakalpādivāsinām ||
narakāṇaṃ ca sarveṣaṃ śroṇibandhendrakotkaraḥ |
prakīrṇakapramāṇādyā budhyante gaṇitena te ||
prāṇinaṃ tatra saṃsthānaṃ āyur aṣṭaguṇādayaḥ |
yātrādyaḥ saṃhitadyaś ca sarve te gaṇitaśrayaḥ ||
bahubhiḥ vipralāpaiḥ kiṃ trailokye sacarācare |
yatkiñcid vastu tat sarvaṃ gaṇitena vinā na hi ||

3 Incommensurability in Hindu Mathematics

The incommensurability of the circumference and diameter of a circle has been a puzzling problem that kept many brilliant minds engaged for centuries. In fact, astronomers and mathematicians of almost all the major ancient civilizations across the globe have been pondering over this problem. Āryabhaṭa (b. AD 476) in his *Āryabhaṭīya*, one of the earliest works completely devoted to study of mathematics and astronomy that is extant today, presents the value of the ratio of the circumference to the diameter of a circle as follows:

> Four added to hundred and [the result] multiplied by eight, and this added to 62,000 is 'close to' (*āsanna*) the circumference of a circle whose diameter is twice 10,000 (*ayuta-dvaya*).[12]

The ratio mentioned above is none other than the value of π. Expressing it in modern mathematical notation, we have

$$\pi = \frac{62832}{20000} = 3.1416. \quad (1)$$

It turns out that the above value presented by Āryabhaṭa is correct to four decimal places. While commenting upon the word *āsanna* appearing in the above verse, which means *close to/approximate*, Nīlakaṇṭha Somayājī in his *Āryabhaṭīya-bhāṣya* observes:

> The relation between the circumference and the diameter was expressed. ... Approximate. This value (62832) was stated to be nearly the circumference of a circle having a diameter of 20,000. 'Why then has

[12] Āryabhaṭa, *Āryabhaṭīya*, *Gaṇitapāda* 10: *caturadhikaṃ śatam aṣṭaguṇaṃ dvāśaṣṭis tathā sahasrāṇām | ayutadvayaviṣkambhasyāsanno vṛttapariṇāhaḥ* ||

an approximate value been mentioned here leaving behind the actual value?' It is explained [as follows]. Because it (exact value) cannot be expressed. Why?[13]

Explaining as to why the exact value cannot be stated, Nīlakaṇṭha continues:

> If a certain unit of measurement (*māna*) with which the diameter (*vyāsa*) is specified [is just an integer and] has no [fractional] part (*niravayava*), the same measure when employed to specify the circumference (*paridhi*) [of a circle] will certainly have a [fractional] part (*sāvayava*) [and cannot be just an integer]. Again if certain [other] measure when employed to specify the circumference has no [fractional] part, the same measure when employed to specify the diameter will certainly have a [fractional] part [and cannot be an integer]. Thus when both [the diameter and the circumference] are measured by the same unit, they cannot both be specified [as integers] without [fractional] parts. Even if you go a long way (i.e., keep on reducing the measure of the unit employed), the fractional part [in specifying one of them] will only become very small. A situation in which there will be no [fractional] part (i.e, both the diameter and circumference can be specified in terms of integers) is impossible, and this is what is the import [of the expression *āsanna*].[14]

---

[13]Nīlakaṇṭha, *Āryabhaṭīyabhāṣya*, part I, pp. 41: *...paridhivyāsayoḥ saṅkhyāsambandhaḥ pradarśitaḥ| ...āsannaḥ, āsannatayaivāyutadvaya-saṅkhyaviṣkambhasyeyaṃ paridhisaṅkhyokta| kutaḥ punaḥ vastavīṃ saṅkhyām utsṛjya āsannaiva ihoktā? ucyate| tasyā vaktum aśakyatvāt| kutaḥ?*

[14]Ibid, pp. 41-42: *yena mānena mīyamano vyāsaḥ niravayavaḥ syat, tenaiva mīyamānaḥ paridhiḥ punaḥ sāvayava eva syāt| yena ca mīyamānaḥ paridhiḥ niravayavaḥ tenaiva mīyamāno vyāso 'pi sāvayava eva; iti ekenaiva*

Obviously what Nīlakaṇṭha is trying to explain here is nothing but the incommensurability of the circumference and the diameter of a circle. Particularly, the last line of the above quote, where Nīlakaṇṭha clearly mentions that, however small you may choose your unit of measurement to be, the two quantities will never become commensurate, is indeed remarkable.

By this, of course, we do not try to impress upon the readers that Nīlakaṇṭha has proved the incommensurability of circumference and diameter. Making a statement that two quantities are incommensurable is quite different from proving them to be so. But the very fact that such an explicit statement exists not only provides the necessary base but also forms a concrete evidence to refute the false projections that Hindus could not make a distinction between the commensurable and the incommensurable.

4 What constitutes Proof ?

Unlike a precise mathematical problem, the above question does not have a definite or sharply defined answer. However, in general, proof could be defined as *an evidence or argument adduced in order to convince oneself/others regarding the truth of an assertion.* Depending upon whether the assertion is a mathematical result, or a hypothesis based on statistical data, or a statement related to physical phenomenon, the nature and structure of proof widely varies. It also varies with a variety of other factors such as the discipline in which it is being adduced and the audience to which it is adduced and the 'rigour' with which it is expected to be adduced and so on.

The standards of rigour are generally set by those who are considered to be the 'leaders' of a particular discipline, at a par-

---

mīyamānayoḥ ubhayoḥ kvāpi na niravayavatvaṃ syāt| mahāntam adhvānaṃ gatvapi alpavayavatvaṃ eva labhyaṃ| niravayavatvaṃ tu kvapi na labhyaṃ iti bhāvaḥ|

ticular point of time, not to mention the 'social acceptance' required by a proof. For instance, what may be considered a proof by a philosopher may not be acceptable to a physicist and what is acceptable to a physicist may not be acceptable to a mathematician and so on. Even amongst the philosophers some hold the view that proof is a mind-independent abstract object, whereas some others consider it to be purely a mental construction. There are a few others, belonging to the Wittgensteinian tradition, who believe it to be a linguistic convention.

We mention this not to create the impression that proof is completely 'subjective', but only to drive home the point that it is not truly 'objective' either. In other words, there is no unique yardstick to measure (i) what constitutes a proof or (ii) what defines the validity of a proof. In the same vein, the question as to how to arrive at a proof also defies a simple answer. All these things depend upon the discipline, the purpose, the audience, the referee, and the like, to mention a few. Hence, it would be indecorous to conclude that there has been no notion of proof whatsoever in civilizations other than the Greek.[15]

According to the Platonist view, 'proof is a mind-independent abstract object, eternal, unchanging, not located in space-time, and evidently causally inert.'[16] It is quite evident from the above description that proof is 'not' something that is created by a mathematician but is some abstract 'ideal' thing that is discovered by him, perhaps by deductive reasoning from some 'obvious-truths', the so-called axioms. It would be quite instructive to cite Reuben Hersh in this context. Discussing the views of Platonists he observes:

---

[15]Some historians not only deny the existence of proofs in other civilizations, but the existence of science and philosophy as well. See, for instance, Hutten 1952: 15: 'Certainly, without the Greeks we would have neither philosophy nor science today. It was the "Greek miracle" – the upsurge of a feeling for truth and reality – that has made the development ...'

[16]Tieszen 1992: 58.

> Why do mathematicians believe something so unscientific, so far-fetched as an independent immaterial timeless world of mathematical truth?
>
> The mystery of mathematics is its objectivity, its seeming certainity or near-certainity, and its near-independence of persons, cultures and historical epochs ... Platonism says mathematical objects are real and independent of our knowledge. Space-filling curves, uncountably infinite sets, infinite dimensional manifolds—all the members of the mathematical zoo—are definite objects, with definite properties, known or unknown. These objects exist outside physical space and time. They were never created. They never change. By logic's law of the excluded middle, a meaningful question about any of them has an answer, whether we know it or not. According to platonism, a mathematician is an empirical scientist, like a botanist. He can't invent, because everything is already there. He can only discover.[17]

In contrast to this it may be mentioned here that *upapatti* (not necessarily employed in astronomy and mathematics alone, but used in the other branches of philosophy as well) is not considered as a mind-independent, infallible abstract object. It is as much a human construct (*puruṣa-buddhi-prabhava*) as any other thing. Hence *upapatti*-s are liable to be refined, improved and refuted as well, unlike the eternal unchanging nature of proof conceived by Plato. We will see more about *upapatti* and its nature with a few illustrations in section 6.

---

[17] Hersh 1997: 11.

5 Notion of Proof in the Western Tradition

Starting from Plato (4th cent. BC) to Gödel (20th cent. AD), the philosophers and mathematicians in the west, in the process of trying to understand the foundations of mathematics, have developed and maintained notions of proof that differ from one another in the emphasis as well as the nature of the mathematical objects involved in it. This in fact generated a great philosophical debate[18] among the celebrated scholars of those periods. Consequentially, there came into existence some of the major schools of thought such as Platonist, Formalist, Empiricist, Intuitionist and Wittgensteinian.

Without deliberating much on these schools and to drive in the point that is relevant to our present discussion, here we would just like to mention that most of the mathematical discourse in the Greek as well as modern Western tradition is carried out with reference to some axiomatic deductive system. An axiomatic deductive system essentially rests on two pillars: (i) a certain set of statements[19] that are accepted to be true $S_1, S_2, \ldots S_n$ without any further justification and (ii) agreement on certain rules of reasoning, i.e., how one statement 'logically' follows from the other. If these two are not acceptable, then the deductive system would lead to what is known as 'infinite regress'. It has been noted by several scholars that proof in 'western' mathematics is primarily based on deductive reasoning. For instance, Morris Kline observes:

> Whether or not historical research has isolated the relevant factors to explain the Greek preference for deductive reasoning, we do know that they were the first to insist on deductive reasoning as the sole method

[18] Ibid; see also Gerstein 1996.

[19] Not necessarily self-evident.

> of *proof* in mathematics. This requirement has been characteristic of mathematics ever since and has distinguished mathematics from all other fields of knowledge.[20]

The same idea has been aptly put forth, with a certain charm added to it, by Yuri I. Manin, a Russian mathematician, well known for work in algebraic geometry, Diophantine geometry, algorithms and mathematical logic:

> The evolution of commonly accepted criteria for an argument's being a proof is an almost untouched theme in the history of science. In any case, the ideal for what constitutes a mathematical demonstration of a 'non-obvious truth' has remained unchanged since the time of Euclid: we must arrive at such a truth from 'obvious' hypotheses or assertions which have already been proved, by means of a series of explicitly described, 'obviously valid' elementary deductions.[21]

What Manin refers to as 'ideal' and 'unchanged' with reference to mathematical demonstrations (proofs) has been succinctly stated by Davis and Hersh in their recently published scholarly work:

> Abstraction, formalization, axiomatization, deduction – here are the ingredients of proof. And the proofs in modern mathematics, though they may deal with different raw material or lie at deeper level, have essentially the same feel to the student or the researcher as the one just quoted.[22]

Thus as far as the western tradition is concerned, the heart of the mathematical proof lies in axiomatization and deduction,

[20] Kline 1972: 46.
[21] Manin 1977: 48.
[22] Davis & Hersh 1981: 150.

though the laws of deduction are likely to be awesome in their complexity in certain cases. Concluding our philosophical discussion on the nature and notion of proof in the west, we now proceed to carry our discussion on the nature of *upapatti* as presented in the Indian tradition.

6 Concept of upapatti or vāsanā in Indian Tradition

The *upapatti*-s of Indian mathematics, unlike the western tradition, are not formulated with reference to a formal axiomatic deductive system. In other words, *upapatti*-s do not form a part of logical deductions based on a set of axioms. This nevertheless does not mean that *upapatti*-s would be illogical. In the Indian philosophical tradition, they do form a set of coherent logical arguments, primarily of the nature of *anumāna* (inference), that are employed to justify a certain statement or a result. In fact, one of the introductory texts in Vedānta defines *upapatti* as:

> The logical arguments (*yukti*) that are presented to substantiate an idea that is being put forth in a particular context (*prakaraṇa*).[23]

Brahmānanda in his scholarly commentary *Laghucandrikā* on *Advaitasiddhi* of Madhusūdana Sarasvatī, a monumental work on Advaita-vedānta, observes:

> And *upapatti* whose nature is of not being sublated.[24]

Two things are clear from the above definitions: (i) *upapatti* must contain arguments that are not/cannot be sublated by other arguments (with the knowledge that is currently available), and (ii) the arguments presented in *upapatti* need not always be

[23]Sadānanda, *Vedānta-sāra*, p. 44: *prakaraṇapratipādyārthasādhane tatra tatra śruyamaṇa yuktiḥ* |

[24]Madhusūdana Sarasvatī, *Advaita-siddhi*, p. 374: *abādhitattvarūpopapattiś ca* ...

universal in nature, i.e., they could be context specific. Etymologically the word *upapatti* can be derived from the root (*dhātu*) '*pad*', which means 'understanding', with the prefix '*upa*' and suffix '*ktin*' added to it.

upa + pad + ktin = upapatti.

In Indian mathematics, *upapatti* would generally be presented as a palatable mixture of logical argument, geometrical description and mathematical expression interspersed with ordinary sentences. Of course, all these will be in natural language, either in the form of prose or poetry or a mixture of two, and not symbolic.

On many occasions one finds the word *vāsanā* being employed by the Indian astronomers synonymously with the word *upapatti*. The word *vāsanā* as employed in the astronomical and mathematical literature has a completely different connotation from its usage in the philosophical literature. While in the former it is used to refer to logical reasoning/mathematical demonstration, in the latter it refers to 'past impressions' carried by the person.

To our knowledge, it is Caturveda Pṛthūdakasvāmin (c. AD 860) who has employed the word *vāsanā* for the first time, as a title of the commentary. His commentary on *Brāhmasphuṭasiddhānta* is called *Vāsanābhāṣya*. Later many astronomers such as Bhāskara (c. 1150), Āmarājā (c. 1200), Nṛsiṃha (c. 1621) and Kamalākarabhaṭṭa (c. 1658) seem to have adopted this practise. For instance, Kamalākara's commentary on *Sūryasiddhānta* is titled *Sauravāsanā*. Besides including the word *vāsanā* as a part of the title of the commentary, the astronomers keep using it as a part of the text in their commentaries. One often finds the statement *iyam atra vāsanā*, when the commentator is about to begin to explain/demonstrate something. Meaningwise this statement *iyam atra vāsanā* ≡ *atropapattiḥ*.

Both the forms being equivalent, there is hardly any consideration for choosing one over the other. So much so, one finds the same author employing both forms freely interchangeably in his commentaries. However, it must be mentioned that it is hard to find the word *upapatti* being used in the title of the commentary like *vāsanā*. It is equally hard to find the word *vāsanā* being employed in philosophical literature in the sense of reasoning/rationale/demonstration, other than the mathematical and astronomical ones. As with any other word in Sanskrit, the origin of the word *vāsanā* can be traced back to the root (*dhātu*), which happens to be '*vas*' in this case. Among the different meanings that are associated with the root *vas*,[25] the one which suits the most in the present context, is 'to dwell/reside'. With this in mind, the derivation of the word *vāsanā* can be shown as follows:

> That which makes the enunciated principle *reside/stay* [deeply] in the minds of the reader.[26]

Since the arguments/explanations/demonstrations that are presented under the name of *vāsanā* in the commentaries help the reader to convince himself regarding the 'truth' of a certain principle discussed in the primary text, and thereby instill it deeply into his own mind, the name *vāsanā* becomes quite meaningful. Perhaps, keeping this in mind, Bhāskarācārya titled his own commentary on his monumental work *Siddhānta-śiromaṇi* as *Vāsanābhāṣya*. The annotations/super-commentary on the *Vāsanābhāṣya* by Nṛsiṃha Daivajña goes by the name *Vāsanāvārtika*.

Having said so much about the origin and usage of the words *upapatti* and *vāsanā*, we now move on to provide a glimpse of the *upapatti*-s by considering a few examples from the Indian

[25]The root *vas* appears in three conjugations (*gaṇas*) 1, 2 and 10. In the first *gaṇa* it means dwelling/staying (*nivāsa*), in the second covering/shielding (*ācchādana*) and in the tenth it refers to a variety of things which include clinging, piercing and snatching.

[26]*vāsayati = dṛḍhaṃ yojayati, adhyetuḥ manāṃsi pratipāditatattve - iti vāsanā.*

astronomical works. These examples, culled primarily from the works of Kerala astronomers who lived around the sixteenthth century, have been chosen to provide a flavor of the different types of *upapatti*-s that are offered by the Indian astronomers in order to convince/demonstrate the correctness of a particular result or assertion. Of the three examples given below, the first is an *upapatti* in the form of logical reasoning, the second one is an *upapatti* by geometrical demonstration, while the third one is an *upapatti* by mathematical analysis.

6.1 Upapatti in the form of Logical Reasoning:

Here we consider the incisive logical argument adduced by Nīlakaṇṭha in order to deduce the heliocentric motion of Mercury and Venus. Nowadays, even as we undergo schooling, we are all taught that all the planets move around the Sun in elliptical orbit with the latter at one of its foci. Since this information gets registered as a well-established *fact* (law) in the unquestioning mind, the curiosity to carry out any investigation in this direction does not arise. Nevertheless, this was not the situation during/prior to the time of Nīlakaṇṭha (c. 1500). Determining the precise nature of the motion of planets, particularly Mercury and Venus, was quite a challenging problem for at least two reasons: (i) All the data for carrying out analysis had to be procured by making prolonged observations with the unaided eyes, unlike the present day observations carried out with the aid of sophisticated tools controlled by computers, powerful telescopes and cameras. (ii) They would not be visible for observation for long stretches of time (see Fig.1), as more often they either fall in the line of sight of the Sun or would be within the domain of the twilight of the Sun.

Notwithstanding this serious constraint, Nīlakaṇṭha deduces purely on the basis of observed latitudinal variations and logical analysis of the data obtained therefrom, and pronounces two sig-

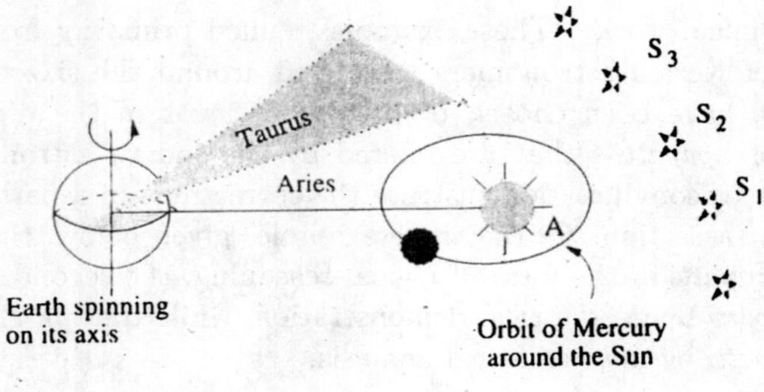

Figure 1: Motion of Mercury around the Sun.

nificant facts: (i) that their orbit does not circumscribe the Earth and (ii) what was referred to as the *śīghrocca* by the earlier scholars is none other than the planet itself.[27] The line of argument based on which Nīlakaṇṭha has made this pronouncement in his monumental work *Āryabhaṭīya-bhāṣya* is furnished below:

> Now he (Āryabhaṭa) explains the nature of the orbits and their locations for Mercury and Venus . . . In this way for Mercury the increase of the latitude occurs only for 22 days and then in the same number of days the latitude decreases to zero. Thus the Mercury moves on one side of the plane of ecliptic (*apamaṇḍala*) only for 44 days. . . .
> The latitudinal motion is said to be due to *śīghrocca*. How is this appropriate? Is it not a fact that the latitudinal motion of a body is dependent only on the motion of that body and not due to the motion of something else? True it is. The latitudinal motion of one body cannot happen due to the motion of some

[27]For more details, see Ramasubramanian et al 1994; see also Sriram et al 2002.

> other body. Therefore [we must conclude that] Mercury goes around in its orbit in 88 days only. ...
> However, this [picture] does not seem to be appropriate. Because, we see it going around [us] only in one year and not 88 days. True. The period in which Mercury moves around the celestial sphere (*bhagola*) is in one year only.
> This is what is being stated: the orbits of Mercury and Venus do not circumscribe the Earth. The Earth is always outside their orbit. Since their orbit is always confined to one side of the [geocentric] celestial sphere, in completing one revolution, they do not go around the twelve *rāśi*-s. For them also the mean Sun is the *śīghrocca*.[28]

The above set of passages, clearly present the logical reasoning based on which Nīlakaṇṭha arrives at this very important conclusion that the orbits of the inner planets (Mercury and Venus) are also eccentric around the Sun. Right from the time of Āryabhaṭa there seems to have been no ambiguity regarding

---

[28]Nīlakaṇṭha, *Āryabhaṭiya-bhāṣya*, part III, pp. 8–9: *atha budhaśukrayoḥ bhramaṇaprakāraṃ taddeśaviśeṣaṃ ca darśayati ... nanv evaṃ budhasya dvāviṃśatyaiva ahorātrair vardhamānasya vikṣepasya mahatvanivṛttiḥ syāt; punarhrāsavaśāt tāvadbhireva dinaiḥ śūnyatāpi syāt| evam apakramamaṇḍalād ekapārśve eva gamanaṃ catuścatvāriṃśad dināny eva| ... śīghravaśāc ca vikṣepaḥ uktaḥ| katham etad yujyate ?*
nanu svabiṃbasya vikṣepaḥ svabhramaṇavaśād eva bhavitum arhati; na punar anya-bhramaṇavaśād iti| satyam| na punar anyasya bhramaṇavaśād anyasya vikṣepa upapadyate| tasmād budhaḥ aṣṭāśītyaiva dinaiḥ svabhramaṇavṛttaṃ pūrayati| ...
etac ca nopapadyate| yataḥ ekenaiva saṃvatsareṇa tatparibhramaṇaṃ upalabhyate, naiva aṣṭāśītyā dinaiḥ| satyam| bhagolaparibhramaṇaṃ tasyāpi ekenaiva abdena|
etad uktaṃ bhavati - tayoḥ bhramaṇavṛttena na bhūḥ kabalīkriyate| tato bahir eva sadā bhūḥ| bhagolaikapārśve eva tadvṛttasya parisamaptatvat tadbhagaṇena na dvadaśaraśiṣu caraḥ syat| tayor api vastutaḥ adityamadhyama eva śīghroccam| ...

the fact that the orbits of the other three exterior planets were eccentric around the Sun, and this is quite evident from the calculational procedure. It was only with reference to Mercury and Venus that there was some discrepancy in the procedure adopted for the computation of their longitudes and this discrepancy has been resolved by Nīlakaṇṭha for the first time in the history of astronomy. Nīlakaṇṭha has mentioned in no uncertain terms that their orbits do not circumscribe the Earth and that their motion around the Earth is only due to the motion of the Sun.

Nīlakaṇṭha has also explained the geometrical picture implied by the calculational procedure in several of his other works such as *Siddhānta-darpaṇa*, apart from the *Āryabhaṭīya-bhāṣya*. The important point to be noted from the passages quoted above, particularly with reference to the theme of this paper, is that Nīlakaṇṭha's pronouncement of this important result is not based on obscure theology or faith, but on incisive logical argument (*upapatti*), which in turn is based on the analysis of the observational data.

6.2 Upapatti by Geometrical Demonstration:

As second example we take up the geometrical proof (*upapatti*) given by Nīlakaṇṭha in his *Āryabhaṭīya-bhāṣya* for the summation of an arithmetic series. Āryabhaṭa in his *Āryabhaṭīya*, while discussing the summation of series, has provided a formula for finding the number terms in an arithmetical series, in terms of its sum S, the first term a and the common difference d. The formula is encoded in the following verse:

> Multiplying [the sum of the series][29] by eight and by

[29]The content in the parenthesis is obtained by what is technically known as *anuvṛtti* from the earlier verse. This has been amply clarified by Nīlakaṇṭha at the very beginning of his commentary to this verse in his *Āryabhaṭīya-bhāṣya* (part I, p. 135). He says: *pūrvasūtre sarvadhanasyāpi prakṛtatvāt sarvadhanam atra viśeṣyatvena vivakṣitam* |

> the common difference, increase that by the square of the difference between twice the first term and the common difference. Then take the square root and subtract twice the first term [from that]. Divide this by the common difference, then add one [to the quotient]. Half of that is the number of terms in the series (*gaccha*).[30]

Consider an arithmetical series of the form

$$a + (a + d) + (a + 2d) + (a + 3d) \ldots\ldots + (a + (n - 1)d). \quad (2)$$

Clearly the above series has n terms, with a as the first term and d as the common difference. If S be the sum of the series, then the content of the above verse can be expressed in the form of an equation using modern mathematical notation as follows:

$$n = \frac{1}{2}\left(\frac{\sqrt{8Sd + (2a - d)^2} - 2a}{d} + 1\right). \quad (3)$$

The right hand side of the above equation, though sounding a bit complex, can be shown to have its basis in a specific geometrical construction. This construction/demonstration has been made by Nīlakaṇṭha in his elaborate commentary to the *Āryabhaṭīya* known as *Āryabhaṭīya-bhāṣya*. Before proceeding with the commentary of Nīlakaṇṭha, where he provides *upapatti* for the above relation, we shall explain the term *śreḍhī* as it frequently appears in the context of summation of a series, and has also been employed by Nīlakaṇṭha himself in his commentary repeatedly.

Defining what a *śreḍhī* is, Śaṅkara Vāriyar in his *Kriyākramakarī*, an elucidative commentary on the *Līlāvatī* of Bhāskarācārya, observes:

[30] Āryabhaṭa, *Āryabhaṭıya*, *Gaṇitapada* 20: *gaccho 'ṣṭottaraguṇitad dviguṇādyuttara-viśeṣavargayutāt | mūlaṃ dviguṇādyūnaṃ svottarabhājitaṃ sarūpārdham ||*

> What is this *śreḍhī* ? Here some say: 'The summation [of series] with arbitrarily chosen first term (*ādi*) and successive terms increasing at regular intervals (*niyatottara*) is *śreḍhī*.'[31]

It is clear from the above definition that the word *śreḍhī* is used to refer to the sum of the series. Here the word *uttara* is employed to represent the common difference. If the first term in the series is a and the common difference is d, then it is easy to see that the successive terms in the series can be graphically represented in the form of a *śreḍhī* (steps) as in the case of a staircase. Such a description is explicitly given by Munīśvara in his commentary on the *Līlāvatī*:

> [Here] entities of different sizes, made out of any material, are arranged in the form of steps, because the summation involved here (*tadgaṇanāyāḥ*) is somewhat similar to the steps [of different sizes] placed together. Now commences a different type of counting called *śreḍhīvyavahāra* (operations in series).[32]

The explanations for the term *śreḍhī* presented above is indicated in the form of a diagram (see Fig. 2). In this figure, the n rectangular blocks correspond to the n terms in the series.

Continuing with his commentary, Nīlakaṇṭha in his *Āryabhaṭīya-bhāṣya* gives a detailed description as to how (3) can be understood by means of geometrical demonstration. In the following we provide a brief summary of the discussion made by Nīlakaṇṭha, with a few citations from the text, and their translations. The necessary diagrams and the mathematical details,

---

[31] Śaṅkara Vāriyar, *Kriyākarmakarī*, p. 238: *atha kimiyaṃ śreḍhī nāma | atra kecid āhuḥ 'ader yataḥkutaścit śreḍhī niyatottaraṃ tu saṅkalitam'* | This statement has to be understood by re-arranging the words in the following prose order – *yataḥkutaścid ādeḥ niyatottaraṃ saṅkalitaṃ tu śreḍhī* |

[32] Cited by Radhakantadeva, *Śabda-kalpadruma*, vol 5, p. 171: *bhinnaṃ bhinnaṃ yatkiñcid dravyādikaṃ śreḍhīkriyate; tadgaṇanāyāḥ śreḍhyā miśraprāyatvāt | tadgaṇanāntaram ārabdhaḥ śreḍhīvyavahāraḥ* |

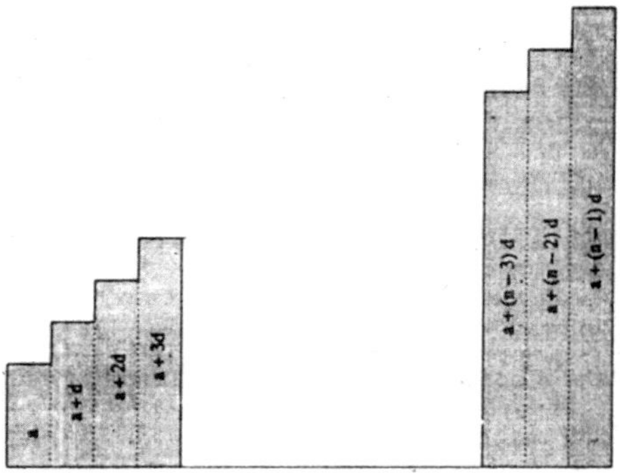

Figure 2: Representation of the terms in an arithmetical series as a *śreḍhī*.

using modern notation, are also furnished to facilitate our understanding of the text. The commentary begins as follows:

> This is what the rationale is. The sum (S) of the series is same as (equivalent to) *śreḍhīkṣetra*. Hence, when it (S) is multiplied by 8, there will be 8 *śreḍhīkṣetra*-s. With them four rectangles have to be constructed. ... These four rectangular figures will result by multiplying the sum of the series by 8. Their lengths (*āyāma*) will be the sum of the last segment and the first one, because the last block and the first one have been attached together. The breadth (*vistāra*) is equal to the number of terms in series (*gaccha*).
> When the sum (S) multiplied by 8 is further multiplied by the common difference (*uttara* d), then all of them (the pieces employed to construct *śreḍhīkṣetra*) are multiplied by the *uttara* as well. Since all the four [rectangles] have been multiplied by *uttara*, [now] we have four rectangular figures whose dimensions have

> been multiplied by *uttara*. The two sides of them (the resulting rectangles) will have the dimension of the product of the *gaccha* and *uttara*, since this has been obtained by placing together *uttara* number of pieces, each having a breadth equal to *gaccha*. The other two sides will have the dimension of the sum of the last term and the first term in the series, since it has been constructed out of figures (blocks/rectangles) having that length.[33]

The procedure for the construction of 4 rectangles from 8 *śreḍhīkṣetra*-s described by Nīlakaṇṭha is as follows. The last piece of one *śreḍhīkṣetra* representing $a+(n-1)d$ should be placed above the first piece representing the first term a of the other *śreḍhīkṣetra*, the last but one over the second, and so on. The resulting rectangular figure (*dīrghacaturaśra*) is shown in Fig. 3. The length and the breadth of the rectangle are also indicated in the figure.

It may be noted that Nīlakaṇṭha started the commentary of this verse with the statement that the sum of the series, $S \equiv$ *śreḍhīkṣetra*. Since two *śreḍhīkṣetra*-s form a rectangle (Fig. 3),

$$\text{Four such rectangles} = 8 \times \textit{śreḍhīkṣetra} \equiv 8S.$$

[33]Nīlakaṇṭha, *Āryabhaṭīya-bhāṣya*, part I, pp. 135–136: *iyam atra vāsanā – sarvadhanaṃ nāma śreḍhīkṣetram eva| atas tasmin aṣṭābhir guṇite 'ṣṭau śreḍhīkṣetrāṇi syuḥ| taiḥ punaḥ catvāri dīrgha-caturaśrāṇi kṣetrāṇi sampādayet| ... tāny etāni catvāri api kṣetrāṇi sarvadhane aṣṭābhir guṇite bhavanti| teṣām āyāmo 'ntyapadamukhayogatulyaḥ, parasparam antyapadābhyāṃ mukhayoḥ saṃśliṣṭattvāt| vistāro gacchatulyaḥ| aṣṭaguṇite sarvadhane punaruttareṇa guṇite tany evottareṇa guṇitāni| tadā teṣāṃ caturṇām api uttareṇa guṇitattvāt tathāvidhāni caturguṇitottarasaṅkhyāni (=catvāri guṇitottara-saṅkhyākāni) kṣetrāṇi bhavanti| ...teṣāṃ ca dve dve parśve gacchottaraghātatulye, gacchatulyavistārair uttaratulyasaṅkhyaiḥ kṣetraiḥ sampāditattvāt| anye tu antyadhanamukhayogatulye, tattulyāyāmaiḥ kṣetraih sampāditattvāt|*

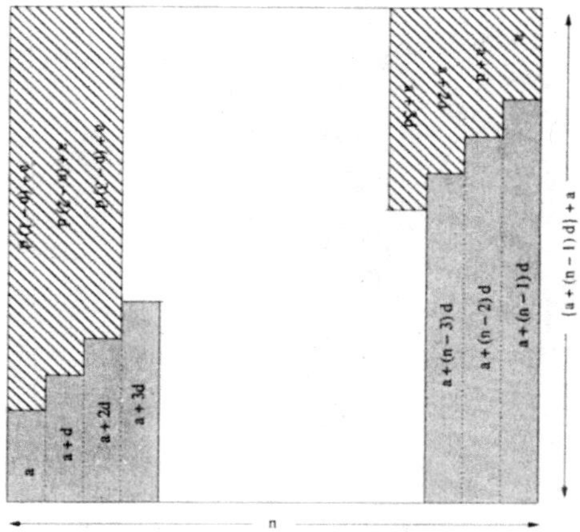

Figure 3: Rectangle formed by combining two *śreḍhīkṣetra*-s.

The expression for *gaccha* given in the *Āryabhaṭīya* (3) includes a term $8Sd$. To get a geometrical representation corresponding to this term, Nīlakaṇṭha suggests that d rectangles with dimensions as indicated in Fig. 3 be placed side by side to form a larger rectangle whose side is nd. The resulting rectangle is shown in Fig. 4.

Proceeding further with the commentary, Nīlakaṇṭha analyses the three possible cases that could arise, and then mentions that in all the cases the longer side should be taken as length (*āyāma*) and the shorter one as the breadth (*vistāra*). The three distinct cases enlisted by Nīlakaṇṭha are:

1. $nd > [2a+(n-1)d]$ nd is the length and $[2a+(n-1)d]$ is the breadth.

2. $nd < [2a+(n-1)d]$ nd is the breadth and $[2a+(n-1)d]$ is the length.

3. $nd = [2a+(n-1)d]$; it would be a square and there is no distinction.

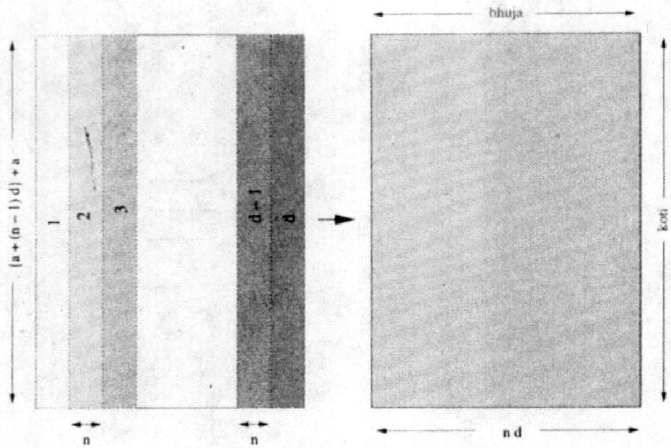

Figure 4: Rectangle formed by placing d rectangles side by side.

He further mentions the convention that the *āyāma* should be taken as *koṭi* and the *vistāra* as *bhujā* in the rectangle that results.[34] Fig. 4 represents the second of the three cases listed above. Then, Nīlakaṇṭha describes the procedure for constructing a square out of the four rectangles obtained above.

> Again with them, let a square be constructed. [The procedure for] that is as follows. Let one among them be placed in the east by laying it along the north-south direction. Then, let the second one be placed in the south by laying it along the east-west direction in such a way that the *bhujā* [of the second rectangle] forms in line with the *koṭi* [of the first rectangle] in the eastern direction. Therefore, a portion of that [second rectangle], whose measure is equal to the difference between the *bhujā* and the *koṭi*, will remain in the south. Then again, let the third one be placed to the

[34]The words *bhujā* and *koṭi*, employed in the Indian mathematical/astronomical literature, denote the sine and cosine of an angle in a right angled triangle multiplied by the hypotenuse.

> west of the second by laying it along the north-south direction in such a way that a portion of the *koṭi* [of the third rectangle] whose measure is equal to the *bhujā* comes in contact with the *bhujā* [of the second rectangle in the west]. Therefore, there a portion of that [third rectangle], whose measure is equal to the difference between the *bhujā* and the *koṭi*, will remain in the north. And let the fourth one be placed to the north of the third by laying it along the east-west direction, in such a way that a portion of the *koṭi* [of the fourth], whose measure is equal to the *bhujā*, comes in contact with the *bhujā* of the third and its (fourth) eastern *bhujā* comes in contact with that portion of the *koṭi* of the first whose measure is equal to the *bhujā*. Therefore, a portion of both [the fourth and the first rectangle], whose measure is equal to the difference between the *bhujā* and the *koṭi*, will remain in the east and the south [respectively]. By doing so, we get a geometrical figure in the form of a square.[35]

The geometrical figure that results by following the above prescription, along with the markers for the direction, is shown in Fig. 5. Here, the four rectangles to be placed one after the

---

[35] Nīlakaṇṭha, *Āryabhaṭīya-bhāṣya*, part I, pp. 136–137: *taiḥ punaḥ samacaturaśraṃ kṣetraṃ saṃpādayet| tac caivam – prathamaṃ teṣv ekaṃ pūrvasyāṃ diśi dakṣiṇottaradiśā nidadhyāt| punas tasya dakṣiṇabhujayā saṃśliṣṭaḥ koṭer bhujātulyaḥ prāgbhāgo yathā syāt tathā dvitīyaṃ dakṣiṇasyāṃ diśi pūrvāparadiśā nidadhyāt| atas tasya bhujākoṭyantaratulyaḥ paścādgato bhāgaḥ pariśiṣṭo bhavati| tṛtīyaṃ punar dvitīyasya paścimabhujāsaṃśliṣṭabhujākoṭitulyakoṭibhāgaṃ paścimāyāṃ diśi dakṣiṇottaradiśa nidadhyat| atas tasya bhujakoṭyantaratulyo bhāga uttarataḥ pariśiṣṭaḥ syāt| caturthaṃ ca tṛtīyottarabhujayā saṃśliṣṭabhujātulyakoṭibhāgaṃ prathamasya bhujā-koṭitulyakoṭibhāgena saṃśliṣṭapurvabhujakam uttarasyaṃ diśi purvaparadiśa nidadhyat| atas tayor api bhujākoṭyantaratulyau bhāgau prāgdakṣiṇataś ca pariśiṣṭau bhavataḥ| evaṃ kṛte tat samacaturaśraṃ kṣetraṃ syāt|*

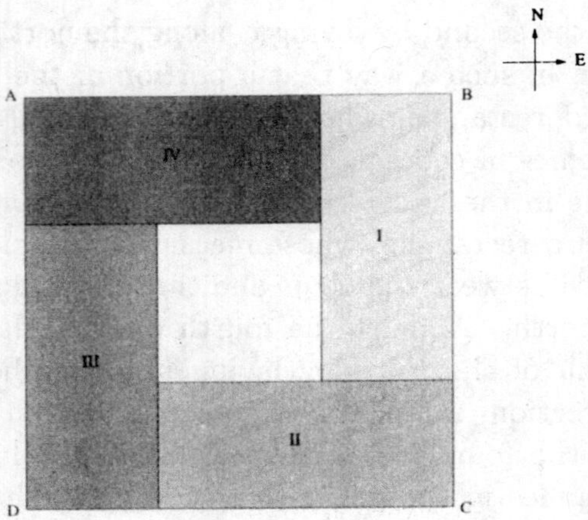

Figure 5: Square formed by placing four rectangles with a void at the centre.

other, in order to get a square are serially numbered. It may be noted from Fig. 5, that there is a void at the centre in the form of a square. With regard to this square Nīlakaṇṭha observes:

> At the centre of it, there will be a portion that remains not-filled whose *bhujā* and *koṭi* have a measure which is equal to the difference between the *bhujā* and the *koṭi*. This is so because, in all the cases, the portion that remains is equal to the difference between the *bhujā* and the *koṭi*. In order to fill that [void] we have to insert the square of the difference between the *bhujā* and the *koṭi* into that. When the square of the difference between twice the first term and the common difference is inserted, that [void] gets plugged in. This is so because the difference between the *bhujā* and the *koṭi* and the difference between twice the first term and the common difference are the same.[36]

[36]Ibid, p. 137: *tasya ca madhye bhujākoṭyantaratulyabhujākoṭikaṃ*

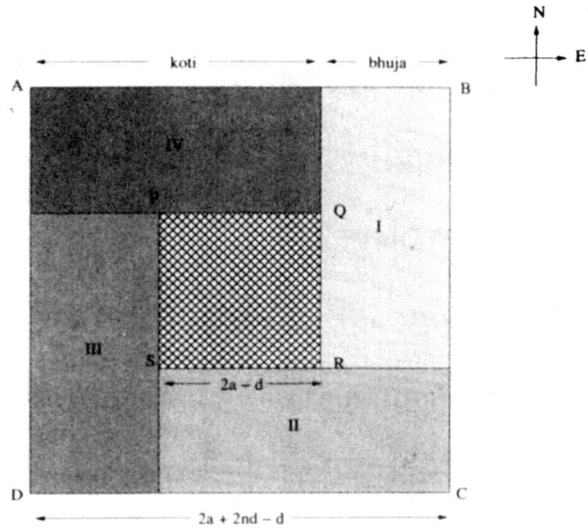

Figure 6: Square formed by placing four rectangles with the void at the centre filled by another square.

The resulting square with the void filled in as described above is depicted in Fig. 6. It is quite clear from the figure that the area of the small square PQRS formed at the centre is numerically equivalent to the square of the difference between *bhujā* and *koṭi*. That is,

$$\text{Area}_{PQRS} \equiv (2a - d)^2. \quad (4)$$

The area of the larger square ABCD is,

$$\begin{aligned} \text{Area}_{ABCD} &= \text{Area}_{PQRS} + \text{Contribution due to four rectangles} \\ &= (2a - d)^2 + (4 \times 2Sd) \\ &= 8Sd + (2a - d)^2. \quad (5) \end{aligned}$$

---

kṣetra(m a)paripūrṇaṃ bhavati, sarvatrāpi bhujākoṭyantaratulyasya bhāgasya pariśiṣṭattvāt| atas tatparipūrtyarthaṃ bhujākoṭyantaravargas tasmin kṣepyo jātaḥ| sa ca dviguṇādyuttaraviśeṣavarge kṣipte kṣipto bhavati| bhujākoṭyantara(sya) dviguṇādyuttaraviśeṣasya ca tulyattvāt|

Considering the fact that the length of the resulting square ABCD is equal to the sum of the *bhujā* and *koṭi*, we have

$$\text{Area}_{ABCD} = (2a + 2nd - d)^2 \tag{6}$$

Equating (5) and (6) we have,

$$(2a + 2nd - d)^2 = 8Sd + (2a - d)^2 \tag{7}$$

With some algebraic manipulation, the above reduces to

$$n = \frac{\sqrt{8Sd + (2a - d)^2} - 2a}{2d} + \frac{1}{2} \tag{8}$$

which is same as (3) given by the *Āryabhaṭīya*.

Thus we find Nīlakaṇṭha providing a brilliant way of proving an algebraic result by means of geometrical demonstration. It is quite plausible that Āryabhaṭa himself had such a geometrical construction in his mind because the tradition of geometrical representation dates back to the period of *Śulva-sūtra*-s (prior to 800 BC). Not being aware of such geometrical demonstrations, a few scholars have been quite dismissive in their remarks.[37] We now move on to highlight the third kind of *upapatti*, namely *upapatti* by mathematical analysis.

6.3 Upapatti by Mathematical Analysis :

It is well known that the Kerala School of astronomers had arrived by the later half of the fourteenth century, if not earlier, at the infinite series expansions for trigonometric functions such

[37] See, for instance, Smith 1913: 'Enough, however, has been stated to show us clearly that the native Hindus, like the Chinese and Japanese, had no interest in or knowledge of demonstrative geometry ... They had interest in mensuration, but they contributed nothing to the theory beyond what the Greeks had already set forth and clearly understood, ...'

as $\sin x$, $\cos x, \tan^{-1} x$, and so on. One of most famous series expansions for π

$$\frac{\pi}{4} = 1 - \frac{1}{3} + \frac{1}{5} - \frac{1}{7} \dots \quad (9)$$

which is generally attributed to Leibniz, is also found in their works. Most of these series expansions, quoted in different commentaries, unanimously point out Mādhava of Saṅgamagrāma (1340-1425) to be the author of them, who predates Leibniz (1664-1716) at least by 250 years. It may be mentioned here that the use of the symbol π in (9) is for the purpose of our own understanding. The Indian astronomers did not represent it that way. Instead, they wrote π as the ratio of *paridhi* and *vyāsa*. Thus, rewriting the above series using Indian terminologies,

$$\frac{\textit{Paridhi}\ \text{(Circumference)}}{\textit{Vyāsa}\ \text{(Diameter)}} = 4 \times (1 - \frac{1}{3} + \frac{1}{5} - \frac{1}{7} \dots). \quad (10)$$

Or,

$$\textit{Paridhi} = 4 \times \textit{Vyāsa} \times \left(1 - \frac{1}{3} + \frac{1}{5} - \frac{1}{7} + \dots + \frac{1}{p} - \dots\right). \quad (11)$$

An ingenious geometrical proof of this equation is to be found in the celebrated text *Yuktibhāṣā* of Jyeṣṭhadeva (c.1530). Though this fact was first brought to the attention of the western scholars in the early 1830s by C. M. Whish,[38] his paper seems to have had no impact almost for a century till Mukunda Marar, C. T. Rajagopal and his associates started publishing on this subject.[39]

It is a well known fact that the series for π given by (9) is an extremely slowly converging series. In fact, one has to consider about 1,00,000 terms in the series to compute a value of π which is accurate to four decimal places.[40] Realizing that the series

[38]The paper was read by Whish on 15, December 1832 and later communicated for publication by the Madras Literary Society and Auxiliary Royal Asiatic Society.

[39]C. T. Rajagopal et al: 1947.

[40]Kline 1972: 439.

in its present form is hopeless for obtaining accurate values of π, Indian astronomers devised ingenious ways to obtain highly accurate values of π using the same series just by finding the partial sum of the series and then applying a correction known as *antya-saṃskāra*. The term *antya-saṃskāra* essentially refers to a rational function which gives an estimate of the remainder terms in the series. The following verse cited in *Yuktidīpikā* of Śaṅkara Vāriyar gives the expression for the infinite series as well as the correction term employed after terminating the series at the desired term and obtaining the partial sum:

> The diameter multiplied by four and divided by unity [is calculated and stored]. Again the products of the diameter and four are divided by the odd numbers like three, five, etc., and the results are subtracted and added successively [to the earlier stored result]. Take half of the succeeding even number as the multiplier (*guṇa* term) at whichever [odd] number the division process is stopped, because of boredom [by the slow converging process]. The square of that [even number] added to unity is the divisor. The ratio has to be multiplied by the product of the diameter and four as [stated] earlier.
> The result obtained has to be added if the earlier term [in the series] has been subtracted and to be subtracted if the earlier term has been added. The resulting circumference is very accurate; in fact more accurate than the one which may be obtained by continuing the division process [with a large number of terms in the series].[41]

[41]Śaṅkara Vāriyar, *Yuktidīpikā*, p. 117:
vyāse vāridhinihate rūpahṛte vyāsasāgarābhihate |
triśarādi-viṣamasaṅkhyābhaktaṃ ṛṇaṃ svaṃ pṛthak kramāt kuryāt ||
yatsaṅkhyayātra haraṇe kṛte nivṛttā hṛtis tu jāmitayā |
tasyā ūrdhvagatā yā samasaṅkhyā taddalaṃ guṇo 'nte syāt ||

When represented in modern mathematical notation, the above verse reduces to

$$\frac{\pi}{4} = 1 - \frac{1}{3} + \frac{1}{5} - \frac{1}{7} \pm \frac{1}{p} \mp \frac{\left(\frac{p+1}{2}\right)}{\left(\frac{p+1}{2}\right)^2 + 1}. \tag{12}$$

The last term in RHS of the above equation is nothing but an estimate of the remainder terms (up to ∞) in the series, having terminated the series at some stage dividing by the odd number p. A detailed analysis of how the mathematicians could have been arrived at this term is explained by Jolly John.[42] His explanation in turn is based on the detailed exposition that is available in the text *Yuktibhāṣā*.[43]

Śaṅkara Vāriyar also presents a more accurate correction term as given below.

$$\frac{\pi}{4} = 1 - \frac{1}{3} + \frac{1}{5} - \frac{1}{7} \pm \frac{1}{p} \mp \frac{\left(\frac{p+1}{2}\right)^2 + 1}{[(p+1)^2 + 4 + 1]\left(\frac{p+1}{2}\right)}. \tag{13}$$

It would suffice to mention here that the expressions for the remainder terms in the equations (12) and (13) are amazingly accurate. A graph of error versus the number of terms considered in the series is shown in Fig. 7. Here the lines with circular and triangular marks denoted as k_1 and k_2 in the figure corresponds to the remainder terms/correction-factors in the equations (12) and (13) respectively. It may be noted from the graph that by merely considering the first 10 terms in the series (N), we are

---

tadvargo rūpayuto hāro vyāsābdhighātataḥ prāgvat |
tābhyām āptaṃ svam ṛṇe kṛte ghane kṣepa eva karaṇīyaḥ ||
labdhaḥ paridhiḥ sukṣmaḥ bahukṛtvo haraṇato 'tisukṣmaḥ syat ||

[42] John, 2002

[43] Jyeṣṭadeva, *Gaṇita-yuktibhāṣā*.

able to get π values that are accurate to 8-9 decimal places. This is indeed a remarkable feat by all standards. Thus we see that Kerala mathematicians have not only arrived at the infinite series expression by the end of fourteenth century but also have found ingenious ways to obtain fast convergent approximations of a very slowly converging series.

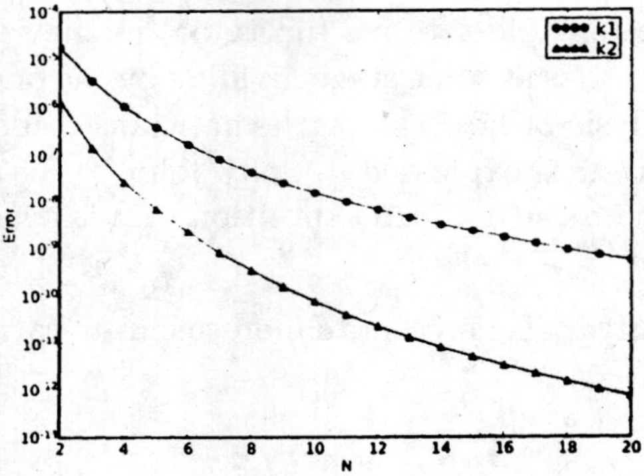

Figure 7: Error in the value of π by considering an estimate of the remainder terms.

7 Concluding Remarks

It has been amply demonstrated that the general picture that emerges from the books on history of mathematics besides being incomplete is also at times misleading. The historians, with the exception of a few, do not seem to have paid enough heed to bring out the non-European contributions to the development of mathematics and scientific thinking.[44]

[44]See, for instance, Katz 2007: 1: '...even as late as 1972, Morris Kline's monumental work *Mathematical Thought from Ancient to Modern Times* contained but 12 pages on Mesopotamia, 9 pages on Egypt, and 17 pages combined on India and the Islamic world (with nothing at all on China) in

It is not uncommon to find downgrading remarks[45] with reference to the contributions made by Hindus, the reasons for which are many and varied. It is hard to believe that such remarks, which of course do not stand scrutiny, could be intentional. But it is equally hard to digest the fact that such statements keep appearing in the books on history of mathematics, as late as the end of the twentieth century, despite the availability of material in English as early as the first half of the nineteenth century.[46]

Coming to think of the reasons for misconceptions, it could be partially due to the ignorance of the actual history and evolution of Indian mathematics and more importantly due to lack of proper understanding of the methodology and tradition of transmission of knowledge in the Indian context. For instance, in the case of astronomy and mathematics the proofs/rationale (*upapatti*-s) are given, not in the primary texts, but in the commentaries, and presumably also by the teachers in the oral discourse. Not being fully aware of these facts, even some of the major historians seem to have developed misconceived notions and ended up making infelicitous remarks in their writings. Such misconceived notions are likely to continue, and the will keep penetrating to deeper and deeper levels unless serious studies are launched into the original source works in Sanskrit along with their commentaries, many of which are lying uncared for in various repositories, and their contents are brought out in the light of modern mathematical language.

It may also be mentioned here that even the celebrated *Āryabhaṭīya-bhāṣya* of Nīlakaṇṭha or the *Vāsanābhāṣya* of

its total of 1211 pages.'

[45]See, for instance, Kline 1972: 189-90: 'Though astronomy was a primary interest in the period of A.D. 200, the Hindus made no significant progress. They took over a minor Hellenistic activity in arithmetical astronomy (of Babylonian origin), which predicts planetary and lunar positions by extrapolation from observed data. ...'

[46]See, for instance, Whish 1834.

Bhāskarācārya or *Buddhivilāsinī* of Gaṇeśa Daivajña have not been studied in toto so far, the fault of which, of course, does not lie so much with Boyer and other historians of the west as much with the native Indians. It is high time to bring into the limelight the contents of these commentaries as they provide a wealth of information with regard to the nature of *upapatti*-s whose understanding may prove to be quite useful in having an alternative epistemology for the future of mathematics.

Acknowledgements

I thank Prof. M. D. Srinivas and Prof. S. M. R. Ansari for their valuable suggestions and comments. I would also like to acknowledge the encouragement and professional guidance I received from Prof. S. R. Sarma in the preparation of this article.

BIBLIOGRAPHY

Primary Texts

Āryabhaṭa, *Āryabhaṭīya* *of Āryabhaṭa with the Commentary of Bhāskara and Someśvara*, ed. Kripa Shankar Shukla, Indian National Science Academy, New Delhi 1976.

Jyeṣṭhadeva, *Gaṇita-yukti-bhāṣā* (*Rationales in Mathematical Astronomy*), Malayalam Text, critically edited and translated into English by K. V. Sarma with Explanatory Notes by K. Ramasubramanian, M. D. Srinivas & M. S. Sriram, vol. 1, Hindustan Book Agency, New Delhi 2008.

Madhusūdana Sarasvatī, *Advaita-siddhi* ed. Anantakrishna Sastri, Parimal Publications, Delhi 1997.

Mahāvīra, *Gaṇitasārasaṅgraha*,
text with translation in Hindi by L. C. Jain, Sholapur 1963 (Jeevaraj Jain Granthamala).

Nīlakaṇṭha, *Āryabhaṭīya-bhāṣya*
in: *The Āryabhaṭīyam of Āryabhaṭācārya with the Bhāṣya of Nīlakaṇṭha Somasutvan*, part I: Gaṇitapāda, ed. K. Sāmbaśiva Śāstrī 1930 (Trivandrum Sanskrit Series 101); part II: Kālakriyāpāda, ed. K. Sāmbaśiva Śāstrī, Trivandrum 1931 (Trivandrum Sanskrit Series 110); part III: Golapāda, ed. Suranad Kunjan Pillai, Trivandrum 1957 (Trivandrum Sanskrit Series 185).

Nṛsiṃha Daivajña, *Vāsanāvārttika*
in: Bhāskarācārya, *Siddhānta-śiromaṇi*, with the auto-commentary *Vāsanā-bhāṣya* and supercommentary *Vāsanāvārttika* by Nṛsiṃha Daivajña, ed. Muralidhara Caturvedi, Sampurnanand Sanskrit University, Varanasi 1981.

Sadānanda, *Vedāntasāra*
ed. G. A. Jacob, Krishnadas Academy, Varanasi 2000.

Śaṅkara Vāriyar, *Kriyākramakarī*
in: Bhāskarācārya, *Līlāvati, with Kriyākramakarī of Śaṅkara and Nārāyaṇa*, ed. K. V. Sarma, Vishveshvaranand Vedic Research Institute, Hoshiarpur 1975.

Śaṅkara Vāriyar, *Yuktidīpikā*
in: *Tantrasaṅgraha of Nīlakaṇṭha Somayājī with Yuktidīpikā of Śaṅkara Vāriyar*, ed. K. V. Sarma, Vishveshvaranand Vedic Research Institute, Hoshiarpur 1977.

Secondary Literature

Boyer, C. B.
1949 *The History of Calculus and its Conceptual Development*, Dover Publications, Inc., New York.

Davis, P. J. & Reuben Hersh

1981 *The Mathematical Experience*, Birkhäuser, Boston.

Gerstein, Larry J.

1996 *Introduction to Mathematical Structures and Proofs*, Springer-Verlag, New York.

Hersh, Reuben

1997 *What is Mathematics, Really?*, Oxford University Press, Oxford.

Hutton, E. H.

1952 *The Origin of Science*, George Allen and Unwin Ltd., London.

John, Jolly

2002 'Derivation of the *saṃskāras* applied to the Mādhava Series in *Yuktibhāṣā*' in: M. S. Sriram, K. Ramasubramanian & M. D. Srinivas (ed.) *500 years of Tantrasangraha*, Indian Institute of Advanced Study, Shimla, pp. 169-182.

Katz, Victor (ed.)

2007 *The Mathematics of Egypt, Mesopotamia, China, India, and Islam: A Sourcebook*, Princeton University Press, Princeton and Oxford.

Kline, Morris

1972 *Mathematical Thought from Ancient to Modern Times*, Oxford University Press, New York.

Manin, Yu. I.

1997 *A Course in Mathematical Logic*, Springer-Verlag, New York.

Rādhākāntadeva

1886 *Śabdakalpadruma*, Baptist Mission Press, Calcutta.

Rajagopal, C. T.

1947 'The sine and cosine power-series in Hindu mathematics,' *Journal of Royal Asiatic Society of Bengal*, XV.1 (1949) 1-13.

1949 'A neglected chapter of Hindu mathematics,' *Scipta Mathematica*, 15 (1949) 201-209.

Ramasubramanian, K., M. D. Srinivas & M. S. Sriram
1994 'Modification of the earlier Indian planetary theory by the Kerala astronomers (c.1500 AD) and the implied heliocentric picture of planetary motion,' *Current Science*, 66.10 (1994) 784-790.

Smith, David E.
1913 'The Geometry of Hindus,' *Isis*, 1.2 (1913) 197-204.

Srinivas, M. D.
2005 'Proofs in Indian Mathematics' in: Gerard Emch et al (ed), *Contributions to the History of Indian Mathematics*, Hindustan Book Agency, New Delhi, pp. 209-250.

Sriram, M. S., K. Ramasubramanian & M. D. Srinivas (ed)
2002 *500 years of Tantrasangrahá*, Indian Institute of Advanced Study, Shimla.

Tieszen, Richard
1992 'What is Proof' in: Michael Detlefson (ed), *Proof, Logic and Formalization*, Routledge, New York 1992, pp. 57-76.

Whish, C. M.
1834 'On the Hindu Quadrature of the Circle, and the Infinite Series of the Proportion of the Circumference on the Diameter exhibited in four Shastras, the Tantrasangraham, Yucti Bhasa, Carana Paddhati and Sadratnamala,' *Transactions of the Royal Asiatic Society of Great Britain and Ireland*, 3.3 (1834) 509-523.

A Comparative Study of the Procedures of Three Astronomers of the Early Sixteenth Century Copernicus, Nīlakaṇṭha Somayājī and Gaṇeśa Daivajña

S. Balachandra Rao

1 Introduction

In the classical Indian astronomical texts, even as in pre-Copernican Europe, the generally followed planetary model is *geocentric*. However, the great Kerala astronomer Nīlakaṇṭha Somayājī (AD 1444-1550) proposed a quasi-heliocentric model in which, while all planets except the earth revolve round the sun, such a solar family itself revolves round the earth. Actually the same model was proposed much later by Tycho Brahe (1546-1601). In the Indian canonical astronomical texts (*siddhāntas*), two epicycles (*manda* and *śīghra vṛttas*) each for the planets and one epicycle (viz., *manda vṛtta*) each for the sun and the moon are prescribed. While the equation due to the *manda* corresponds to obtaining the *true heliocentric* longitude (from the *mean*), the one due to the *śīghra* epicycle results in transforming the true *heliocentric* to the true *geocentric* longitude of a planet.

In contrast, the *heliocentric* model propounded by Copernicus (1473-1546) did not help much in yielding better results than Ptolemy's (2nd cent.) geocentric model. While Copernicus replaced the earth by the sun as the centre of the solar system, he failed to transform all the related kinematic constraints and parameters correspondingly. His relying too much on Ptolemy's results, except the geocentricity, was responsible for his model yielding erroneous results. In fact, the need for fictitious epicycles was successfully got over only after Kepler enunciated his famous laws of planetary motion in which planets move in *elliptical* orbits with the sun at one of the foci.

In the present paper, the accuracy of the epochal positions (*kṣepakas*) and the residual values (*dhruvakas*) for a cycle (*cakra*) of 4016 days, i.e. about 11 sidereal solar years, as given by Gaṇeśa Daivajña in his *Grahalāghava* are investigated. The procedure for computing the planetary position according to the Copernican model is studied and then applied to the case of Jupiter as an example. A comparison of the mean positions of the heavenly bodies according to the three great contemporary astronomers of the earlier part of the 16th century – for a contemporary date of their time – is provided as a test case. The lunar eclipse of 6 November 1500 (Julian), observed by Copernicus, is worked out by a *Grahalāghava* (*GL*) procedure. Two famous transits of Venus, of 1631 and 2004, are worked out by modified *GL* and *siddhāntic* procedures.

2 Revised Manda Peripheries

In classical Indian astronomical texts, the equation of the centre of a celestial body is determined by using the periphery (*paridhi*) of its *manda* epicycle. However, these values need updating.

In Table 1, the proposed peripheries (in degrees) for the different celestial bodies are given using the current values of the eccentricities of the orbits of bodies.

Table 1: Peripheries of Manda Epicycles

Planet	*Periphery (Deg)*		*Coefficient of Equation of Centre*					
			MIN			MAX		
	MIN	MAX	D	M	S	D	M	S
Sun	11.80781	12.31284	1	52	45	1	57	34
Moon	36.8085	42.22932	5	51	29	6	43	15
Mercury	109.8002	184.7195	17	28	30	29	23	56
Venus	4.869	4.952738	0	46	29	0	47	17
Mars	59.30061	74.92371	9	26	16	11	55	28
Jupiter	32.69004	36.89168	5	12	10	5	52	17
Saturn	37.41842	43.03509	5	57	19	6	50	57

3 The Case of Mercury and Venus

The traditional Indian astronomical texts have always treated Mercury and Venus differently from the remaining *tārāgrahas*, viz. Mars, Jupiter and Saturn, in the context of determining their *true* positions.

(i) While the *mean* positions of the superior planets are taken as they are, in the case of the inferior planets Mercury and Venus two special points called Mercury *śīghrocca* and Venus's *śīghrocca* are considered.

(ii) The position of the mean Sun is itself taken as the positions of both mean Mercury and mean Venus. Again, while working out the *śīghra* equation, the argument of the relevant sine function is taken, for example in the case of Mercury as $(B - R)$ according to the *Sūryasiddhānta* convention, where B and R are respectively the Mercury *śīghrocca* and the mean Sun.

In the case of the superior planets, the order of the terms in the argument is reversed. For example, for Jupiter, the argument in the sine term of the *śīghra* equation is $(R - G)$ where G is the mean position of Jupiter. For the superior planets the mean Sun is considered as their *śīghrocca.*

Nīlakaṇṭha points out in his *Tantrasaṃgraha* that it is incorrect to have a differential treatment to the inferior and superior planets and that the sun is the common centre for the *śīghra* equation to all the planets. This is truly a remarkable breakthrough in the history of mathematical astronomy in general and in Indian astronomy in particular.[1] In fact, Nīlakaṇṭha's innovation, prompted by his *paramaguru* Parameśvara (1380-1460), is highly suggestive of a *heliocentric* model of planetary motion much before Copernicus.

Following the innovation introduced by Nīlakaṇṭha, we propose the consideration of the *śīghra* anomaly in the same way for *all* the planets, namely

$$\textit{śīghra kendra} = \textit{śīghrocca} - \text{Mean planet}$$

(in the *Sūryasiddhānta* style) where the *śīghrocca* is the mean sun for *all* the planets.

(iii) In the case of Mercury, the major reason why its true position, calculated according to *siddhāntas*, goes generally off the mark is that the *manda* periphery taken for Mercury *śīghrocca* by the *siddhāntas* is far below its actual modern value.

The *manda* periphery as prescribed in the *Sūryasiddhānta* varies from 28° to 30° for Mercury. But actually, as pointed out in Table 1, the periphery of Mercury's *manda* epicycle should vary from about 109°.8 to about 184°.7. The coefficient of the *manda* equation depends on the eccentricity e of the planet's orbit. In fact, the coefficient, to a first approximation is given by $2e$. In the

[1] See Ramasubramanian et al.

case of Mercury, $e = 0.205656$ currently and hence the co-efficient of the *manda* equation turns out to be about 23°.566. In the improved values for the parameters (vide Table 1) suggested by us even higher powers of e up to e^5 and the first two terms in the expansion for the equation of centre are considered. Accordingly, for the beginning of AD 2000, the variation of the periphery of the *manda* epicycle is from $109^0\ 50'46''$ to $184°\ 47'43''$ (depending on the varying *manda* anomaly). Correspondingly, the coefficient of the *manda* equation varies from about 17°.48 to 29°.41. In fact, our ancient Indian astronomers had not taken note of the fact that among the planets known to them, Mercury's orbit has the largest eccentricity. This lapse explains why Mercury's true position always remained an enigma to them despite all the *bīja-saṃskāras* introduced by them. Of course, now after the discovery of the three trans-saturnine planets, Pluto's orbit has the largest eccentricity (0.2488723) while the immediately next is Mercury's orbit (0.205656).

4 Constants of Grahalāghava vis-à-vis Modern Values

In his *Grahalāghava* (*GL*), Gaṇeśa Daivajña used some constants called *dhruvakas* and *kṣepakas*. The *dhruvakas* are the residual constants for different heavenly bodies, being the balance of mean motion (in longitude) in excess of integral multiples of 360° over a cycle (*cakra*) of 4016 civil days (nearly 11 sidereal solar years). The *kṣepakas* are the mean longitudes of the bodies at the epoch, 19 March 1520, the mean sunrise (Ujjain). The *dhruvakas* as given by the *GL* are compared with the values obtained by modern computation in Table 2.

We observe from the last column that the difference between the values of the *dhruvakas* of the bodies according to *GL* and the modern computations is extremely small.

Table 2: Dhruvakas for a Cycle of 4016 days

Body	*GL Dhruvaka* (*Nir.*) DG	*Modern Dhruvaka* (*Nir.*) DM	*Difference Modern – GL* (DM – DG)
1. Sun	−1°49′11″	−1°47′38″	1′33″
2. Moon	−3°46′11″	−3°44′37″	1′34″
3. Mandocca	−272°45′0″	−272°45′17″	−0′17″
4. Rāhu	−212°50′0″	−212°49′0″.5	0′59″.5
5. Mars	−55°32′0″	−55°29′2″.64	2′57″.36
6. Mercury*	−123°27′0″	−123°22′23″	4′37″
7. Jupiter	−26°18′0″	−26°18′20″.91	−0′20″.91
8. Venus*	−44°02′0″	−44°03′1″.43	−1′1″.43
9. Saturn	−225°42′0″	−225°37′34″.4	4′25″.6

The *dhruvakas* obtained in column 3 of Table 2, according to modern computations, are our recommended *bījas* for *dhruvakas*.

5 Copernicus' Model for Planetary Motion

While Copernicus' heliocentric model was truly a great breakthrough in science, note the following statements by N. M. Swerdlow and Otto Neugebauer:

(i) 'With the wisdom of hindsight, we know that Copernicus' objections (against Ptolemy) were ill-founded and that Ptolemy's model was the single most important step towards a correct understanding of planetary motion prior to Kepler.'[2]

(ii) '... at no point, however did he (Copernicus) question the soundness of Ptolemy's models for representing the apparent motions of the planets, and so at no time did he carry out

[2]Swerdlow & Neugebauer, p. 293.

the analysis that Ptolemy had, and that Kepler did later, to determine what really constituted an approximate model for the planets.'[3]

(iii) 'The recovery of planetary theory of the astronomers of the *Maragha school* . . . is not only of great interest in itself but has also demonstrated that much of what had been taken for Copernicus' own planetary theory is actually of medieval Arabic origin, was transmitted to western Europe in the 15th century.'[4]

Prior to Copernicus, the Arab astronomers of the Marāgha school suggested various planetary models, different from the Ptolemaic geocentric model. These models of the Marāgha school yielded better results than Ptolemy's. One such model given by Mu'ayyad al-Dīn al-'Urḍī (d. *ca* 1266) and Quṭb al-Dīn al-Shīrāzī (1236-1311) is shown in Fig. 1. This model is of course geocentric. The Copernican heliocentric model is superimposed on Ptolemy's model in Fig. 2

5.1 Model of al-'Urḍī and al-Shīrāzī

AB: Apsidal line (joining apogee and perigee)

$e_1 = OM' = \frac{3}{2}e$, where e = eccentricity of Ptolemy's model ($e = OM$)

R : Radius of circle with M' as centre

r' : Radius of epicycle: $r' = \frac{e_1}{3} = \frac{1}{3}(\frac{3}{2}e) = \frac{1}{2}e$

C_1 : Centre of epicycle

[3]Ibid, p. 77.

[4]Ibid, p. 290.

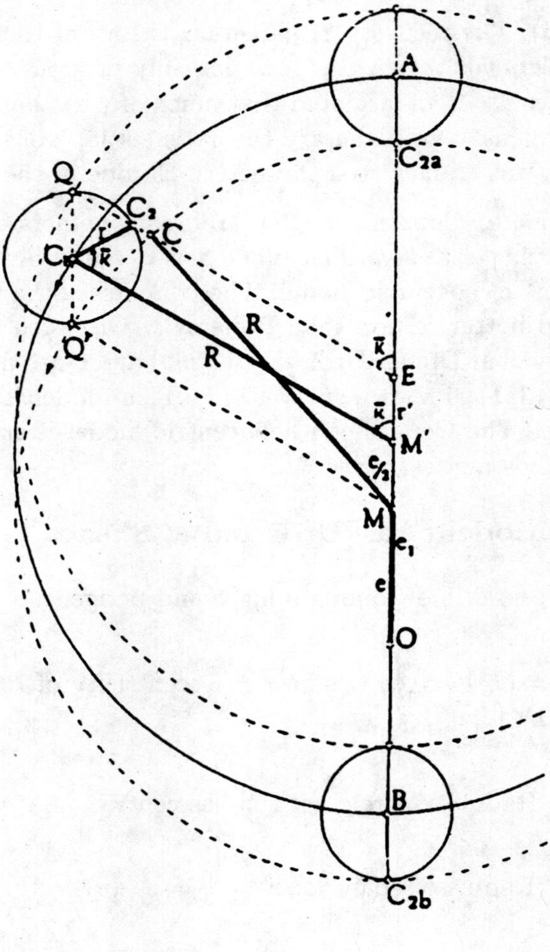

Figure 1. Models of al-'Urḍī and al-Shīrāzī

C' : Centre of epicycle in Ptolemy's model

K : Eccentric anomaly Angle AEC_2

$K = 0$ when C_2 coincides with C_{2a}

When C_1 is at $A(k=0)$

$$OC_{2a} = (M'A + OM' - AC_{2a}) = R + e_1 - r'$$

$$= R + \tfrac{3}{2}e - \tfrac{1}{2}e = R + e$$

$$OC_{2b} = (M'B - OM' + BC_{2b}) = R - e_1 + r'$$

$$= R - \tfrac{3}{2}e + \tfrac{1}{2}e = R - e$$

This agrees with Ptolemaic model.

5.2 Model of Copernicus (superimposed on Ptolemy's Model)

The earth O of Fig. 1 is replaced by the Mean Sun, S and C_2 by the planet P as shown in Fig. 2.

6 Copernicus' Procedure for a Planet's True Longitude

Based on Figs. 1 and 2, Copernicus' procedure is demonstrated with an example in which Jupiter's true tropical longitude is computed.

True Longitude of Jupiter (By Copernicus' Procedure)

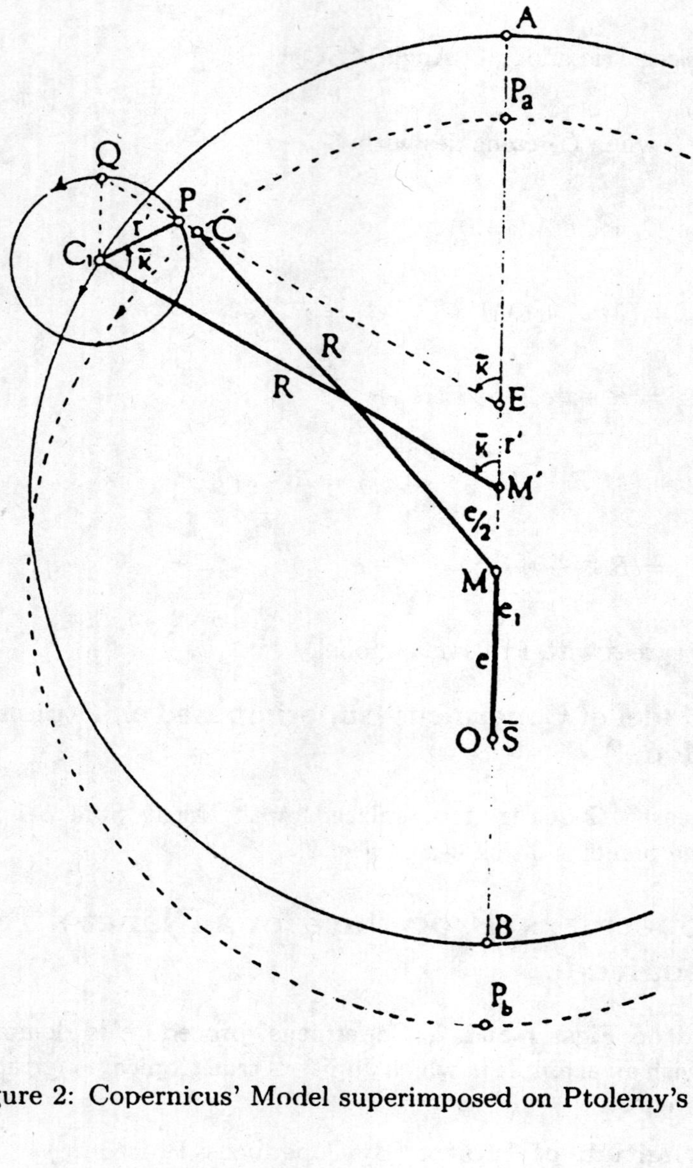

Figure 2: Copernicus' Model superimposed on Ptolemy's Model

Date: 19 February 1473 (J) at 16^{h} 48^{m} at Torun (Poland): Long. 18°37′ E; Lat: 53°01′ N. Christian days (from epoch 1/1/1 AD) CHD = 5,37,697

1. Precession of Equinox, $\pi = 26°47'$

2. Mean anomaly $\bar{\alpha} = 99°56'30''.83$

3. Mean sidereal longitude $\bar{\lambda}^{*} = 211°49'32''$

4. Sidereal Apogee $\lambda^{*}_{A} = 153°45'$

5. (i) $\bar{S}C = \sqrt{R^2 + e_1^2 + 2R\, e_1 \cos \bar{k}} = 10,428.04391$

   (ii) $a_1 = \sin^{-1}\left[\dfrac{e_1 \sin \bar{k}}{\bar{S}C}\right] = 3°0'55''$

   (iii) $\bar{S}P = \sqrt{\bar{S}C^2 + (r')^2 - 2\bar{S}C.r' \cos(\bar{k} - a_1)} = 10,282.24291$

   (iv) $a_2 = \sin^{-1}\left[\dfrac{r' \sin(\bar{k} + a_1)}{\bar{S}P}\right] = 1°3'28''.52$

6. $C_{3(\bar{k})} = a_1 + a_2 = 4°04'23''$

7. True Anomaly $\alpha = \bar{\alpha} + C_{3(\bar{K})} = 104°01'$

8. According to *De Revolutionibus* for Jupiter

   $r = 1916,\ R_0 = 10,548,\ R_{180} = 9542$

   (i) Now $C_m = \sin^{-1}\left(\frac{r}{R_0}\right) = 10°33'24''$

   (ii) $C_M = \sin^{-1}\left(\frac{r}{R_{180}}\right) = 11°35'0''.74$

   (iii) $C_M - C_m = 1°01'37''$

9. $C_{4(\bar{K})} = \dfrac{C_{\max(\bar{K})} - C_m}{C_M - C_m} = \dfrac{C_{\max(\bar{K})} - 10.5567}{1.02694}$

   Now $C_{\max} = \sin^{-1}\left(\frac{r}{R_{(\bar{K})}}\right)$

Taking $R_{(\bar{K})} = \bar{S}P = 10,282.24291$,

$C_{\max(\bar{K})} = \sin^{-1}\left(\frac{1916}{10,282.24291}\right) = 10°44'21''.5$

therefore, $C_{4(\bar{K})} = 0°10'40''.25$

10. We have $R_0 = 10,458$, $r = 1916$, $\alpha = 104°01'$, $R_{180} = 9542$

(i) $\rho_0 = \sqrt{R_0^2 + r^2 + 2R_0 r\cos\alpha} = 10,165.35665$

(ii) $\rho_{180} = \sqrt{R_{180}^2 + r^2 + 2R_{180} r\cos\alpha} = 9266.317469$

(iii) $C_{5(\alpha\ \min)} = \sin^{-1}\left[\frac{r\sin\alpha}{\rho_0}\right] = 10°32'13''.37$

(iv) $C_{7(\alpha\ \max)} = \sin^{-1}\left[\frac{r\sin\alpha}{\rho_{180}}\right] = 11°34'22''.29$

(v) $C_6 = C_7 - C_5 = 1°02'08''.92$

11. $C_{(\alpha,\bar{K})} = C_{5(\alpha)} + C_{4(\bar{K})} \cdot C_{6(\alpha)}$
$= 10°43'16''.55$

12. $\Delta' = \alpha - C_{(\alpha,\bar{K})} = 93°17'43''.45$

13. True sidereal longitude of Jupiter
$\lambda^* = \bar{\lambda}^*_{sun} - \Delta' = 218°27'16''.5$
where, mean siderial longitude of Sun, $\bar{\lambda}^*_{sun} = 311°45''$

14. True Tropical longitude of Jupiter.
$\lambda = \lambda^* + \pi = 245°14'16''.5$

7 Procedure of Contemporary Indian Astronomers of the 16th Century

We have provided in Table 3 the *kṣepakas* (reduced to *sāyana*) of Gaṇeśa Daivajña's *Grahalāghava* for his epoch, namely 19 March 1520, mean sunrise (at Ujjayinī). The same are compared with the *sāyana* positions computed according to Nīlakaṇṭha Somayājī and the modern procedures.

We observe that the values of Gaṇeśa and Nīlakaṇṭha are close to each other as also to the modern values. This establishes the accuracy of both Gaṇeśa's and Nīakaṇṭha's procedures and the authenticity of their observations.

The procedures of Copernicus are used to obtain the positions and anomalies of planets for the *GL* epoch. We observe that Copernicus' values differ appreciably from those by modern procedures.

Table 3: *Kṣepakas* (Epochal positions) of GL

19 March 1520, mean sunrise at Ujjayinī *GL Ayanāṃśa* = 16°38′

Body	*Grahalāghava*		*Nīlakaṇṭha sāyana*	*Copernicus tropical*	*Modern tropical*
	nirayaṇa	*sāyana*			
Sun	349°41′	6°19′	6°24″	5°18′45″	6°01′23″
Moon	349°06′	5°44′	5°53′	2°53′43″	5°32′24″
Rāhu (Node)	27°38″	44°16′	44°38′	-	44°06′25″
Mars	307°08′	323°46′	322°58′	321°42′50″	322°44′14″
Mercury śīghra kendra	269°33′	269°33′	265°38′	-	261°13′59″
Jupiter	212°16′	228°54′	227°32′	227°19′	232°13′38″
Venus Kendra	230°09′	230°09′	228°22′44″	-	228°48′14″
Saturn	285°21′	301°59′	300°56′	307°21′ 50″.21	304°51′07″
Sun's Apogee	78°	94°38′	94°22′52″	98°17′	94°41′44″
Moon's Apogee	167°33′	184°11′	-	199°07′	182°9′02″
Mars's Anomaly	187°08′	-	186°20′	194°33′	168°49′27″
Mercury's Anomaly	220°19′	-	*229°58′	232°52′09″	275°0′55″
Jupiter's Anomaly	32°16′	-	30°54′	39°48′45″	39°30′33″

* Nīlakaṇṭha gives Mercury's apogee as about 219° (*GL* value: 210°).

8 Lunar Eclipse according to *GL*

The lunar eclipse of 6 November 1500 (Julian) is mentioned by Copernicus in his *De Revolutionibus.* The circumstances of this eclipse, observed by Copernicus, are worked out according to the *Grahalāghava.*

At the mean sunrise at Ujjain [i.e. 6 A.M. (LMT) ≡ 6^h 27^m AM (IST)] Nirayaṇa (siderial) longitudes:

True Sun:	217°07′46″
True Moon:	37°19′11″
Rāhu (Node):	42°28′16″

Instant of Opposition: 5^h 36^m 35^s (LMT) ≡ 6^h 03^m 35^s (IST)

At the instant of opposition (6^h 03^m 35^s IST) we have

True Sun:	217°06′46″	*Nirayaṇa* (sidereal)
True Moon:	37°06′46″	
Rāhu (Node):	42°28′19″	

Moon's latitude: – 0°25′13″

Moon's angular diameter (*bimba*): 10.3213 *aṅgulas.*

i.e., Moon's semi-dia = 15′.48195

Shadow's angular diameter (*chāyā-bimba*): 25.7788 *aṅgulas*

i.e., Shadow's semi-dia = 38′.6682,

śara of Moon = 8.4218 *aṅgulas*

Grāsa = $\frac{1}{2}$ (*candra-bimba*+ *chāyā-bimba*) – *śara*

i.e. *Grāsa* (Obscuration) = 9.628262 *aṅgulas*

	LMT	IST	Duration
Sparśa (Beginning):	$4^h03^m02^s$	$4^h30^m02^s$	
Madhya (Middle):	$5^h36^m35^s$	$6^h03^m35^s$	$3^h15^m41^s$
Mokṣa (End):	$7^h18^m43^s$	$7^h45^m43^s$	

Summary of the Eclipse

Pramāṇa (Magnitude) $= \frac{9.628262}{10.3213} = 0.93285$

8.1 A Comparison of Circumstances according to Copernicus and Gaṇeśa

Lunar Eclipse of 6 November 1500 (Julian)

	Particulars	*Gaṇeśa*	*Copernicus*
1.	Ins. of Oppositon	0^h34^m (GMT)	0^h39^m (GMT)
2.	Moon's Latitude	25′13″ S	31′ S
3.	Moon's semi-dia	15′.48	15′.83
4.	Shadow semi-dia	38′.67	41′.66
5.	Obscured part (*Grāsa*)	28′.88	26′.5
6.	Duration of the eclipse	$3^h15^m41^s$	3^h22^m

The mean half-interval (*madhya-sthiti-ardha*) is 1^h 38^m according to Gaṇeśa (modern value: 1^h 35^m) and 1^h 41^m according to Copernicus.

9 Transit of Venus

The transit of Venus on 7 December 1631 (Gregorian) is of immense historical importance. In fact, it was the first transit of Venus after the advent of the telescope. While it was not visible in India, the event was missed in Europe since the sky was overcast.

Example 1: Venus Transit of 7 December 1631(G)

Computation according to modified *GL* procedure

Bheda* (or *Antar*) *Grahayuti

At the mean sunrise at Ujjayinī: 6 A.M. (LMT):

Mean Sun: 235°48′18″ ; Mean Venus: 55°01′25″

Sun's Mean Daily Motion: 59′08″ ; Venus' Mean Daily Motion: – 96′08″

At 9^h30^m A.M. (LMT):

True Sun: 235°10′18″ ; Sun's True Daily Motion: 61′

Manda corrected Venus: 54°37′55″

Venus' *manda* corrected Daily motion: 97′08″

Range of Venus' Retrograde Motion (*vakragati*):

śīghra kendra = 165° to 195° (Bhāskara II)

At the Instant of True Conjunction of Venus & Sun i.e, at 9^h51^m 36^s (LMT):

True Venus = True Sun = 235°11′12″

Venus' True Daily Motion = −37′ (Retrograde)

Sun's Ang. Dia = 32′30″; Venus' Ang. Dia ≈ 1′

Corrected Latitude of Venus, *śara* = 13′12″

Amount of Obscuration, *grāsa* = 3′33″

Half-duration of Transit, *sthiti* = 6|18 Gh ≡ 2^h 31^m 30^s

Half-duration of Totality, *marda* = 5|15 Gh ≡ 2^h 06^m 15^s

Summary of the Transit

Example 2: Venus transit of 8 June 2004

		LMT	IST
Beginning of Transit (Ext. Ingress)	:	$7^h\ 20^s\ 06^s$	$7^h 47^m\ 06^s$
Beginning of Totality (Int. Ingress)	:	$7^h\ 45^m\ 21^s$	$8^h\ 12^m\ 21^s$
Middle of Transit (Least ang. dist.)	:	$9^h\ 51^m\ 36^s$	$10^h\ 18^m\ 36^s$
End of Totality (Int. Egress)	:	$11^h\ 57^m\ 51^s$	$12^h\ 24^m\ 57^s$
End of Transit (Ext. Egress)	:	$12^h\ 23^m\ 06^s$	$12^h\ 50^m\ 06^s$

We watched with great interest and curiosity the exciting phenomenon of Venus transit on 8 June 2004 over the TV and also its reflected image on the telescope. In fact, in our lifetime this was the first Venus transit. For the recently occurred famous Venus transit (for the world in general) we have

1. Instant of conjunction of the Sun and Venus: $14^h\ 8^m$ (IST)

At the instant of conjunction we have

2. True Sun = True Venus = $77°53'32''$ (*sāyana*, tropical)
3. True daily motion: SDM = $0°57'23''$, PDM = $-37'36''$
4. Latitude of Venus, $\beta = -11'$
5. Parallax of the Sun, $\text{PAR}_1 = 8''.659262$
6. Parallax of Venus $\text{PAR}_2 = 30''.44077$
7. Node of Venus = $76°43'12''$ (*sāyana*)
8. Angular semi-diameters:
   $\frac{\text{SDIA}}{2} \equiv 946''.8672$, $\frac{\text{PDIA}}{2} = 28''.86874$
9. VRKNG = $-\frac{(57'23''+37'36'')}{60} = -1'.5830556$ per *nāḍī*
   [VRKNG: *Vyarka (graha) nāḍīgati*]= $\frac{(\text{PDM}-\text{SDM})}{60}$
10. $D = \text{PAR} + \frac{(\text{SDIA} + \text{PDIA})}{2} = 16'.769612$
11. $D' = \text{PAR} + \frac{(\text{SDIA-PDIA})}{2} = 15'.807321$
12. $\lambda = \beta \times \frac{204}{205} = 10'.946341$

13. Since $|\lambda| < D$, the transit is *possible* and since $|\lambda| < D'$, the transit is *total*
14. VPG = True Venus − Node = $1°10'19''$

    [VPG: *Vipātagraha*]
15. $\dot{m} = \text{VRKGN} \times \frac{206}{205} = 1'.5907778$
16. Correction to middle of the transit $= \frac{99}{100}\left(\frac{|\lambda|}{10\dot{m}}\right)$

    $= 0.6812313$ *nāḍī* $= 16^m.35$

    Since VPG is in the first quadrant, the above correction is subtractive. Therefore,

    Middle $= 14^h\ 08^m - 16.^m35 = 13^h51^m.65$
17. Half-duration, HDUR $= \frac{\sqrt{D^2-\lambda^2}}{\dot{m}} = 3^h\ 11^m\ 40^s$
18. Half-duration of totality, THDUR $= \frac{\sqrt{(D'^2)-\lambda^2}}{\dot{m}} = 2^h\ 52^m\ 3^s.01$

Summary of the Transit

(1) Beginning of the transit BEGG $= 10^h\ 40^m$ (Ext. Ingress)
(2) Beginning of totality BEGGT $= 10^h\ 59^m$ (Int. Ingress)
(3) Middle (Least ang. dist.) $= 13^h\ 52^m$
(4) End of the totality. ENDT $= 16^h\ 44^m$ (Int. Egress)
(5) End of the transit END $= 17^h\ 03^m$ (Ext. Egress)

(Timings are in Indian Standard Time, IST).

Remark: The transits of Venus occur periodically in the months of December and June over a cycle of 8, 121.5, 8 and 105.5 years, i.e. a total cycle of 243 years.

10 Conclusion

In this paper we have made a comparison, though briefly, of the models and computational procedures of three great contemporary astronomers of the early 16th century: Copernicus, Gaṇeśa Daivajña and Nīlakaṇṭha Somayājī.

Although the Copernican model is heliocentric, its computational procedures do not yield better results than those of Gaṇeśa and Nīlakaṇṭha despite the fact that the latter ones are geocentric.

Bibliography

Primary Texts

Āryabhaṭa I, *Aryabhaṭiya*
with the commentary of Nīlakaṇṭha Somasutvan, ed. K. Sambasiva Sastri, University of Kerala, Trivandrum 1957.

Bhāskara II, *Karaṇakutūhala*
(a) with the commentary *Gaṇaka-kumuda-kaumudī* of Sumatiharṣa, Bombay 1989.
(b) with English Tr. and Notes by S. Balachandra Rao & S. K. Uma, *Indian Journal of History of Science*, 42.1–2 (2007) i-xv, S1-S108; 43.1 (2008) S109–S150; 43.3 (2008) S151–S220.

Gaṇeśa Daivajña, *Grahalāghava*
(a) with the commentary of Mallāri and Viśvanātha and a Hindi commentary by Kedarnath Joshi, Motilal Banarsidass, Varanasi 1981.
(b) with an English Exposition and Mathematical Notes by S. Balachandra Rao & S. K. Uma, *Indian Journal of History of Science*. 41.1–4 (2006) i-xii, S1–S415.

Sūryasiddhānta
tr. E. Burgess, edited by Phanindralal Gangooly with an Introduction by P.C. Sengupta, Motilal Banarsidass, Delhi 1989.

Varāhamihira, *Bṛhatsaṃhitā*
with English tranlation and Notes by M. Ramakrishna Bhat, Motilal Banarsidass, Delhi 1981.

Varāhamihira, *Pañcasiddhāntikā*
with English Translation and Notes by T. S. Kuppanna Sastri, critically edited with Introduction and Appendices by K.V.Sarma, PPST Foundation, Madras 1993.

Secondary Literature

Balachandra Rao, S.
2000 *Ancient Indian Astronomy: Planetary Positions and Eclipses*, B.R.P.C. Ltd., New Delhi.

Kuppanna Sastry, T. S.
1989 *Collected papers on Jyotisha*, Kendriya Sanskrit Vidya Peetha, Tirupati.

Ramasubramanian, K., M. D. Srinivas & M. S. Sriram
1994 'Modification of the earlier Indian Planetary Theory by the Kerala Astronomers (c. 1500 A.D.) and the implied Heliocentric Picture of Planetary Motion,' *Current Science* 66.10 (25 May 1994) 784-790.

Shylaja, B. S.
2004 *Transit of Venus*, BASE and Navakarnataka Pubn., Bangalore.

Shylaja, B. S. & H. R. Madhusudhan
1999 *Eclipse*, University Press, Hyderabad.

Sriram, M. S., K. Ramasubramanian & M. D. Srinivas (ed)
2002 *500 years of Tantrasangraha*, Indian Institute of Advanced Study, Shimla.

Swerdlow, N. M. & O. Neugebauer
1984 *Mathematical Astronomy in Copernicus's De Revolutionibus*, ed. G. J. Toomer, Springer-Verlag, New York.

Why did Sanskrit Mathematics ignore Asakṛt Methods?

KIM PLOFKER

1 Introduction: The Organization of Mathematical Knowledge

Sanskrit mathematical sciences, like other classical Sanskrit *śāstrās* or fields of learning, generally recognized a traditional normative structure handed down from early works, while in practice also accepting a good deal of autonomy on the part of individual authors in how they chose to select and organize their subject matter. This combination of tradition and flexibility raises the question of how Indian mathematical scientists perceived disciplinary boundaries. What determined an author's decision to assign a particular mathematical topic to one traditional category rather than another, or to reject the classification assigned to it by an earlier mathematician, or simply to omit it entirely from his discussion of mathematics?

So far, this question has not been widely investigated, and the Sanskrit sources provide few direct answers to it. It is seldom that an Indian mathematician explains the details of his decisions about the construction of his text. We are not told, for instance, why Brahmagupta's mathematical chapters do not discuss the geometry of the sphere, or why Mahāvīra's treatise identifies multiplication and division instead of addition and subtraction as the first of the canonical fundamental arithmetic operations, or why Bhāskara II includes formulas for the sphere with those for the circle in his section on plane geometry. The expositions added to mathematical treatises by commentators are usually equally silent about such issues. Generally, mathematicians' motivations for their choices of disciplinary and subject boundaries can only be tentatively reconstructed from the content of their works.

An interesting illustration of the puzzles of disciplinary boundaries within Indian mathematics emerges from the computational techniques known in Sanskrit works as *asakṛt* (literally 'not once') rules: i.e., what modern mathematics calls iterative numerical approximations. Such iterative rules are widely used in Sanskrit mathematical astronomy (*jyotiṣa* or *jyotiṣa-gaṇita*), but never described in textbooks treating mathematics or computation in general (*gaṇita*). Yet *asakṛt* methods are not intrinsically astronomical: they can be applied to any mathematical problem whose closed-form solution is intractable (and where a suitable iterative approximation can be found). What was it about them that put them definitively within the discipline of *jyotiṣa* rather than *gaṇita*? The investigation of this question requires us to look more closely at the relationship between the two sciences and at the nature of the *asakṛt* rules themselves.

2 Mathematics, Astronomy, and Iterative Methods

The nature of the original genetic link between *jyotiṣa* and *gaṇita* is rather unclear. The first surviving detailed treatments in Sanskrit of mathematics in general (as opposed to, say, the altar-building geometry preserved in ancient ritual texts) appear in designated chapters of *jyotiṣa* texts, a century or so before the first known mathematics treatises proper. And throughout the entire known history of classical Sanskrit *gaṇita* works, most of the authors writing on *gaṇita* wrote on *jyotiṣa* as well. This may indicate that *gaṇita* as a recognized *śāstra* in its own right originally spun off from the *śāstra* of *jyotiṣa*. If so, however, it was not long before *gaṇita* or computation *per se* began to be perceived as a fundamentally broader and more comprehensive subject than its parent discipline. The classic statement of the all-pervading nature of mathematics as the abstract essence of universally applicable quantification is the description in the ninth-century *Gaṇitasārasaṅgraha* of Mahāvīra:

> In all these transactions which relate to worldly, Vedic or [other] similarly religious affairs, calculation is of use. In the science of love, in the science of wealth, in music and in the drama, in the art of cooking, and similarly in medicine and in things like the knowledge of architecture; In prosody, in poetics and poetry, in logic and grammar and such other things, and in relation to all that constitutes the peculiar value of [all] the [various] arts, the science of computation is held in high esteem. In relation to the movements of the sun and other heavenly bodies, in connection with eclipses and the conjunctions of planets, and in connection with the *tripraśna* and the course of the moon—indeed in all these [connections] it is utilized.[1]

The first explicit discussion of the relationship between *gaṇita* and *jyotiṣa* appears to be that in the commentary *Āryabhaṭīyabhāṣya* of Bhāskara I in the early seventh century.[2] The base-text by Āryabhaṭa specifies three subjects comprehended in *jyotiṣa*, namely *gaṇita*, *kālakriyā* or timekeeping, and *gola* or the sphere. Bhāskara's commentary defines these concepts, explaining *gaṇita*

[1] Mahāvīra, *Gaṇitasārasaṅgraha*, p. 2, verses 1.9–12.

[2] A more detailed study of this discussion was given by Keller.

as 'figures, shadows, series, equations, the pulverizer [linear indeterminate equations], etc.'[3]

He goes on to address in more detail the issue of what knowledge is subsumed under *gaṇita*:

> Here, this word '*gaṇita*' expresses '*gaṇita* in its entirety'. Because of this meaning '*gaṇita* in its entirety', although [one] says [specifically] 'figures-*gaṇita*' and 'planet-*gaṇita*', because of the non-differentiation of planet-*gaṇita* from figures etc., and because of the non-differentiation of timekeeping and spherics from *gaṇita*, he [i.e., Āryabhaṭa] calls [it] '*gaṇita*' [*per se*].[4]

So mathematics as a whole was clearly considered from an early period to embrace all the computations of *jyotiṣa* as well as those in other fields.

As noted above, however, this did not prevent texts on *gaṇita* from omitting certain mathematical techniques employed in *jyotiṣa*, such as the *asakṛt* or iterative methods. Most of these took the form of what are now known as 'fixed-point' approximations, where a solution to an intractable equation is found by first guessing an approximate value of the desired solution, and then using the guessed value to solve a related equation that gives a more accurate approximate value.[5] This new value is then plugged

[3]Bhāskara I, Commentary, p. 5 (on verse 1.1): *gaṇitaṃ kṣetracchāyāśreḍhīsamakaraṇakuṭṭākārādikam.*

[4]Ibid, p. 6: *atrāyaṃ gaṇitaśabdo 'śeṣagaṇitābhidhāyī tasmād aśeṣagaṇitābhidhāyitvād yathā kṣetragaṇitaṃ bravīty evaṃ grahagaṇitam api grahagaṇitasya ca kṣetradyavyatiriktatvāt kālakriyāgolayoś ca gaṇitāvyatiriktatvād gaṇitaṃ nigadatīty etāvad eva* [...].

[5]Other basic iteration techniques like the false-position method and the secant method, which use two initial approximate values instead of the one initial approximation employed by most fixed-point methods, also appear in Indian astronomy texts, but for brevity's sake they are not discussed here.

back into the same equation, which is solved again to produce a still more accurate value, and so on until the successive approximations converge, with the required degree of precision, to the desired solution. A simple example of this technique was used to solve what is now known as 'Kepler's equation', although similar forms of both the equation and its iterative solution were used centuries before Kepler in Indian and Islamic astronomy.[6]

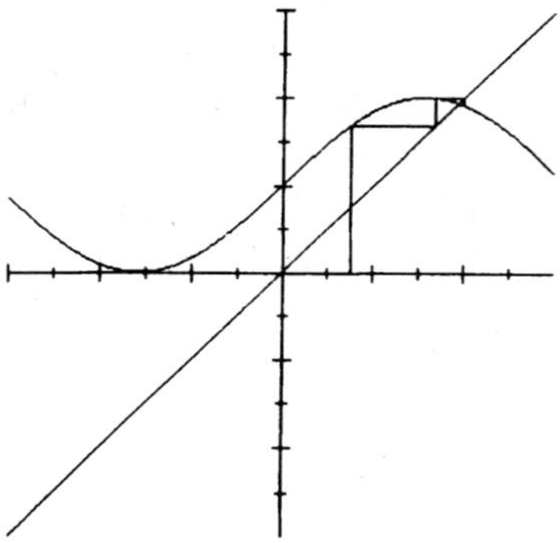

Figure 1: An iterative solution of the Kepler equation $x = 1 + \sin x$.

Kepler's equation involves two given quantities α and β and a desired quantity x, which are related by the expression

$$x = \alpha + \beta \sin x. \tag{14}$$

This equation cannot be solved directly for x, but it can be solved iteratively by assuming some initial approximate value x_0, using it to compute a new approximate value $x_1 = \alpha + \beta \sin x_0$, which is then used to find $x_2 = \alpha + \beta \sin x_1$, and so forth. After some number n of iterations, when the value x_n is not detectably different from the previous $x_{(n-1)}$, the iteration is said to have converged to the desired *fixed point* $x_n = x$. The steps of such a procedure

[6]These earlier versions are described in more detail in Plofker 2002; the story of their recognition as forms of Kepler's equation is told in Dutka 1997.

are represented graphically in Figure 1: the zigzag line starting at some initially guessed value on the horizontal x-axis proceeds through each of the successive approximate values, finally reaching its fixed point at the intersection of the curve and the $y = x$ line, where $x = 1 + 1 \cdot \sin x$.

3 An Example of an Asakṛt Rule in Jyotiṣa

The above explanation and example, of course, are very anachronistic; Sanskrit texts do not talk about the conditions affecting solvability of equations or graphical representations of them. The standard approach is to identify the problem to be solved and then supply a rule or algorithm for solving it. Iteration is indicated merely by specifying that the rule should be followed repeatedly. A more true-to-life example (although still contaminated, for ease of exposition, by modern diagrams and notation) is shown in what follows.

The problem in question involves an astronomical computation for finding the distance of a planet at some given point in its (circular) orbit about the earth, if the diameter of the orbit and its eccentricity (i.e., the displacement of the center of the orbit from the center of the earth) are known. The standard trigonometric solution to this problem is quite straightforward, and can be explained in terms of the quantities shown in the diagram in Figure 2. If the earth is at E and the planet at P, and the planet's eccentric orbit is centered at C a known distance EC from the earth, then we imagine a second circle the same size as the orbit but centered at E, with radius EM equal and parallel to CP. The so-called 'mean anomaly', or angular distance $\angle ACP = \angle AEM$ between the planet and its apsidal line AE, is given.

If we take $CP = EM = 1$, we can solve for the desired distance EP in the right triangle AEP using modern trigonometric functions, as follows. The horizontal leg of the triangle, AP, is

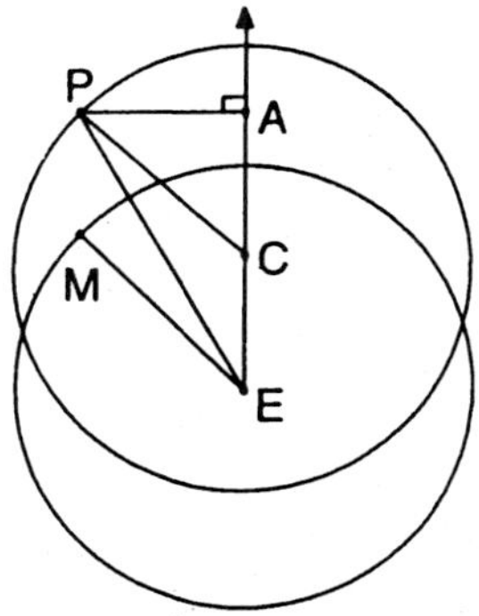

Figure 2: Finding the geocentric distance EP of a planet

just the sine of the known angle $\angle ACP$, and the vertical leg AE is the known eccentricity EC plus the cosine AC of $\angle ACP$. Then the hypotenuse is easily found by the 'Pythagorean' theorem:

$$EP = \sqrt{\sin^2 \angle ACP + (\cos \angle ACP + EC)^2}. \qquad (15)$$

But this solution is actually an oversimplified version of the computations prescribed in many *jyotiṣa* texts, whose models display more complicated physical features than the simple circles shown here. To handle their complexity, iterative solutions are sometimes required. For instance, a rule in the *Mahābhāskarīya* of Bhāskara I requires the eccentricity EC to change depending on the planet's distance from the earth, rather than remaining fixed. The effect is to squeeze the orbit into an elongated oval rather than a circle.[7] This means that we can no longer solve

[7]This is the planetary model that is popularly if somewhat inaccurately described as the ancient Indian equivalent of modern elliptical planetary orbits. It is actually more closely related to an astronomical device known as the equant, which is used to reduce the inaccuracy of the simple eccentric model. The relation of this 'pulsation' of the eccentric orbit to the equant is mentioned in Duke 2005.

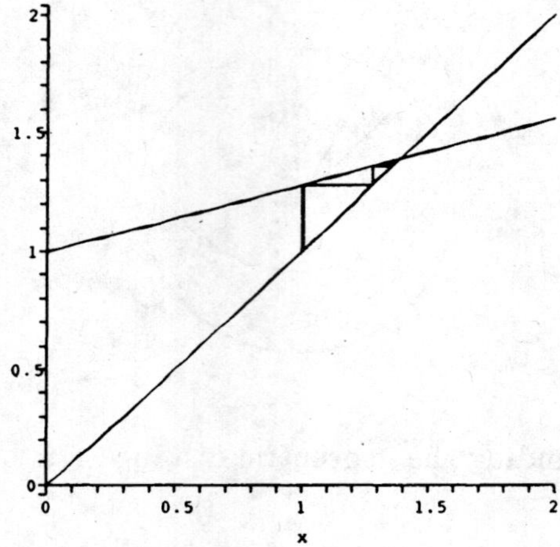

Figure 3: Iteration of equation 16 for planetary distance

directly for the geocentric planetary distance EP, since the eccentricity EC itself now depends on EP. The core of Bhāskara's algorithm is given in the following verse:

> When one has multiplied the last result [for EC] by the hypotenuse [EP], it is divided by the Radius [CP]. [The quotient] should be added to or subtracted from the previous Cosine [$\cos \angle ACP$] until the hypotenuse becomes equal [to its previous value].[8]

[8]Bhāskara I, *Mahābhāskarīya*, p. 196, verse 4.20: *karṇenāntyaphalaṃ hatvā niṣkambhārdhena labhyate | pūrvakoṭyāṃ dhanārṇaṃ syād yāvat karṇaḥ samo bhavet.* Here, the word *antyaphala* which would literally be interpreted as 'last equation of center', i.e., the angle ($\angle ACP - \angle AEP$), is evidently intended to mean the sine of the maximum equation of center, namely the eccentricity EC. This is shown by the fact that in the preceding verse, the same *antyaphala* is combined with $\cos \angle ACP$ to give the vertical leg of the triangle whose hypotenuse is EP.

In other words, according to this form of the rule, the planetary distance EP is expressed by

$$EP = \sqrt{\sin^2 \angle ACP + (\cos \angle ACP + EP \cdot EC)^2}, \qquad (16)$$

which clearly cannot be solved for EP directly. But if an initial guess for EP is plugged into the right side of equation 16 and successive values are computed iteratively, the desired fixed value for the distance quickly emerges.

This is illustrated in Figure 3, where x along the horizontal axis represents EP and the desired fixed point, as before, falls at the intersection of the (almost flat) curve of the function in equation 16 with the straight line $y = x$. The iterative path zigzagging upwards from an initial guess of $EP = 1$ proceeds very rapidly to the fixed point.

4 Other 'Non-Canonical' Methods in Gaṇita Texts

As the above examples illustrate, iterative approximation can be a handy mathematical tool for attacking equations that cannot be solved directly. The fundamental *asakṛt* trick of starting with a guessed wrong answer and repeating the same calculation until a fixed right answer emerges is apparently unique to *jyotiṣa* treatises. Of course, there do exist other repetitive procedures in mathematical texts, such as computing the digits of a square-root or cube-root, or grinding out greatest common divisors from coefficients in a 'pulverizer' or linear indeterminate equation. But no mathematics author ever explains how to construct an iterative algorithm (or even instructs the reader to perform one iteratively) or how such an approximation works.

On the surface, this omission seems to contradict the avowed universalist claims of mathematicians such as Bhāskara and Mahāvīra. If, as they assert, *gaṇita* embraces all forms of calculation, and *asakṛt* procedures are a significant form of calculation, then why do *gaṇita* texts not treat it?

We might speculate that the technique of iteration is simply too broad and vague to be successfully classified among mathematical topics. After all, what is iteration? Clearly, it is not a fundamental arithmetic operation (*parikarma*) like addition or division; and it is not one of the canonical applications or practices (*vyavahāra*) such as series, figures and the like. Nor does it fit in with particular types of equations or other such standard topics in algebra. Were *asakṛt* methods perhaps disqualified just for being insufficiently specific?

Against this speculation we must set the puzzling fact that some other similarly vague and general computational methods did attain a recognized identity and status in *gaṇita* textbooks. Let us consider in particular the mathematical concepts known as 'inversion' and 'method of an assumed quantity', which also are neither fundamental operation nor application nor equation. They are explained by Bhāskara II in the *Līlāvatī* as follows:

> Now, the rule of operation for the procedure of inversion... In finding a quantity [i.e., an operand] when [the result] is given, make a divisor [into] a multiplier, a multiplier a divisor, a square a square-root, a square-root a square, a negative [quantity] a positive [one], [and] a positive [quantity] a negative [one]...
>
> Now, the rule of operation for methods of assumption [of some arbitrary quantity]... Any desired number is multiplied, divided, or decreased and increased by fractions. The given quantity, multiplied by the desired [number] and divided by that [result], is the [required] quantity; [that] is called the operation with an assumed [quantity].[9]

[9] Bhāskara II, *Līlāvatī*, pp. 42–45, verses 48–51: *atha vyastavidhau karaṇa-*

The first of these procedures, inversion, is a rule for finding an unspecified operand when the final answer is given. E.g., if some quantity multiplied by 6 and increased by 4 gives the answer 16, what is the quantity? The trick, as Bhāskara explains, is to invert the given operations: start with the answer 16 and subtract the addend 4, and then divide by the multiplier 6: that is, $16 - 4 \div 6 = 2$.

The method of an 'assumed quantity' is simply what we know (or what our forebears knew, at least) as 'false position'. For instance, if we are told that some quantity multiplied by 4 and increased by half the resulting product equals 18, instead of trying to solve for the unknown quantity directly, we could just guess some value for it—say, 1—and see what answer we get when we follow the prescribed manipulations. In this case, $(1 \cdot 4) + 1/2\,(1 \cdot 4) = 6$, which is too small for the given answer 18. But we can find the ratio between the right and wrong answers, and use it to scale the wrong operand up to the correct value: in this case, 6 is to 18 as 1 is to 3, and indeed the value 3 gives the right answer in the original problem.

It is difficult to see any reason why the basic concept of *asakṛt* techniques could not have been explained and illustrated by mathematicians in a similar way to these 'inversion' and 'false position' methods. We still do not seem to have found any obvious technical or conceptual difference in *asakṛt* rules to explain their exclusion from *gaṇita.*

5 Conclusion: A Question of Certainty?

Does the reason for the placement of *asakṛt* methods outside the disciplinary boundaries of *gaṇita* proper perhaps go deeper

sūtraṃ [...] *chedaṃ guṇaṃ guṇaṃ chedaṃ vargaṃ mūlaṃ padaṃ kṛtim* | *ṛṇaṃ svaṃ svam ṛṇaṃ kuryad dṛśye raśiprasiddhaye* || [...] *atheṣṭakarmasu* [...] *karaṇasūtraṃ* [...] *iṣṭarāśiḥ kṣuṇṇo hṛto 'ṃśai rahito yuto vā* | *iṣṭāhataṃ dṛṣṭam anena bhaktaṃ rāśir bhavet proktam itīṣṭakarma.*

than subject classification and topical structure, into fundamental ideas of the nature of mathematical thought? For fixed-point iterative methods, despite their mathematical usefulness, also possess the suspect quality of being unreliable, sometimes in ways that are very difficult to understand. That is, the iterated calculations that are supposed to result in a fixed right answer sometimes fail to do so. And it is hard to see how their failures could be confidently understood and explained without sophisticated mathematical tools, some of which have emerged only in the past few decades.

A brief sketch of one such untrustworthy rule will illustrate this problem.[10]

Specified first by Lalla in about the eighth century, this algorithm computes the sun's altitude above the horizon in a particular direction, when the time of year and the observer's terrestrial latitude are known. We will not go through the geometry of the situation or the details of the algorithm, but instead skip directly to the pictorial interpretation of how the iteration works, shown in Figure 4.

The diagram on the left represents the successive steps of the computation for a time close to the winter solstice and a latitude corresponding to central India. Here the iterative path, instead of zigzagging directly to the desired fixed point at the intersection of the curve and the $y = x$ line, spirals around and around the fixed point as it approaches slowly. Perhaps dozens of repeated calculations will be required to reach the step where the successive values cease to be perceptibly different. The behavior of the graph on the right, representing the situation for the same time at a north-Indian latitude, is even worse: starting from an initial guess quite close to the desired fixed point, the iteration

[10]The history of this rule in Indian astronomy, and the larger question of Indian awareness of convergence problems with iterative approximations in general, are discussed in more detail in Plofker 2004.

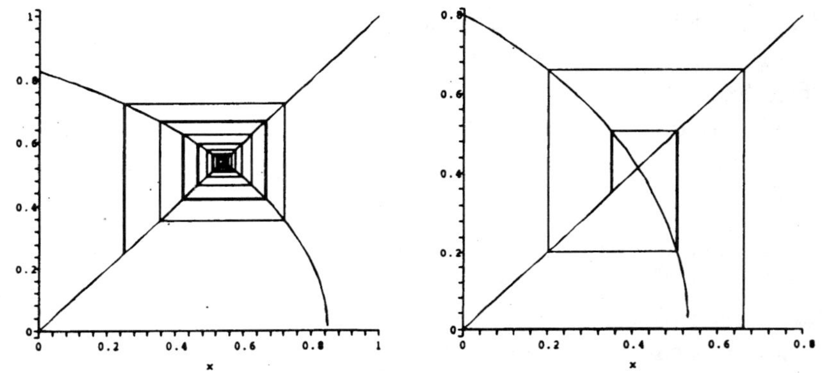

Figure 4: Iterations that converge only very slowly (L) or diverge (R).

path spirals *away* from the point rather than towards it, finally falling off the curve entirely and failing to produce any usable answer at all.

It is not immediately obvious, even with modern diagrams to help us, why the same iterations performed on the same algorithm with only slightly different parameters should sometimes differ so wildly in their results. To medieval mathematicians perceiving iteration only as sequences of numbers, its failures must have been often, if not always, inexplicable.

Was this mysterious behavior the reason, or one of the reasons, that Indian mathematicians did not discuss *asakṛt* rules in the context of *gaṇita*? Although recently renewed interest in the epistemology of Sanskrit mathematics has led to more scrutiny and discussion of concepts like proof and verification in Indian contexts, we are still far from knowing all the details of how mathematicians set criteria for testing and accepting mathematical knowledge. We know that several *jyotiṣa* works exhorted their readers to study the geometry underlying their algorithms, in order to acquit themselves well in learned debates and to be 'free from doubt' about their answers.[11] Was there a minimum threshold for certainty or comprehensibility in accepted *gaṇita* knowledge that *asakṛt* rules, however indispensable in applied calculation, simply failed to attain?[12]

This conundrum never attracted much attention in the earlier historical study of Sanskrit mathematics, perhaps due in part to the influence of a similar pattern in the history of the modern mathematical tradition. Western mathematics too refrained, until the early modern period, from formally analyzing iterative approximation methods, although they had been occasionally used at least since Hellenistic times. This neglect was probably due to the influence of Hellenistic notions of mathematical 'rigor' or detailed deductive proof, which is difficult to apply to the dynamical characteristics of iterative techniques. Such techniques were therefore excluded from the realm of recognized mathematical subjects in the Greek corpus and its descendants, and their exclusion in other mathematical traditions consequently seemed natural. But there is no reason for present-day historians to assume that Indian mathematicians followed Greek epistemological norms, even if it is somewhat daunting to realize, upon shedding that assumption, how remarkably little we still know about the epistemological norms that Indian mathematicians devised for themselves.

---

[11] A survey of such statements and their implications for Indian ideas of mathematical proof is presented in Srinivas 2005.

[12] If this is so, it raises equally puzzling questions about how the threshold of certainty was reached for various topics in some solidly recognized *gaṇita* fields, such as the use of the 'cyclic method' of Jayadeva and Bhāskara II for solving second-degree indeterminate equations, a method whose validity was not conclusively proved even in modern mathematics until a couple of centuries ago.

Bibliography

Primary Texts

Āryabhaṭa, *Āryabhaṭīya of Āryabhaṭa with the Commentary of Bhāskara and Someśvara*, ed. Kripa Shankar Shukla, Indian National Science Academy, New Delhi 1976.

Bhāskara I, *Mahābhāskarīya of Bhāskarācārya with the Bhāṣya of Govindasvāmin and the Super-Commentary Siddhāntadīpikā of Parameśvara*, ed. T. S. Kuppanna Sastri, Government Oriental Manuscripts Library, Madras 1957.

Bhāskara I Commentary in: *Āryabhaṭīya of Āryabhaṭa with the Commentary of Bhāskara and Someśvara*, ed. Kripa Shankar Shukla, Indian National Science Academy, New Delhi 1976.

Bhāskara II, *Līlāvatī of Bhāskarācārya* with the commentaries *Buddhivilāsinī* by Gaṇeśa Daivajña and *Līlāvatīvivaraṇa* by Mahīdhara, ed. V G. Āpaṭe, Pune 1937 (Ānandāśrama Sanskrit Series 107).

Mahāvīra, *Gaṇitasārasaṅgraha* ed. & tr. M. Rangacharya, Government Press, Madras 1912.

Secondary Literature

Duke, Dennis

2005 'The Equant in India: the Mathematical Basis of Indian Planetary Models,' *Archive for History of Exact Sciences* 59 (2005) 563-576. For a computer-animated representation of the model, visit http://people.scs.fsu.edu/dduke/pingree2.html.

Dutka, Jacques

1997 'A Note on Kepler's Equation,' *Archive for History of Exact Sciences* 51 (1997) 59-65.

Keller, Agathe

2007 'Qu'est-ce que les mathématiques? les réponses taxinomiques de Bhāskara, un commentateur, mathématicien et astronome indien du VIIème siècle', in: Phillipe Hert and Marcel Paul-Cavalier (ed.), *Sciences et Frontiéres: délimitations du savoir, objets et passages*, Éditions Modolaires Européennes, Fernelmont (Belgium) pp. 29-61.

Plofker, Kim

2002 'Use and Transmission of Iterative Approximations in India and the Islamic World' in: Y. Dold-Samponius et al. (ed.), *From China to Paris: 2000 Years of Transmission of Mathematical Ideas,* Steiner, Stuttgart, pp. 167-186.

2004 'The Problem of Sun's Corner Altitude and Convergence of Fixed-Point Iterations in Medieval Indian Astronomy' in: C. Burnett et al. (ed.), *Studies in the History of Exact Sciences in Honour of David Pingree*, Brill, Leiden, pp. 552-586.

Srinivas, M. D.

2005 'Proofs in Indian Mathematics' in: Gerard Emch et al. (ed.), *Contributions to the History of Indian Mathematics*, Hindustan Book Agency, New Delhi, pp. 209-250.

Yantrarāja at Edinburgh On a Sanskrit Astrolabe made for Maṇirāma in AD 1644

SREERAMULA RAJESWARA SARMA

1 Introduction

As a highly sophisticated and versatile observational and computational instrument, the astrolabe held a pre-eminent position among the pre-modern astronomical instruments.[1] It was employed for measuring the altitude of the sun in the daytime and that of several bright stars at night; it was also used for measuring heights and distances in land survey. More important still, it can simulate the motion of the heavens at any given locality and time. It can also be used as an analog computer for solving numerous problems in spherical trigonometry. Therefore, the astrolabe was rightly termed as the 'universe within one's palm.' Writing in 1428 at Naimiṣāraṇya, Rāmacandra Vājapeyin declares that if one knows the science of the astrolabe well, the entire universe

[1]On the history and function of the astrolabe, see, inter alia, Michel 1947, Hartner 1985, Gibbs & Saliba 1984, Turner 1985, King 1987. See also Khareghat 1950.

will become comprehensible like the myrobalan fruit on one's own palm (*karāmalakavad*).[2]

Though the astrolabe was invented in Hellenistic Greece around the second century BC, it was the Islamic world which preserved this Greek knowledge, elaborated upon it and then disseminated it eastwards up to India and westwards up to England. In fact, the astrolabe is thought to have been a major vehicle through which the Greek science of astronomy was transmitted to Europe, together with Arab innovations. Thus the astrolabe held sway over the medieval world, transcending the boundaries of geography, culture and language.

In his *India*, al-Bīrūnī claims to have composed a manual on the astrolabe in Sanskrit verse.[3] The work does not survive, but it is quite probable that al-Bīrūnī had brought the astrolabe with him and taught its working principles to his Hindu interlocutors at Multan in the first quarter of the eleventh century. With the establishment of the Sultanate in Delhi in the next century, Muslim scholars began migrating to Delhi in great numbers. Some of these scholars brought astrolabes and employed them for teaching astronomy and also for astrological purposes. Since astronomy formed a regular part of Muslim education, the ability to use the astrolabe was expected of every good scholar. A few thirteenth century astrolabes from the Middle East, which must have been

[2]Rāmacandra Vājapeyin, *Yantraprakāśa*, 1.11 (MS folio 3r):
sulabhākhyayantarājaṃ sāvayavaṃ pūrvam eva pravadāmi |
yasmin karāmalakavad vidite viditaṃ bhaved viśvam ||
'First I shall describe the king of instruments called *Sulabhā* together with its components. If this instrument is understood [well], then the universe will become comprehensible like the myrobalan fruit on one's own palm.'

[3]Cf. Al-Bīrūnī 1964: I.137: 'Most of their books are composed in *Śloka*, in which I am now exercising myself, being occupied in composing for the Hindus a translation of the books of Euclid and of the Almagest, and dictating to them a treatise on the construction of the astrolabe, being simply guided herein by the desire of spreading science.'

brought here by the immigrant scholars, are still extant in Indian collections.[4]

In the latter half of the fourteenth century, Fīrūj Shāh Tughluq promoted the study of the astrolabe. He not only got several astrolabes manufactured at Delhi— probably for the first time in India—, he also encouraged the composition of manuals on the construction and use of the astrolabe both in Persian and in Sanskrit.[5] During the next five hundred years, a large number of astrolabes were manufactured in India with Arabic/Persian legends. These are generally classified as Indo-Persian astrolabes. I have discussed this class of astrolabes in several publications.[6]

The astrolabes and the Persian manual commissioned by Fīrūj do not survive any more, but the Sanskrit manual named *Yantrarāja* which this monarch sponsored is extant. It was written in 1370 by a Jaina monk, Mahendra Sūri, who was a leading astronomer at the Tughluq court.[7] Mahendra was so impressed by the versatile functions of the astrolabe that he called it *Yantrarāja*, king of instruments, and it is under this name that the instrument is known in India. Subsequent Hindu and Jaina astronomers were no less enthusiastic about this remarkable instrument imported from the Islamic world. Thus, for example, Viśrāma, in his *Yantraśiromaṇi* (composed in 1615), extols the

[4] In Indian collections, there are three Kufic astrolabes which were originally produced in the Middle East. (i) An astrolabe made by al-Sarrāj Damishqī in 623 AH/AD 1226 is now at the Salar Jung Museum, Hyderabad; cf. Sarma 1996: 23-24; (ii) Another astrolabe made by the same al-Sarrāj Damishqī in 626 AH/AD 1228-9 (CCA 3765) is at the Rampur Raza Library; cf. Dube 1928; Sarma 2003: 25-33; (iii) An anonymous astrolabe is in the Archaeological Museum, Red Fort, Delhi. Kaye assigns it to ca. AD 1289; cf. Kaye 1921: Astrolabe A, pp. 2-5 and Pl. 1 and 2.

[5] See Sarma 2000.

[6] Sarma 1992, 1994, 1996a, 1996b, 2003.

[7] Mahendra Sūri, *Yantrarāja*. On this text, cf. Pingree 1978: 626-28; Plofker 2000.

astrolabe as the lord of instruments (3.56: *yantreśvara;* 3.61: *yantrendra*).[8]

The response of the Indian *jyotiṣīs* towards the astrolabe was twofold: first, between 1370 and 1870, some fifteen manuals were composed in Sanskrit on the construction and use of the astrolabe. Second, this activity of composition was accompanied by the manufacture of astrolabes on which the legends and numbers were engraved in Sanskrit language and in Devanāgarī script.[9] I classify this group as 'Sanskrit astrolabes'.[10] Today there are extant some 100 Sanskrit astrolabes in various collections all over the world.

This impressive number of Sanskrit manuals and Sanskrit astrolabes produced during the half millennium from 1370 to the end of the nineteenth century makes it abundantly clear that the Indian *jyotiṣīs* were greatly impressed by this versatile instrument. But the earliest surviving Sanskrit astrolabes are from the seventeenth century. I have identified some nine specimens produced in that century.

2 Maṇirāma's Astrolabe

By a happy coincidence, one of these nine early Sanskrit astrolabes is preserved in the Royal Museum of Scotland (Acc. No. 1986.20) in the city of Edinburgh where the 13th World Sanskrit Conference was held. The Museum acquired the astrolabe in 1986 at an auction held by Christie's of London.[11] As one of the earliest extant Sanskrit astrolabes, this specimen is important for the history of the astrolabe in India. Therefore, in this paper, I

---

[8] Viśrāma, *Yantraśiromaṇi*, pp. 112-113.

[9] They also reworked several Arabic-Persian astrolabes with additional legends in Sanskrit. These will be discussed in a future publication.

[10] Sarma 1999a, 1999b.

[11] See Christie's Catalogue 1986: 66, item no. 358. There are several errors in the description printed in the catalogue. These will be mentioned at the appropriate places below.

shall first describe this astrolabe in detail and then try to situate it within the history of the astrolabe in India.

2.1 Ownership and Provenance of the Astrolabe

The astrolabe was made by an unnamed artisan for one Maṇirāma in 1644. On the front side of the suspension bracket, there are two inscriptions engraved one below the other (see Figs. 1 and 5). Both are in Sanskrit language and in Devanāgarī characters. The first inscription in three lines reads thus : *Saṃvat* 1700 *caitra kṛṣṇaikādaśyāṃ maṇirāmeṇa kāritaṃ*, 'caused to be made by Maṇirāma on the 11th day of the dark half of [the month] Caitra in Saṃvat [year] 1700.' It means that an astronomer named Maṇirāma prepared the technical design and got it made for his own use by a metal worker whose name is not recorded. The date translates to 2 April 1644.

Christie's consultant read the Saṃvat year 1700 as 1900. There is no apparent reason for this mistake because the digit 7 is quite clear. Even elsewhere in the astrolabe, 7 and 9 are clearly distinguished by the engraver. This will be evident by comparing it with the numerical symbols appearing on the circular scale immediately below the crown, where the numbers 7 and 9 occur several times. Based on their consultant's decipherment, Christie's announced it as a nineteenth century product in their catalogue. But when I studied the astrolabe in August 1993 in connection with my project of cataloguing extant Indian astronomical instruments,[12] I immediately saw that it was older by 200 years than it was thought to be; I also realised that it was one of the earliest surviving Sanskrit astrolabes.

Below this inscription, there is a second inscription, in a different hand and cut more deeply into the metal: *śrīlīlānāthajyotirvido* [']*yam*, 'this [instrument is the property] of the illustrious as-

[12]On this project, see Sarma 1994.

trologer (*jyotirvid*)[13] Līlānātha'. He must be a subsequent owner, but we do not know when he lived. On the plate calibrated for the latitude of Jodhpur (see Fig. 4), there is an addition, where the writing resembles the calligraphy of this line and is cut likewise more deeply than the rest. This too must have been an addition caused to be engraved by Līlānātha. The addition reads *nepāle* [']*pi*, 'also in Nepal,' that is to say, the plate could be used also in Nepal, or more precisely in the capital city Kathmandu. The modern values for the latitudes of Jodhpur and Kathmandu are 26;18° N and 27;42° N respectively. Therefore, it was a reasonable approximation to say that these two cities lie on the same latitude. Līlānātha's addition on this plate suggests that he may have been from Kathmandu and may have used it there. If this hunch is correct, then this would be the only known astrolabe that was ever used in Nepal.

About Maṇirāma, the original owner of the astrolabe, we have no other information. But it is quite certain that the astrolabe, like many other early extant Sanskrit astrolabes, was produced in Gujarat. It is a neatly crafted piece made of brass with a diameter of 128 mm. There are some lacunae in execution. For some unknown reason, the astrolabe was left unfinished in three respects. (i) On the inner side of the mater the astrolabe maker drew a grid but did not fill it in with the geographical gazetteer. (ii) On the back, a grid was drawn likewise on the upper right side quadrant, but was not filled in. (iii) The upper left quadrant was left completely blank, where a sine-cosine graph is generally engraved.

Now I shall describe the different components of this astrolabe and their functions; thereafter I shall attempt to situate this astrolabe within the seventeenth century traditions of astrolabe manufacture in India.

---

[13] *Jyotirvid*, 'knower of the celestial luminaries,' is a common title of astrologers.

2.2 The Front

The main body of the astrolabe, called mater, consists of a thick circular plate with an upraised rim all around. It is surmounted by a triangular piece like a crown.[14] A shackle and a ring are added to the top of the crown so that the astrolabe can be suspended in a vertical plane for observation. In the present specimen, the ring and the shackle are missing: otherwise the astrolabe is in a good state of preservation. The main body (*koṣṭhakāgāra, āgāra*),[15] the rim (*pālī, parikhākāra-vṛtta*) and the crown (*kirīṭa*) are cast as a single piece (Fig. 1). The rim carries a double band of scales. While the inner and narrower band is graduated in single degrees, the outer band is calibrated in groups of 6° and numbered separately for each quadrant from 6 to 90, starting from the east and west points and reaching up to the south and north points.[16]

The crown is high and solid, rising above the circumference of the body by 46 mm. The left and right profiles of the crown are artistically contoured with a succession of lobes. A hole is bored in each of the two top lobes. These holes have no real function. They were made as decorations in Kufic astrolabes of the thirteenth century, and were occasionally emulated by later astrolabe makers. There is another hole at the very top of the crown. Into this was inserted the shackle, which is now missing.

[14]The triangular suspension bracket on the top of the main circular body of the astrolabe is called in Arabic *kursī*, 'throne,' in an allusion to the *Āyah al-Kursī*, 'Verse of the Throne,' at Qur'ān 2.255 ('His Throne doth extend/Over the heavens/And the earth'). Sanskrit writers, however, see in it the *kirīṭa*, 'crown', because of its position on the top of the main body and also because of its shape and ornamentation.

[15]This and the following Sanskrit terms for the different parts of the astrolabe are taken mainly from Mahendra Sūri's *Yantrarāja* and from the *Yantrarājavicāra-viṃśādhyāyī* (a Sanskrit rendering of Nāṣir al-Dīn al-Ṭūsī's celebrated Persian work, the *Bist Bab*).

[16]In Arab cartography, the south is shown at the top. The same convention is followed in the astrolabes as well.

The meridian (south-north line) drawn on the body is extended on to the crown on both the sides. Otherwise the back of the crown is blank. The front of the crown bears the two inscriptions mentioned above.

2.3 The Rete

In the space created inside the upraised rim, there are inserted a number of circular discs. On the top is a perforated plate, generally known as rete (*bhacakrapatra, bhapatra*).[17] The rete contains the ecliptic and a star map with pointers indicating the positions of some bright stars. Beneath the rete are to be found a series of plates (*akṣāṃśapatra, akṣapatra*)[18] which are specific to particular terrestrial latitudes and display stereographic projections of the local horizon, equal altitude circles or almucantars, azimuth circles, hour curves etc. When the rete is correctly set and made to rotate upon the plate of a particular latitude, the astrolabe simulates the motion of the heavens above the localities situated on that latitude.

The rete in our astrolabe has a diameter of 108 mm (Fig. 2). It contains the circles representing the tropic of Capricorn, the equator and the ecliptic, one inside the other. The outer circumference of the rete is constituted by the tropic of Capricorn and the centre by the north pole. The tropic of Capricorn is not completely represented; the upper part where it touches the ecliptic tangentially is not shown. Likewise the equator is not fully shown. Only a small part of the equatorial belt is shown below

---

[17]Because the openwork resembles the spider's web, it is called *ᶜankabūt* (spider) in Arabic and 'rete' (net) in Latin. As against this, the Sanskrit expressions *bhacakra-patra*, lit. 'the disc of the stellar region' and *bha-patra*, 'disc of the stars,' are more meaningful.

[18]The plate is called *ṣafīḥa* (pl. *ṣafa'iḥ*) in Arabic, and 'plate', 'disc', 'tablet', 'tympan' in English. Once again the Sanskrit terms *akṣaṃśapatra* and *akṣapatra*, lit. 'latitude plate or disc', are more expressive than the Arabic or English terms.

Figure 1: The front of the astrolabe with the two inscriptions on the crown. This and the following photos courtesy of the National Museums of Scotland, Edinburgh.

the ecliptic. Here it is distorted in the middle to join an upturned tulip flower (for decorative reasons). The equinoctial bar is complete and plain without any counter changes. The ecliptic circle (*krāntivṛtta*), placed off centre, is fully represented. It is divided into 12 unequal divisions to represent the signs of the zodiac, which are named, but not always correctly inscribed: *meṣa, vṛsa, mithūna*, (sic! read *mithuna*), *karka, siṃha, kanā* (sic! *kanyā*), *tulā, vṛścaka* (sic! *vṛścika*), *dhana* (*dhanuṣ*), *makara, kumbha, mīna*. Each sign is further subdivided into 6° and the divisions are numbered as 6, 12, 18, 24, 30. In the bevelled edge of the ecliptic ring, these are further halved to form divisions of 3° each. The divisions are not always uniform.

On both sides of the ecliptic, there are several points to represent the bright stars to the south and north of the ecliptic. The points are joined by a tracery representing vines, leaves and tulip-like flowers. Some tips of leaves and flowers constitute star pointers (*nakṣatra-cañcu*), but not all. The maker aimed at mirror symmetry so that the rete rotates smoothly around the central pin.

Of these pointers, 12 are named. On these pointers the names of the respective stars are engraved in abbreviated form, obviously due to shortage of space. Seven of these are situated outside the ecliptic circle (i.e. to the south of the ecliptic; these stars consequently have southern latitudes) and five inside (i.e. to the north of the ecliptic; these stars have northern latitudes). Interestingly these abbreviated forms of the star names are followed by certain numbers, e.g. *ro 8*, meaning *rohiṇī* 8. *Rohiṇī* or α Tauri is the fourth lunar mansion, then why 8 after the name? It took me some time to realise that 8 is the serial number assigned to this star by Mahendra Sūri in his *Yantrarāja*. This work contains a catalogue of 32 stars together with their longitudes and latitudes for the use of astrolabe makers.[19] Of these 32, Maṇirāma

[19] Mahendra Sūri, *Yantrarāja*, 1.22-39, pp. 25-28; see Pingree 1978: 628,

chose just 12 stars for his astrolabe. More would have cluttered the rete. But by adding Mahendra's serial numbers to the star names of his astrolabe, Maṇirāma is conferring a canonical status to Mahendra's work. Indeed it deserves this status. It was extensively read throughout the centuries; we know of at least 100 surviving manuscripts of this work.[20]

In the ecliptic circle, at the first point of Capricorn, a small projecting tip is formed. This is the point where the ecliptic touches the tropic of Capricorn. This point or mark is called the head (lit. face) of Capricorn (*makarānana*).[21]

Leaving aside the tropic of Capricorn, the ecliptic circle, the star pointers and the tracery joining all these and thus supporting the frame, the rest of the plate is cut out so that through the resulting gaps the lines and graduations on the plate below can be read. On the north point of the rete at the intersection of the meridian, there is a knob. It is the handle to facilitate the rotation of the rete around the centre (*bha-patra-bhrāmaka-kīla*). The named stars and their identification are shown in Table 1.

The engraver, by mistake, interchanged the names of two stars. What is labelled as *kṛtti* 5 (=*kartitakara*, β Cassiopeiae) does in fact point to the star *Samudrapakṣī* (ι Ceti), and that which is inscribed as *samu* 32 pertains to *kartitakara*, β Cassiopeiae.[22] Otherwise, the star pointers are correctly positioned

---

Table XI.3.

[20]Cf. Pingree 1981: 393-95; Pingree 1994: 296; see also Sarma 2000: 144.

[21]There is no exact English equivalent; European astrolabes do not have a prominent tip. The Arabic word is *murī' ra's al-jadī*, lit. 'head of Capricorn'. In Sanskrit, it is called the 'face' of Capricorn (*makarānana, makarāsya*).

[22]Incidentally the name of this star is translated also as *rañjitakara*, which is actually the correct rendering of the Arabic name *al-kaff al-khaḍīb*, 'dyed hand,' i.e. a hand dyed with henna (*lawsonia inermis*); cf. Savage-Smith 1985: 147. But Mahendra Sūri renders it as *kartitakara*, probably thinking that a hand which is red must have been stained by blood from a cut! These are the pitfalls of trans-cultural translations.

Figure 2: The rete of the astrolabe with the named star positions

for the time when the astrolabe was made.

There are 8 more pointers which are not named. These are α Leporis, β Gemini, α Corona Borealis, α Librae, α Lyrae, ζ Cygni, δ Capricornis, δ Aquarii. Notable among these is *Abhijit* (α Lyrae, Vega). In the Islamic tradition this star is named *al-nasr al-wāqiʿ* ('falling eagle'), which expression degenerated to

'Vega' in European languages. In the Islamic tradition, this star cluster is seen as a falling eagle. In this context, there developed a tradition of depicting the position of this star with a pointer shaped like a bird. The earliest surviving example is to be found in a Byzantine astrolabe of 1062,[23] but there must be earlier Islamic prototypes for this.[24] In any case, this bird-shaped star pointer is right in the middle of the rete of our astrolabe, but is not named. The bird and its surroundings in our astrolabe rete have a further significance, which will be discussed later.

In 1990, these star positions were examined by Ronald Torode, who had devised 'A Mathematical System for identifying the Stars of an Astrolabe and Finding its Age.'[25] Applying this system to the star pointers of our astrolabe, he came to the following conclusion: 'The positions indicated by the pointers were compared with the positions of the same stars given in a recent nautical almanac, the difference in ecliptic longitude being attributed to precession and so to the age of the instrument. A date was calculated from each pointer ... and the mean calculated as AD 1640.'[26] It should be noted that this happened before I had deciphered the inscription in 1993 and found that it was made in 1644. In 1990, the Museum was still under the impression that the instrument was made in 1843 as Christie's consultant opined. Therefore Torode thought that the 200 hundred years' difference between his estimate based on the star positions and the alleged date of the astrolabe 'suggests some inaccuracy in the making of

[23]Gunther 1976: No. 2, pp. 104-108, Fig. 57.

[24]David King, however, observes that 'Vega as a bird appears for the first time in a Byzantine astrolabe of 1062 (Museo dell 'Età Christiana, Brescia) which is free of Islamic influence. No contemporary Islamic astrolabe has this feature, no surviving Islamic astrolabe from the period 900-1100 shows it. Muslim astrolabists may have borrowed this feature later from Greek astrolabes or come up with the idea independently;' cf. King 1993: 29-52, esp. 30.

[25]Torode 1989.

[26]The Museum kindly provided me a copy of Torode's report.

this instrument.'

But now we know that the difference is just four years which is negligible. This shows that Maṇirāma must have computed the longitudes of these stars afresh by adding precession up to his time. Therefore, our astrolabe is reasonably accurate for the time it was produced.

2.4 The Plates

Below the rete are stacked six plates (*akṣāṃśapatra, akṣapatra*) each with a diameter of 108 mm (Figs. 3 and 4). While the rete can rotate around the central pin, the plates have to stay firmly in position, providing the steady reference points to the variable positions of the rete. For this purpose, all these plates are endowed with a projecting bit at the top (southern point) which goes into a slot cut into the side of the rim.

Each face of these plates is calibrated for a different terrestrial latitude. While making observations, the observer chooses the face of the plate which is meant for his own location and places it on the top of the other plates, so that the rete rotates just above this one. Then the plate represents the observer's location on the surface of the earth, while the rete, when rotated to the appropriate angle (according to specific rules) represents the starry heavens above the observer at the given point of time.

The outer periphery or circumference of the plate is constituted, as in the case of the rete, by the diurnal circle or tropic of Capricorn (*makarāhorātravṛtta*). Inside this, at appropriate intervals are drawn the diurnal circle of Aries and Libra (*meṣāhorātravṛtta*) which is the same as the equator, and inside this the diurnal circle of Cancer (*karkāhorātravṛtta*). All the three circles have the same centre.

Then the oblique horizon, i.e. horizon (*kṣitija*) pertaining to the terrestrial latitude, is drawn as an arc cutting across the three circles mentioned above. Above the horizon and parallel to it are drawn equal altitude circles or almucantars (*unnatāṃśavṛttas*). On the plates of our astrolabe, these are drawn for each 6° and labelled as 6, 12, 18, ... 78, 84, 90 along the periphery on the left hand side as well as on the right.

The semi-circular space below the horizon is divided into 12 equal divisions by means of arcs. These divisions are numbered from 1 to 12, starting from the western horizon, and represent the twelve unequal or seasonal hours of the day and also of the night, as counted from sunset. In Islamic culture, the day commences from sunset, from which the hours of the day are counted. Thus our astrolabe is designed for measuring seasonal hours in Islamic fashion; but it cannot measure equal hours of 60 minutes each, nor equal *ghaṭīs* of 24 minutes each, though it is possible to measure both these types of time units by drawing the appropriate curves. Some of the Mughal astrolabes indeed contain lines for measuring such time units. But Sanskrit astrolabes generally have only hour lines (for equal hours, or unequal hours, or both) but never *ghaṭī* lines, in spite of the fact that the Hindus reckoned in equal *ghaṭīs*.

Besides these, Indo-Persian astrolabes contain azimuth lines. But these are not drawn on the plates of our astrolabe.

In the space between the horizon and the tropic of Cancer are engraved three items of data: the locality for which this face of the plate is calibrated, its latitude and the duration of the longest day at this latitude (*paramadina*) in *ghaṭīs*. Thus on the plate for Delhi, the inscription reads as follows:

Ḍhillī *paramadina*
28/39 34/35

It means that the latitude of Delhi is 28; 39° N and that the duration of the longest day at this latitude is 34 *ghaṭīs* and 35

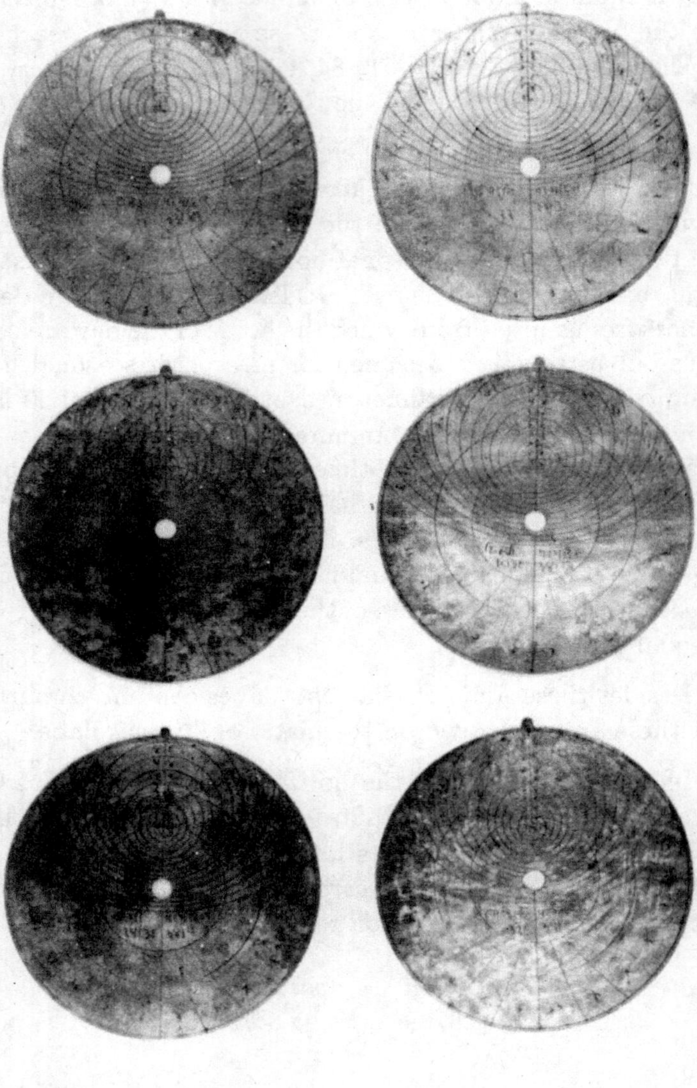

Figure 3: The six plates, obverse

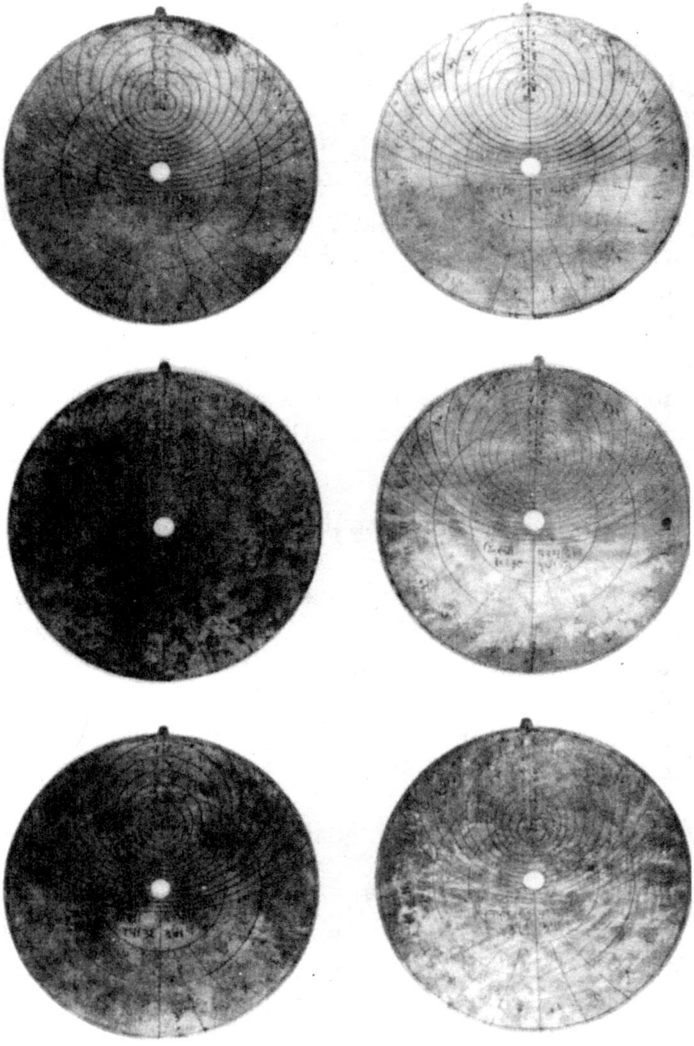

Figure 4: The six plates, reverse

palas (= 13^h 50^m).

The geographical data given on the 12 sides of the 6 plates is shown in Table 2. Accordingly, the plates are calibrated for 12 different localities, ranging from Devagiri in the south (lat. 20;34° N) to Kāśmīra in the north (lat. 35° N). The plates are locality specific rather than latitude or climate specific. Usually among the plates, there is included a special plate, one face of which is calibrated to the latitude 66°30′ (= 90 − obliquity = 90 −23°30′). On this the ecliptic coordinates of the star pointers on the rete are measured. It is called *ṣafīḥa mīzān al-ᶜankabūt*. The other face contains sets of multiple horizons, which can be used for taking observations at latitudes for which no plate is available. Such a special plate was not made for this astrolabe though it can be seen in some other Sanskrit astrolabes of the seventeenth century.

2.5 Geographical Gazetteer

Usually a geographical gazetteer is engraved on the inner side of the mater. Maṇirāma also intended to have a gazetteer engraved on his astrolabe, for which purpose ten concentric circles were drawn (Fig. 5). But for unknown reasons, the blank spaces have not been filled in. As we shall see, there are other areas on the back which were not filled in.

2.6 The Back of the Astrolabe

The back of the astrolabe (Fig. 6) is divided into four quadrants by the vertical and horizontal diameters. The outer periphery of the top left quadrant contains a double-banded scale as in the front, the inner band displaying single degrees, and the outer band groups of 6°. These are numbered as 6, 12, 18 ... 78, 84, 90, starting from the east point and going up to the south point. This is the scale on which the altitude of the sun or of some bright star is measured by means of the alidade, which is

Figure 5: The inner side of the body with an empty grid; alidade and pin.

pivoted at the centre. In Fig. 6, the alidade is pointing to 61° on the scale. The alidade (*bhujā, vedhapaṭṭī*) is 110.5 mm long. It is solidly built and is without any graduations. The two sighting vanes (*dṛṣṭikā-śakala*) have one hole (*chidra*) each through which the sighting is done. A pin holds the alidade in position and also the plates and the rete on the other side. This pin represents the celestial north pole and is accordingly called in Sanskrit *meru-kīla* or *dhruva-kīla*.

In the front of the astrolabe, the pin is held in position by a transverse wedge (*tiryak-kīla*) which is inserted into the hole in the pin. In Islamic astrolabes this wedge is generally shaped like a horse and is called the horse (*aśva-mukha-kīla*), but ours is a plain one with a thicker end for a better grip.

Normally the four quadrants at the back contain various trigonometric and astrological tables, though the configuration of the tables varies from astrolabe to astrolabe. Usually, the top quadrant at the left contains a sine grid or cosine grid, or both, so that the angle of altitude measured by the alidade can be converted directly into the corresponding sine or cosine. In the present astrolabe, this place is blank. In the quadrant on the top right, there are concentric arcs, creating eight bands alternately broad and narrow. Each pair appears to form a particular scale. The top two are divided into 15 cells each; the next two into 13 cells each, the next two into 10 cells each; and the last two into 6 cells each. But these cells are not filled. Probably this grid was meant for a table as in the two quadrants below, but it was left empty.

The quadrant on the lower right has inscribed on it a table of declinations for each 2° from 1° to 89°. The table is inscribed upside down, i.e. starting from the circumference and going down up to the centre, in four concentric rows. Around the hole near the centre is the label *krāntayaḥ*, 'declinations'. This table of declinations is derived also from Mahendra's *Yantrarāja*; or more exactly, from Malayendu's commentary on the *Yantrarāja*, where he introduces this table with the words: *atha rāśitrayasya paramakrāntikoṣṭakāḥ sāntarā likhyante*, 'now will be written the tables of maximum declination for three signs (=90°) together with their differences.'[27] In this table, the declinations are given for each degree from 1° to 90°; the maximum obliquity being 23;35°. The declinations are in minutes and seconds; these are followed

[27] Mahendra Sūri, *Yantrarāja*, pp. 7-9

Figure 6: The back of the astrolabe with the tables; note that the alidade is pointing to 61° on the altitude scale.

by the differences (*antara*) between each two successive values of declinations. On our astrolabe, this table is abridged for the purpose of engraving in the following manner. The values are given not for each degree but for each 2 degrees and the differences are omitted. While Malayendu gives the declinations in minutes and seconds of arc, the astrolabe has them in degrees, minutes and seconds. The table is carefully engraved on the very small area of the astrolabe, but there are some errors. These are indicated at the appropriate places in the footnotes. The table is reproduced as Table 3. The first row shows the degrees of solar longitude, and the next three rows display respectively the corresponding degrees, minutes and seconds of the sun's declination.

The quadrant on the lower left contains a table of shadow lengths for a gnomon of 12 digits (*aṅgulas*). This too was engraved in four rows, starting from the outer periphery and reaching up to the centre. Around the hole at the centre is the label: *dvādaśāṃgulaśaṃko*[*ś*] *chā*[*yāḥ*], 'shadows of the gnomon of 12 *aṅgulas*.' The first row shows the degrees of solar altitude, for each 2° from 1° to 89°; the second and third rows the corresponding lengths of the gnomon shadow in *aṅgulas* and their sexagesimal submultiples. The table is reproduced as Table 4.

2.7 Tables of Declinations and of Shadow Lengths on Astrolabes

Such tables on the back of an astrolabe are a very unusual feature not met with on any Islamic astrolabe. But they occur on other Sanskrit astrolabes besides the present one. In an astrolabe made for Indrajī in 1673,[28] the lower left quadrant is filled with a table of declinations. This too was taken from Malayendu's commentary on the *Yantrarāja*. Here the declinations are given for

[28]The astrolabe is now in the Pitt Rivers Museum of Ethnology at Oxford, acc. no. 1893.4514. For a brief description, see Gunther 1923: 198-99; see also Gunther 1976: No. 79, p. 211, fig. 110.

each 6°; the values are in minutes and seconds as in Malayendu's commentary. An identical table is engraved on the lower left quadrant of an anonymous astrolabe.[29] A much larger table with declinations (in degrees, minutes and seconds) for each degree of arc from 1° to 90° is engraved on the two lower quadrants at the back of an astrolabe made by Vīrabhadra in 1805.[30] In 2002, the auction house Skinner, Bolton, Mass., offered a Sanskrit astrolabe for sale. It was made by Cakrapāṇi in 1625 (*Saṃvat* 1682 *Mārgaśīrṣa Śuklapakṣa* 1 Sunday = 20 November 1625). The back of this astrolabe is covered by a badly engraved table of gnomon shadow lengths for each degree of solar altitude.[31] I suspect the gnomon used here is one of seven units (*saptāṅgula-śaṅku*) while the table in our astrolabe is meant for a gnomon of 12 units (*dvādaśāṅgula-śaṅku*). Thus these tables are not a unique feature of our astrolabe but occur in other Sanskrit astrolabes as well. At the moment, I am unable to say how and where this custom originated, except to record this as a deviation from the standard Indo-Persian astrolabes.

2.8 Pattern of the Rete

A large majority of the Indo-Persian astrolabes were produced by a single family of astrolabe makers from Lahore.[32] Maṇirāma's

[29]This astrolabe is now preserved in the Victoria & Albert Museum, London, and is accessioned under I.M.407 and IPN 2467.

[30]Now in the National Museum of American History, Washington D.C. It is described and illustrated in Gibbs & Saliba 1984: 181-184, figs. 121-123, esp. fig. 123.

[31]Skinner Catalogue 2002: item no. 244, pp. 38-39. The catalogue says: 'This appears to be a mater started by Sri Cahrapani (sic!) but not completed which was then restarted later by someone else for an unknown purpose as the markings on the back do not seem to be related to the uses of an astrolabe.' The late Professor David Pingree, who deciphered the astrolabe in 2002 for Skinner, kindly sent me his full notes from which it is evident that the markings on the back are shadow lengths.

[32]Sarma 1994b.

astrolabe and other Sanskrit astrolabes produced in the seventeenth century differ from the Lahore astrolabes in several respects, including the configuration on the back as mentioned in the previous section. The Lahore astrolabes display a large number of stars on their retes, and these are joined by very decorative floral traceries.[33] In contrast, the Sanskrit astrolabes have a much smaller number of stars, about half the number. While no two retes look alike in Lahore astrolabes, most of the contemporary Sanskrit astrolabes display a rete similar in pattern to Maṇirāma's astrolabe.

The distinctive pattern of the rete is as follows. From the circle of Capricorn, from the east-west bar and so on, arise what look like leaf clusters or tulip-like flowers with two or more outstretched petals, the tips of which point to different bright stars. In the centre, there is a characteristic pattern. The star *Abhijit* (α Lyrae, Vega) in the form of a bird appears to be seated in a cage. In our astrolabe, it is not named. Above the cage, there is a rounded M-like figure. The lower tips of the M-figure terminate in the star pointers of *Dhanuḥśarāgra* (α Opiuchi) and *Śravaṇa* (α Aquilae). Tentatively I call this 'Bird in the Cage' pattern. This pattern occurs in several Sanskrit astrolabes of the seventeenth century. Therefore, in this respect, as also in others, these Sanskrit astrolabes must be following a tradition which is clearly different from that of the Lahore astrolabes.

The same pattern of the rete also occurs in a massive (diameter 402 mm, thickness 13 mm, about 5 kg in weight) bilingual (Arabic-Persian and Sanskrit) astrolabe produced in the 11th regnal year of Jahangir (= 1616 AD).[34] The maker's name is

[33] For example, an astrolabe made by Ḍiyā' al-Dīn Muḥammad of the Lahore family in 1073 AH/AD 1662 has 43 stars in the rete; cf. Gingerich 1982; while another astrolabe made by the same astrolabist in 1060 AH/AD 1650 displays as many as 53 star positions; cf. Savage-Smith 1992: 22-23.

[34] This astrolabe is preserved in the Sarasvati Bhavan Library of the Sanskrit University at Varanasi.

recorded in Persian as 'a. . . w'; in the absence of diacritical points, it is indecipherable. But the name is followed by the suffix 'pandit'. As I shall argue in my forthcoming study of this astrolabe, he must be a Brahmin apprentice of a Muslim master astrolabe maker. Unfortunately we do not know who this master was; but he represents a tradition which is markedly different from that of the much more famous Lahore family of astrolabe makers who produced more than 125 astrolabes that survive. However, the majority of the surviving seventeenth century Sanskrit astrolabes and some more of other periods, follow the style of the bilingual astrolabe of 1616. Hence it is important to find its antecedents, which elude me so far.

2.9 Workmanship of the Sanskrit Astrolabes

The other notable aspect in which Sanskrit astrolabes differ from the Indo-Persian astrolabes is in the matter of workmanship. The Islamic astrolabes, whether in India or outside, were crafted by people who were both astronomers as well as artisans. The same person made the technical design and then executed it from brass sheets. In the Hindu context, the design was drawn by a Brahmin astronomer (who was usually not a good draughtsman), and the actual manufacture was done by a brass worker who may not even be literate. Therefore, the calligraphy is generally of poor quality, often with orthographic errors. The Brahmin astronomers may be good in the theoretical aspect of astronomy and mathematical computations, but there has not been a tradition among them of draughtsmanship as is evident from the almost total absence of diagrams in astronomical and mathematical manuscripts. This dichotomy between the theoretician (*śāstrin*) and the artisan (*śilpin*) is more pronounced in the case of astronomical instrument making, because this craft never developed into a hereditary tradition as other craft forms like sculpture did.

Therefore, notwithstanding the great enthusiasm shown by the Sanskrit *jyotiṣīs* towards the astrolabe, the specimens they got made were far from being precision instruments like the Islamic prototypes; at the most, they could be used as good teaching tools. Nevertheless, the testimony the *yantrarājas* offer to the intellectual exchanges that took place between the Islamic and Sanskrit traditions of astronomy and, more particularly, to the receptivity of Indian *jytotiṣīs* towards, and their appreciation of, foreign scientific notions cannot be underestimated. Among these *yantrarājas*, the one made for Maṇirāma in 1644 is an outstanding specimen.

Acknowledgements

For facilitating my study of the Sanskrit astrolabe which forms the subject of this paper and for providing the photographs published here, I am highly grateful to Dr Alison Morrisson-Low, Principal Curator, History of Science and Photography, National Museums of Scotland, Edinburgh.

Table 4: Stars named in the star map in the order of increasing longitude, read clockwise from the vernal equinox.

S. No.	Star Name as engraved on the rete	Full Form	Identification	Common Name
1[35]	*kṛtti* 5	*kartitakara*	β Cassiopeiae	Caph
2	*manu* 7	*manuṣyapārśva*	α Persei	Mirfak
3	*ro* 8	*rohiṇī*	α Tauri	Aldebaran
4	*ā* 14	*ārdrā lubdhaka*	α Canis Maioris	Sirius
5	*lu* 16	*lubdhakabandhu*	α Canis Minoris	Procyon
6	*ma* 17	*maghā*	α Leo	Regulus
7	*kāka* 19	*kākaskandhapakṣa*	γ Corv	Gienah
8	*ci* 20	*citrā*	α Virginis	Spica
9	*svā* 21	*svātī*	α Bootis	Arcturus
10	*dhanu* 26	*dhanuḥśarāgra*	μ 12 Sagittari	
11	*śrava* 28	*śravaṇa*	α Aquilae	Altair
12	*samu* 32	*samudrapakṣī*	ι Ceti	

[35] By mistake, the engraver interchanged the labels of 1 and 12.

Table 5: Geographical Data on the Plates

S.No.	City *nagaranāma*	Latitude *akṣāṃśa*	Longest day *paramadina*	Modern Name	Modern latitude N	Modern longitude E
1a	Devagiri	20;34°	33;[0]4 *gh*	Daulatabad	19;57°	75;15°
1b	Dhākā	23°	33;41 *gh*	Dhaka	23;43°	90;26°
2a	Vuḍhānapura	21°	33;21 *gh*	Burhanpur	21;17°	76;16°
2b	Khambhāici	22°	33;30 *gh*	Khambhaich (Cambay)	22:19°	72;39°
3a	Yodhapura Nepāle[']pi[36]	26;51°	34;16 *gh*	Jodhpur Kathmandu	26;18° 27;42°	73;04° 85;12°
3b	Ajamera	26;34°	34;[0]9 *gh*[37]	Ajmer	26;27°	74;42°
4a	Kurukṣetra	30°	34;48 *gh*	Kurukshetra	29;59°	76;49°
4b	Ḍhillī[38]	28;39°	34;35 *gh*	Delhi	28;38°	77;12°
5a	Āgarā	26;27°	34;14 *gh*	Agra	27;10°	78;05°
5b	Kāśī	25;36°	34;[0]5 *gh*	Varanasi	25;20°	83;00°
6a	Kāśmīra	35°	35;34 *gh*	Kashmir (Srinagar)	34;06°	74;51°
6b	Lāhora[39]	32°	35;[0]6 *gh*	Lahore	31;37°	74;26°

[36] Added by another hand; see # 1.1 above.

[37] The latitude of Ajmer (26;34°) lies between those of Agra (26;27°) and Jodhpur (26;51°); therefore the duration of the longest day at Ajmer (34;9 sic!) should also be between those of Agra and Jodhpur, namely between 34;14 *gh* and 34;16 *gh*.

[38] Christie's Catalogue 1986: 66 reads it wrongly as Dhisi.

[39] Christie's Catalogue 1986: 66 reads it wrongly as Sahore.

Table 6: Table of Declinations

The first row displays the degrees of the solar longitude, the next three rows show respectively the degrees, minutes and seconds of the sun's declination.

1	3	5	7	9[40]	11	13	15	17	19	21	23	25[41]	27	29
0	1	1	2	3	4	5	5	6	7	8	8	9	10	11
24	11	59	47	11	22	9	56	43	29	14	59	44	27	11
0	59	54	40	30	42	48	37	2	2	36	36	5	54	3

31	33	35[42]	37	39	41	43	45	47	49[43]	51	53	55	57	59
11	12	12	13	14	15	15	16	17	17	18	18	19	19	20
43	35	15	55	34	13	50	26	0	34	6	38	7	36	3
28	9	59	55	59	1	2	1	48	49	53	2	50	19	20

61	63[44]	65	67	69	71	73	75	77	79	81	83	85	87	89
20	20	21	21	21	22	22	22	22	23	23	23	23	23	23
28	52	15	36	55	13	29	44	56	7	16	23	29	32	34
57	1	35	34	54	37	42	1	35	27	32	50	18	58	47

[40]This is actually the value for 8°; the correct value for 9° is 3;35,18.

[41]Malayendu: 9;44,4.

[42]Malayendu: 12;55,59.

[43]Malayendu: 17;34,29.

[44]Malayendu: 20;53,1.

Table 7: Table of Gnomon Shadows

The first row shows the solar altitude in degrees, the second and third rows the corresponding lengths of the gnomon shadow in *aṅgulas* and their sexagesimal submultiples.

1	3	5	7	9	11	13	15	17	19	21	23	25	27	29
687	228	137	97	75	61	51	44	39	34	31	28	25	23	21
38	57	9	44	46	44		46	15	55	16	16	43	41	40

31	33	35	37	39	41	43	45	47	49	51	53	55	57	59
19	18	17	15	14	13	12	12	11	10	9	9	8	7	7
58	28	8	59	48	48	52	0	11	26	43	3	24	46	13

61	63	65	67	69	71	73	75	77	79	81	83	85	87	89
6	6	5	5	4	4	3	3	2	2	1	1	1	0	0
38	6	36	7	34	8	48	12	46	20	54	38	7	36	12

BIBLIOGRAPHY

Primary Texts

Mahendra Sūri, *Yantrarāja of Mahendra Sūri, together with the Commentary of Malayeṅdu Sūri and Yantraśiromaṇi of Viśrāma*, ed. Kṛṣṇaśaṃkara Keśavarāma Raikva, Bombay 1936.

Rāmacandra Vājapeyin, *Yantraprakāśa* MS No.975 of 1886-92, Bhandarkar Oriental Research Institute, Pune.

Viśrāma, *Yantraśiromaṇi*
in: *Yantrarāja* of *Mahendra Sūri together with the Commentary of Malayendu Sūri and Yantraśiromaṇi of Viśrāma*, ed. Kṛṣṇaśaṃkara Keśavarāma Raikva, Bombay 1936.

Yantrarājavicāra-viṃśādhyāyī
[a Sanskrit rendering of Naṣīr al-Dīn al-Ṭūsī's *Bist Bāb*], ed. Vibhūtibhūṣaṇa Bhaṭṭācārya, Varanasi 1979.

Secondary Literature

Al-Bīrūnī
1964 *Alberuni's India: An Account of the Religion, Philosophy, Literature, Geography, Chronology, Astronomy, Customs, Laws and Astrology of India about AD 1030*, tr. Edward C. Sachau, first Indian reprint: New Delhi.

Christie's Catalouge
1986 Christie's South Kensington, *Scientific Instruments, including the Joseph Peter Zallinger Collection of Scientific Instruments and associated books by George Friedrich Brander and other eminent makers*. Thursday, April 17, 1986, at 11.00 a.m. and 2.00 p.m.

Dube, Padmakara
1928 'Astrolabes in the State Library Rampur,' *The Journal of the United Provinces Historical Society*, 4.1 (October 1928) 1-11, Pl. I-IV.

Gibbs, Sharon & George Saliba.
1984 *Planispheric Astrolabes from the National Museum of American History*, City of Washington 1984 (Smithsonian Studies in History and Technology 45).

Gingerich, Owen

1982 'An Astrolabe from Lahore,' *Sky and Telescope*, 63 (1982)

358-360; reprinted in: idem, *The Great Copernicus Chase and Adventures in Astronomical History*, Cambridge, Mass. 1992, pp. 132-138.

Gunther, R. T.
1923 *Early Science in Oxford*, vol. II: Astronomy, Oxford.
1932 *Astrolabes of the World*, Oxford: reprint: Holland Press, London 1976.

Hartner, Willy
1985 'The Principles and Use of the Astrolabe' in: idem, *Oriens-Occidens*, [Vol.I], Hildesheim, pp. 287-311.

Kaye, G. R.
1921 *Astronomical Istruments in the Delhi Museum*, Calcutta.

Khareghat, M. P.
1950 *Astrolabes*, ed. Dinshaw D. Kapadia, Bombay 1950 (M. P. Khareghat Memorial Volume II).

King, David A.
1987 'Astronomical Instrumentation in the Medieval Near East' in: idem, *Islamic Astronomical Instruments*, London.
1993 'Some Medieval Astronomical Instruments and their Secrets' in: Renato G. Mazzolini (ed), *Non-Verbal Communication in Science prior to 1900,* Firenze.

Michel, Henri
1947 *Traité de l'astrolabe*, Paris.

Pingree, David
1978 'History of Mathematical Astronomy in India' in: *Dictionary of Scientific Biography,* vol. 15, ed. Charles G. Gillespie, New York 1978, pp. 533-633.
1981 *Census of the Exact Sciences in Sanskrit,* series A, vol. 4, Philadelphia.
1994 *Census of the Exact Sciences in Sanskrit,* series A, vol. 5, Philadelphia.

Plofker, Kim

2000 'The Astrolabe and Spherical Trigonometry in Medieval India,' *Journal for the History of Astronomy*, 21 (2000) 37-54.

Sarma, Sreeramula Rajeswara

1992 'Astronomical Instruments in Mughal Miniatures,' *Studien zur Indologie und Iranistik,* 16-17 (1992) 235-276; reprinted in Sarma 2008: 76-121.

1994a 'Indian Astronomical and Time-measuring Instruments: A Catalogue in Preparation,' *Indian Journal of History of Science*, 29.4 (1994) 507-528; reprinted in Sarma 2008: 19-46.

1994b 'The Lahore Family of Astrolabists and their Ouvrage,' *Studies in History of Medicine and Science,* 13.2 (1994) 205-224; reprinted in Sarma 2008: 191-222.

1996a *Astronomical Instruments in the Salar Jung Museum,* Salar Jung Museum, Hyderabad.

1996b 'The *Ṣafīḥa Zarqāliyya* in India' in: Josep Casulleras and Julio Samsó (ed), *From Baghdad to Barcelona: Studies in the Islamic Exact Sciences in Honour of Juan Vernet,* Barcelona 1996, pp. 718-735; reprinted in Sarma 2008: 223-239.

1999a '*Yantrarāja*: The Astrolabe in Sanskrit,' *Indian Journal of History of Science,* 34 (1999) 145-158; reprinted in Sarma 2008: 240-256.

1999b 'Kaṭapayādi Notation on a Sanskrit Astrolabe,' *Indian Journal of History of Science,* 34 (1999) 273-287; reprinted in Sarma 2008: 257-272.

2000 'Sulṭān, *Sūri* and the Astrolabe,' *Indian Journal of History of Science,* 35 (2000) 129-147; reprinted in Sarma 2008: 179-198.

2003 *Astronomical Instruments in the Rampur Raza Library,* Rampur Raza Library, Rampur.

2008 *The Archaic and the Exotic: Studies in the History of Indian Astronomical Instruments*, New Delhi.

Savage-Smith, Emilie

1985 *Islamicate Celestial Globes: Their History, Construction and Use*, Washington, D.C.

1992 'Celestial Mapping' in: J. B. Herley & David Woodward (ed), *Cartography in the Traditional Islamic and South Asian Societies* (*The History of Cartography*, Vol. II, 1), Chicago, pp. 12-70.

Skinner Catalogue

2002 Skinner, *Science & Technology featuring Mechanical Music,* Sale 2133, April 13, 2002, Bolton.

Torode, R. K. E.

1989 'A Mathematical System for identifying the Stars of an Astrolabe and finding its Age,' *Astrolabica N° 5: Etudes 1987-1989*, éditées par A. J. Turner, Paris 1989, pp. 53-76.

Turner, A. J.

1985 *Astrolabes, Astrolabe-related Instruments*, Rockford 1985 (The Time Museum, Catalogue of Collection, vol. I, part 1).

The Muhūrtalakṣaṇa: A Brief Text on Time of Day, Gnomonic Shadow and Divination from Java, compared to the Inscriptions and the Sanskrit Ātmajyotiṣa

Amrit Gomperts

Introduction

The subjects of mathematical astronomy, calendar reckoning, keeping the time of day, divination and astrology are interrelated and belong to the field of *jyotiṣa*. In the Old Javanese inscriptions, there are several *jyotiṣa* elements. So far, however, no *jyotiṣa* texts have come down to us from ancient Java. For the interpretation of *jyotiṣa* aspects in the inscriptions, we have had to rely on Sanskrit texts and computational methods from India. Therefore, there are still uncertainties in our interpretations of the *jyotiṣa* data in such inscriptions. I had already given up the idea that texts on *jyotiṣa* elements in the inscriptions survived from ancient Java until I came across the *Muhūrtalakṣaṇa*. The brief *jyotiṣa* text consists of Sanskrit *śloka*-s with an adaptation into Old Javanese that I translated into English (see Appendix 1).

In Old Javanese inscriptions, the smallest recorded unit of time is *muhūrta* that has a duration of 48 minutes. In the inscriptions (AD 1000-1500), the *muhūrta*-s are designated with Sanskrit-derived names which De Casparis identified,[1] drawing up the list of Sanskrit *muhūrta* names appearing in Old Javanese inscriptions.[2] They originate from the Sanskrit text *Ātmajyotiṣa* that is also known as the *Brahmakāśyapasaṃvāda*, *Atharvavedajyotiṣa* or *Ātharvaṇajyotiṣa*.[3] In the *Muhūrtalakṣaṇa*, the names of the *muhūrta* hours are identical to those in the *Ātmajyotiṣa*. Furthermore, *muhūrta* is also a divinatory concept that denotes the auspicious moment for the commencement of an activity, such as building a house, starting a journey, wearing a new garment or the exact suitable moment for performance of marriage, thread-investiture and others of the sixteen rites.[4] Therefore, the importance of the *Muhūrtalakṣaṇa* will be obvious. Did Javanese astronomers-cum-astrologers use the text for the divinatory aspects associated with diurnal time in Old Javanese inscriptions?

In the field of Sanskrit literature, many *jyotiṣa* texts have not yet been explored. The Sanskrit texts of the *Ātmajyotiṣa* and *Muhūrta-lakṣaṇa* are related but the Indian text is not an identical prototype.[5] The *Ātmajyotiṣa* itself is a rare text.[6] It deals with *jyotiṣa* related to *gṛhya*, 'domestic rituals,' and *saṃskāra*, 'purificatory ceremonies'. According to D. Pingree, it is a rather

---

[1] De Casparis 1978:54.

[2] Cf. Kane 1958: 539, n. 539.

[3] Raghavan 1966:46, 69.

[4] Panse 1957: iii.

[5] Datta (1924) and Abhyankar (1951:119, 182-195) published the Sanskrit text of the *Ātmajyotiṣa*. Poucha (1948:283-284) translated the section on *muhūrta* into French.

[6] The *Ātmajyotiṣa* uses a deviating scheme of *nakṣatra* astrology. In the text, there are occasional references to the zodiac signs but the subject is not discussed. Furthermore, the *Ātmajyotiṣa* does not deal with planetary astrology (Kane 1958:532-534, 579; Abhyankar 1951:19).

late text of unknown provenance.[7] The text borrows verses from the *Manusmṛti*. Moreover, *Ātmajyotiṣa* 13.5-11 is found in the *Reṇukārikāḥ* commentary (AD 1266) on the *Pāraskaragṛhyasūtra* which is a text on domestic rituals. Śrīpati-bhaṭṭa's *Jyotiṣaratnamāla* 7 (*c.* AD 1050) corresponds to the section on *muhūrta* in the *Ātmajyotiṣa* but the names or sequences of three *muhūrta* hours differ.[8] Cogently, the final *śloka* of the *Ātmajyotiṣa* states that it is a text on astrology in the Śaunaka tradition of the *Brahmaveda* (i.e. *Atharvaveda*) to which two titles of the *jyotiṣa* text refer, *Ātharvaṇa*, 'belonging to the tradition of the *Atharvaveda*'.

Editing the Sanskrit text of the *Muhūrtalakṣaṇa* poses similar problems to those found in other Sanskrit texts from Java or Bali. Moreover, analysis of Sanskrit, Javano-Sanskrit and Old Javanese texts on grammar and phonetics from Java and Bali reveals important deviations from and erratic interpretations of Pāṇini's description of Sanskrit. For the edition of the Javano-Sanskrit *śloka* we need a better understanding of the generative isolect. After repeated copying of vulnerable palm-leaves and because of a lack of understanding of Sanskrit phonology, the spelling of the Indian Sanskrit has drifted away from the original. In the Sanskrit text, a few *śloka*-s or even merely feet may still seem original Indian Sanskrit. In nearly all cases, a Javanese author probably recomposed *śloka*-s in Javano-Sanskrit. Moreover, the Sanskrit text of the *Muhūrtalakṣaṇa* was transmitted in a more corrupt version than its Old Javanese adaptation. Therefore, I have not edited the Sanskrit text of the *Muhūrtalakṣaṇa* but relied mainly on the Old Javanese text.

[7]Personal communication from D. Pingree (Gomperts 2001:115-116).
[8]Raghavan 1966:46.

The Legend

The first part of the Old Javanese text of the *Muhūrtalakṣaṇa* runs parallel to *Ātmajyotiṣa* 1.1-3. It relates the episode in which Kāśyapa asked Brahma for an explanation of the units and the division of diurnal time. The last three feet of *Ātmajyotiṣa* 1.1 literally recur in the first Sanskrit *śloka* of the *Muhūrtalakṣaṇa*: 'Kāśyapa asked [Brahman, the self-existent,] the teacher, the ancestor of the universe, who is comfortably seated in Brahman's universe' (see Appendix 1).

Muhūrtalakṣaṇa 1.4 lists the names of the *muhūrta*-s:

No.	Sanskrit *muhūrta* hours in the *Ātmajyotiṣa*	*Muhūrta* hours and number of times appearing in the Old Javanese inscriptions, AD 800-1500	*Muhūrta* hours in the Old Javanese text *Muhūrtalakṣaṇa*
1	*Raudra*	*Rodra* (2×)	*Rodra*
2	*Śveta*	*Śveta, Sveta* (5×)	*Śveta, Śvaita, Śvetta*
3	*Maitra*	-	*Maitra*
4	*Arabhaṭa* (or *Sārabhaṭa*?)	- -	*Arabhāṭa*
5	*Sāvitra*	*Sāvitri* (2×)	*Savitri*
6	*Vairājya,*	*Vairājya, Vairajya, Verajya, Vairojya* (6×)	*Vairājya Verrājya, Vairajya*
7	*Viśvāvasu*	*Visabasu* (1×)	*Viśvavasu*
8 .	*Abhijit*	-	*Abici(t)*
9	*Rauhiṇa*	-	*Rohaṇa*
10	*Bala*	*Bala* (1×)	*Bāla*
11	*Vijaya*	*Vijaya, Vījaya* (2×)	*Vijaya, Vijāya*
12	*Nairṛti*	*Neriti* (1×)	*Nairiti, Neriti*
13	*Vāruṇa*	*Baruṇa* (1×)	*Vāruṇa, Varūṇa*
14	*Saumya*	*Somya* (2×)	*Somya*
15	*Bhaga*	*Bago* (1×)	*Bhāga*

In the *Muhūrtalakṣaṇa*, to my current knowledge, the listed names of the *muhūrta*-s and their sequence are unique to the *Ātmajyotiṣa*.[9] Moreover, the entire collection of *muhūrta* names in Old Javanese inscriptions, included as one list of names in the table below for both day and night *muhūrta*-s, appears in

[9] Cf. Türstig 1980:149-153; Panse 1957:165-166.

the *Ātmajyotiṣa* only.[10] The divergences from the original Sanskrit names reflect common Old Javanese and Javano-Sanskrit phonology and orthography.

The names of the *muhūrta* hours appear in Old Javanese inscriptions in the period AD 840-1473. However, there are five inscriptions with dates between AD 840 and AD 933 which are later copies (see Appendix 1). The *muhūrta* hours were probably added later to their calendrical dates.[11]

Divinatory Aspects of the Muhūrta Hours

The second part of the *Muhūrtalakṣaṇa* describes the astrological aspects associated with the *muhūrta* hours. I will compare the text with the *Ātmajyotiṣa.*

The names of the *muhūrta*-s have meanings or presiding Hindu deities which refer to the astrological character of the respective hours. For example, the character of *Bhaga* expresses the hour of happiness with women and conjugal felicity. The *Ātmajyotiṣa* states that one should engage with girls and women or wives, which the text of the *Muhūrtalakṣaṇa* repeats in a different phrasing. The divinatory section would seem closer to an Indian prototype than the first part. Although the second part of the *Muhūrtalakṣaṇa* diverges both in wording and divinatory aspects from the *Ātmajyotiṣa*, for the purposes of my thesis I will outline the similarities.

In the *Ātmajyotiṣa* 2.2.b, *Śveta* is an auspicious hour for *kṛṣi*, 'ploughing, working on the land' The Sanskrit part of the *Muhūrtalakṣaṇa* quotes the Sanskrit word which, in a Javanese context, in the text is rendered correctly as 'working in a *sawah*

[10] Gomperts 2001:111.
[11] Gomperts 2001:116-117.

or wet rice-field'.

Both the *Ātmajyotiṣa* 2.8, the Sanskrit and Old Javanese texts of the *Muhūrtalakṣaṇa* agree that the *muhūrta* hour *Abhijit* is favourable for all kinds of activities. During *Abhijit*, the *Ātmajyotiṣa* relates a union of the four castes. The words of the Sanskrit foot that refer to the castes appear identically in the Sanskrit text of *Muhūrtalakṣaṇa* 2.8c. However, in the *Muhūrtalakṣaṇa*, there is no corresponding Old Javanese wording on the castes.

According to *Ātmajyotiṣa* 2.5, during the *muhūrta Sāvitra*, it is auspicious to perform a tonsure ritual and hold an *upanayana* ceremony. On the basis of the belief in reincarnation during the ceremony, a *brāhmaṇa* boy is reborn through his investiture with the sacred thread or *upanayana* by an older *brāhmaṇa*. In the Sanskrit text of the *Muhūrtalakṣaṇa*, the words 'tonsure' and *upanayana* reappear. However, the corresponding Old Javanese phrase reads: 'oneself [could] perform a religious ritual with the *dvija* or twice-born'.

There are more similarities between the two Sanskrit texts. For example, identical verbal forms in the *Ātmajyotiṣa* recur in the Sanskrit text of the *Muhūrtalakṣaṇa*.[12] The Sanskrit *hastiśikṣa* means the art of training elephants that, according to the *Muhūrtalakṣaṇa* 2.2, is favoured during the *Śveta* hour. However, in the *Ātmajyotiṣa* 4.8, it appears in a different section, on the seven weekdays (Skt. *vāra*). In fact, most of the descriptions of activities that are favourable to the *muhūrta* in the *Muhūrtalakṣaṇa* that differ from those in the *Ātmajyotiṣa* appear at other places in the latter text. Hence, it may have been possible that a Javanese author composed the Sanskrit text of the

[12] A few similar Sanskrit verbal forms are the 3rd singular optatives *kārayet*, *yojayet* and *kurvīta*.

Muhūrtalakṣaṇa on the basis of the *Ātmajyotiṣa*.

The astrological doctrine of the *Ātmajyotiṣa* and other Sanskrit texts, such as Varāhamihira's *Bṛhatsaṃhitā* (*c.* AD 550), is to determine a combination of the *jyotiṣa* cycles for a specific moment of time. The Indian *jyotiṣa* doctrine also existed in ancient Java. Moreover, in Old Javanese texts, the lexeme *pet* has the connotation 'to predict by astrological computations', as in Mpu Triguṇa's *Kṛṣṇāyana* (AD 1204) 3.1cd:[13]

> *lagna mvaṅ śubha-kala len tithi pinet de saṅ mahā-jyotiṣa* |
> *nakṣatrāhayu Rohiṇī Vijaya-sajñaniṅ muhaurtāṅĕne* ||
> 'The ascendant (Skt. *lagna*), the auspicious time and the day of the lunar month (Skt. *tithi*) but also the virtuous lunar asterism (Skt. *nakṣatra*) *Rohiṇī* and the spirit of the *muhūrta* (hour) having the name *Vijaya* [as an appropriate combination of astrological cycles] were determined (O.J. *pet*) by the great astrologer.'

The astrological characteristics fit in with Mpu Triguṇa's preceding narration. After Kṛṣṇa caused the disappearance of the king of the Yavana-s through the fiery eye of the sage Muchukuṇḍa, Kṛṣṇa enters the capital of Dvāravatī as the victorious king.

Varāhamihira, *Bṛhatsaṃhitā* 15.2, states that the *nakṣatra*, 'lunar asterism', *Rohiṇī* presides over kings.[14] Hence, in the *Kṛṣṇāyana*, the lunar asterism emphasizes Kṛṣṇa's acquired kingship over the city of the Yavana-s after the defeat of their king. In agreement with *Muhūrtalakṣaṇa* 2.11, the *muhūrta* of *Vijaya* underlines Kṛṣṇa's hour of victory over the king of the Yavana-s.

[13]Santoso 1986:65.
[14]Bhat 1992, 1:185.

Mpu Triguna's statement that a combination of *lagna*, 'ascendant', and *muhūrta* was computed (O.J *pet*) will provide the basis for the rest of this article.

Gnomonic Shadow

The end of the first section of the *Muhūrtalakṣaṇa* prescribes the shadow length of a gnomon and the corresponding *muhūrta* hours. Although the wording in the Sanskrit *śloka* in the *Muhūrtalakṣaṇa* 1.5 differs from *Ātmajyotiṣa* 1.6-1.12, the passages are related. The measures of shadow length are identical.

The Sanskrit term for gnomon is *śaṅku* that, in connection with time, appears in a few other Old Javanese texts.[15] In the *Muhūrtalakṣaṇa*, however, there is neither a Sanskrit nor an Old Javanese term for gnomon. For the Sanskrit unit of length *aṅgula*, 'digit', the text employs the Old Javanese term *tampak*, 'trace' Moreover, the *Muhūrtalakṣaṇa* omits an essential astronomical detail, the height of the gnomon. According to the *Ātmajyotiṣa* 1.5ab, the height of the gnomon is 12 *aṅgula*-s which is the standard Indian gnomon in *jyotiṣa* texts. The scheme of shadow lengths is crude and does not involve spherical trigonometry.

In both the *Ātmajyotiṣa* and the *Muhūrtalakṣaṇa*, the cycle of the fifteen *muhūrta* hours starts at sunrise. It refers to the *audayika* or sunrise system in Indian astronomy which was adopted in ancient Java. Both the *Ātmajyotiṣa* and the *Muhūrtalakṣaṇa* do not take into account the varying declination of the sun. However, al-Bīrūnī's account in Arabic, *India* (AD 1030-1031), provides an explanation with almost identical shadow lengths.[16] He states that the length of the shadows at noon should be added to the tabulated shadow lengths. In such a way, gnomonic shadow

[15] Cf. Zoetmulder 1982, 2:1671.

[16] Sachau 1910, 1:338-342.

Muhūrta hour before noon	*Muhūrta* hour after noon	*Al-Bīrūnī*, AD 1030/1031 shadow lengths (in digits)	*Muhūrtalakṣaṇa* & *Ātmajyotiṣa* shadow lengths (in digits)
1.	15.	noon shadow length + 96	96
2.	14.	noon shadow length + 60	60
3.	13.	noon shadow length + 12	12
4.	12.	noon shadow length + 6	6
5.	11.	noon shadow length + 5	5
6.	10.	noon shadow length + 3	4
7.	9.	noon shadow length + 2	3
8.		noon shadow length	noon shadow length

could provide a scheme for the determination of *muhūrta* hours in both India and Java. We will explore this in greater detail later.

The *Muhūrtalakṣaṇa* omits the statement in *Ātmajyotiṣa* (1.1. 11) that the cycle of the fifteen *muhūrta*-s is repeated after sunset. The night *muhurta*-s, therefore, could not have been determined by shadow lengths. In agreement with Mpu Triguṇa's testimony, they were computed. Moreover, al-Bīrūnī's comment shows that there were two views on the lengths of *muhūrta* hours. First, gnomonic shadow causes *muhūrta* hours of varying lengths, starting and ending times. We can compute them with astronomical software.[17] Second, according to Indian astronomy in general

[17]The formula for the sun's altitude θ above the horizon is: $\theta = ATAN$ $\{12/[s + ABS(n)]$. $ABS(n)$ is the absolute value of the noon shadow length n. It is determined from the relation: $n = 12/[TAN(90° + \varphi - \delta)]$. A mean geographical latitude and longitude of the finding places of the inscriptions has been taken near the city of Jombang in East Java: φ = S 7°.5, E 112°.25. For the converted dates, their corresponding declinations δ, their respective shadow lengths s corresponding to their *muhūrta* and noon shadow lengths n

and the Old Javanese text *Brahmāṇḍapurāṇa* (late tenth century AD), the unit of *muhūrta* is an hour with a fixed length of 00^h 48^m (cf. Zoetmulder 1982, 2:1154). Therefore, we also could adopt a mean *muhūrta* time:

1. *Raudra* (06^h00^m - 06^h48^m), 2. *Śveta* (06^h48^m - 07^h36^m), ... 15. *Bhaga* (17^h12^m - 18^h00^m);

Moreover, in the inscriptions, daytime and nocturnal *muhūrta*-s have identical names but they are not differentiated:

1. *Raudra* (18^h00^m - 18^h48^m), 2. *Śveta* (18^h48^m - 19^h36^m), ... 15. *Bhaga* (05^h12^m - 06^h00^m).

Therefore, we need an additional *jyotiṣa* cycle, the *lagna* that I will discuss in the next section.

Lagna and Mathematical Astronomy

The concept of *lagna* or ascendant also is a measure of diurnal time. Therefore, in agreement with Mpu Triguṇa's testimony, we can use *lagna* to identify a daytime or a nocturnal *muhūrta*. For the computation of the times of *lagna*, we have to use methods from *siddhānta* texts.

The Sanskrit term *lagna* appears in only three inscriptions from Java: the Stone of Sañjaya from Canggal (Central Java, AD 732), the Stone of Dinoyo (East Java, AD 760), and the Copper Plate of Těrěp I (East Java, AD 1032). Between AD 760 and AD 1032, there are no references to *lagna* in inscriptions that are not later copies.[18] Hence, the concept of *lagna* was reintroduced in

lead to a time of day for the sun's altitude θ that is computed with the Dialist's Companion (see http://sundials.org/publications/dcomp/dcomp.htm).

[18]Cf. Damais 1955; Gomperts 2001:116-117.

the same inscription as the *muhūrta* appeared for the first time in an original inscription from East Java in AD 1032.

The inscription of Tĕrĕp I literally states that *Mṛcchika-rāśi lagna*, 'the ascendant has the zodiac sign Scorpio'. In all other inscriptions after AD 1032, the term *rāśi* appears without the term *lagna*. The term *rāśi* does not appear in connection to other *jyotiṣa* cycles in the inscriptions.[19] From the syntax of the *jyotiṣa* elements in the inscriptions, *rāśi* would implicitly refer to the concept of *lagna* which also seems likely from the statistical analysis below.

The computation of *lagna* is based upon Indian mathematical astronomy as expounded in Sanskrit *siddhānta* and *karaṇa* texts. No such texts have come down to us from Java or Bali.

According to Eade and Gislén,[20] Indo-Javanese mathematical astronomy originates from Lāṭadeva's lost text *Sūryasiddhānta* ('SurS') as partly preserved in Varāhamihira's *Pañcasiddhāntikā*.[21] However, the latter actually is a *karaṇa* text because it employs the local epoch 21 March 505. Moreover, in his *Nāgarakṛtāgama* or *Deśavarṇana* (AD 1365) 43.1bc, the Old Javanese poet Prapañca explicitly refers to the beginning of the Kaliyuga with the numerical chronogram of 3179 years before the Śaka era.[22] Its first reference appears in Brahmagupta's *Brahmasphuṭasiddhanta* 1.26-27 (AD 628) and Bhāskara I's *Laghubhaskarıya* 1.4.[23] For the beginning of the Kaliyuga, all later Sanskrit *siddhanta* texts employ the number of 3179 years before the Śaka era. Hence, it seems likely that the Indo-Javanese tradition of mathematical astronomy relied upon

[19] Cf. Eade and Gislén 2000:203-220.
[20] Eade and Gislén 2000:1-3.
[21] Neugebauer and Pingree 1970-1971; cf. Billard 1971.
[22] Robson 1995:55, 120-121.
[23] Sharma 1966:295, 296.

unidentified Indian *siddhānta* texts dating from the period AD 628-1032. In this article, for practical reasons, I have used Dr. Michio Yano's software for the more recent Saura tradition of the *Sūryasiddhānta*.[24]

The unequal durations are an important aspect of *lagna*. They are caused by the unequal spacings of the Indian and originally Greek parameters for angular separation between the zodiac signs in the plane of the ecliptic that vary between 27.8 and 32.3 arc degrees. They are called right ascensional differences (Skt. *caradala*, *carakhaṇḍa*). In the geographical latitude of Java (*c.* 7°5′ S), for example, the times of zodiac signs in the ascendant vary between $01^h\ 45^m$ and $02^h\ 10^m$. Moreover, from the information given by the former Dutch civil administrator of Grěsik in 1820-1822, A. D. Cornets de Groot Sr., we know that the Indo-Javanese astronomers used the Indian parameters for right ascensional differences.

Dilating on the discussion of the calendar in the *Grěsik Records*, Cornets de Groot describes the Indo-Javanese and Islamic Javanese calendars. Discussing the Indo-Javanese solar months and their calendar, he states that they were determined by a gnomon

[24]In 1997, Dr. Michio Yano of Sangyo Kyoto University developed the computer programme PANCANG2. His programme is based on the *Sūryasiddhānta* that was composed by an anonymous author of the Saura tradition of Indian mathematical astronomy in *c.* AD 800 and Raṅganātha's commentary of AD 1603 (tr. Burgess 1860). The text became enormously popular in south and northeast India after c. AD 1200 (Pingree 1981:23-24). We do not know whether or not the Saura tradition of the *Sūryasiddhānta* reached Java. However, within the context of this article, another *siddhānta* text would not lead to fundamentally different results. PANCANG2 calculates with the correct Indian parameters for right ascensional differences, true sunrise and a southern hemispherical latitude (cf. Eade and Gislén 2000:203). Details of the MS-DOS software can be found in Gomperts (2001:97, n.6). The accuracy of starting and ending times of the *lagna* is in order of 10^m ($\varphi = -7^\circ.5$ for Java, without *bīja*).

and he lists their respective durations that actually represent the numbers of the Indian right ascensional differences.[25]

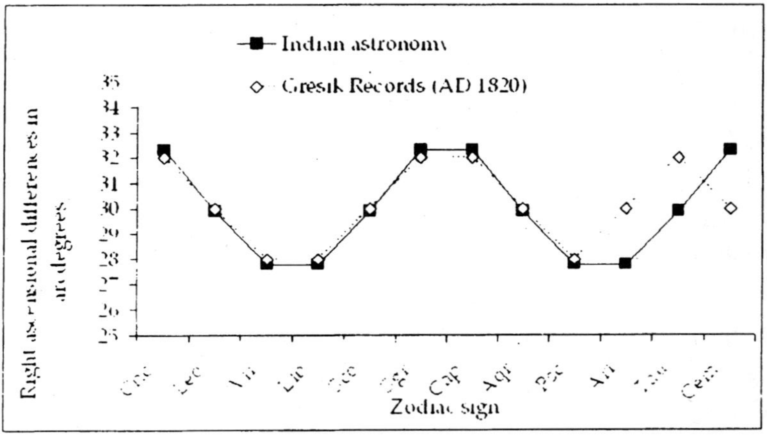

In Indian mathematical astronomy, solar shadow lengths and *lagna* are conceptually interwoven because they both concern computations that involve gnomonic shadow. However, the In-

[25]According to the *Grēsik Records* (ms. KITLV H 379, p. 197) for the Indian-derived gnomon, the sequence of the lengths of the solar months is (from the first to the twelfth month respectively): 32, 30, 28, 28, 30, 32, 32, 30, 28, 30, 32 and 30 days (see also Cornets de Groot 1852:347-348). The sequence and the pattern of the first nine numbers represent the rounded integer values of the right ascensional differences of the zodiac signs in Indian astronomy (from Cancer to Gemini): 32.3, 29.9, 27.8, 27.8, 29.9, 32.3, 32.3, 29.9, 27.8, 27.8, 29.9 and 32.3 arcdegrees (e.g. *Pañcasiddhāntikā* 4.30, see Neugebauer and Pingree 1971, 2:11, 16). Although the Grēsik scheme for the solar months is not correct, the right ascensional differences were used to determine the lengths of the Indian solar months in combination with a gnomon. The total sum of the Grēsik parameters is 362 which shows that the last three ascensional differences (Aries to Gemini) were modified because the total sum has to be equal to 360 arcdegrees.

dian algorithms have actually been formulated from the point of view of an observer on the equator or in the northern hemisphere. For the length of the respective diurnal times of the twelve zodiac signs, an astronomer initially had to determine the geographical latitude of Java in the Southern hemisphere (*c.* 7°5′ S) with an accurate gnomon and subsequently compute *lagna*. Thus, by analogy to Indian algorithms (cf. Neugebauer and Pingree 1971, 2:16-17, 23-24), the Indo-Javanese astronomers would have developed a mathematical relation between longitude of *lagna* (λ_{lagna}), longitude of the sun (λ_{sun}) and a function (f) of the shadow lengths at any time (s) and at noon (n):

$$\boxed{\lambda_{lagna} = \lambda_{sun} + f(s;n)}$$

This is the unknown mathematical relation that would have been unique to the geographical latitude of Java and Indo-Javanese astronomy.

Analysis of Time of Day in 21 Inscriptions from Java, AD 1000-1500

In this section, I will argue that *lagna* reflects time of day more correctly in the inscriptions than does *muhurta*. *Lagna* basically coincided with the rhythm of daily life in Java.

Only a few inscriptions mention both *lagna* and *muhūrta*. Cogently, only those inscriptions that permit consistent conversion of calendrical and *jyotiṣa* cycles into an AD date can be used for analysis.[26] The daylight or nocturnal *muhūrta* that is closest in time to *lagna* is taken (see Appendix 2). The analysis is based on the midpoints of the *lagna* and those of the mean *muhūrta* times.

For the analysis of 24-hour time data, circular statistics is

[26] Cf. Damais 1955; Eade and Gislén 2000.

particularly helpful in graphical presentation of daily activity cycles. Time histograms show the peak and the silent moments around the clock which is shown in the next graph.

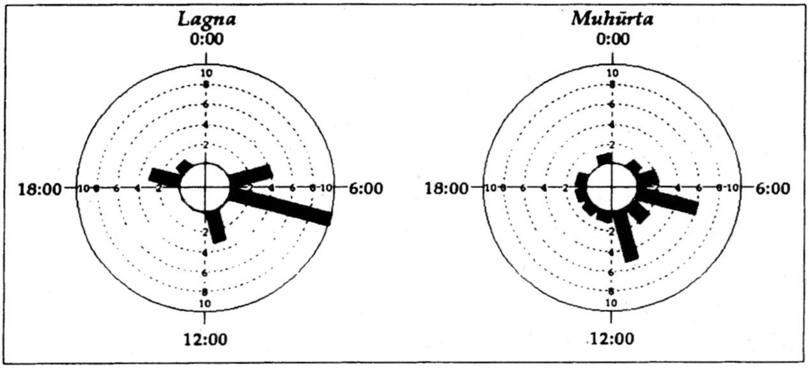

Although the two histograms are not identical graphically, the times of the *lagna* and those of the *muhūrta* seem identical.[27]

[27] Let L and M be the midpoints of the starting and ending moments of the *lagna* and mean *muhūrta* times respectively. In case of large sample statistics, we would expect average differences $(L - M) \approx 00^m$ with a small error. For $n = 21$ inscriptions in Appendix 2, the circular statistics are (Fisher 1993:31, 35-36, 72-73, 75-79):

circular mean $(L - M)$ and its 95% confidence interval	-00^h45^m	-02^h02^m $+00^h32^m$
circular median $(L - M)$ and its 95% confidence interval	-00^h04^m	-03^h11^m $+01^h30^m$

Eade and Gislén (*sic.* 2000:12, 204-205, n. 11) suggest a difference in geographical longitude (Skt. *deśāntara*) between sidereal time at Ujjayinī (E 75°) and a 'notional' Javanese time (E 110°) which, from the data in Appendix 2, should emerge as $(L - M) \approx -02^h20^m$. However, the 95% confidence intervals are large. Errors may have occurred in the original *jyotiṣa* data or in my conversions. Therefore, the circular median is a more suitable estimator than is the circular mean. Moreover, for *muhūrta* 5. *Savitri* and 6. *Vairājya*, there are systematic differences: $-3^h09^m \leq (L - M) \leq -4^h46^m$. Hence, we only can conclude that the times of *lagna* and those of *muhūrta* roughly tend to be the same.

From the two histograms, we see that both the majority of times of the *lagna* and *muhūrta* took place just from before sunset until noon. In both histograms, there is a dominant peak just after sunrise, around 07^h

The *muhūrta*-s have additional peaks around 9^h-11^h. In a third of the total of 21 inscriptions, this is caused entirely by the two *muhūrta*-s 5 and 6 which are all systematically 3^h-5^h later than the times of their corresponding *lagna*-s within a short period AD 1269-1330. Furthermore, from Appendix 2, we can conclude that al-Bīrūnī's scheme for gnomonic *muhūrta* times could be operated in Java because they largely fall within the mean *muhūrta* times. However, the systematic errors in *muhūrta*-s 5 and 6 cannot be ascribed to gnomonic shadow. Both in the *Ātmajyotiṣa* 1.25-6 and the *Muhūrtalakṣaṇa* 2.5-6, the two *muhūrta*-s, 5. *Savitri* and 6. *Vairājya*, are particularly auspicious and very appropriate in the context of issuing charters as related in the inscriptions (cf. Appendix 1). It could perhaps indicate that the divinatory aspects of the *muhūrta* hours were more important than their computed sense of time.

Hence, in five distinctive peaks in the histogram, the *lagna*-s emerge, but the *muhūrta*-s fluctuate around the entire 24-hour clock. Therefore, *lagna* seems to be a better estimator of time of day in the inscriptions than *muhūrta*.

Conclusion

I will correct some of my earlier views.[28] The text of the *Muhūrtalakṣaṇa* fills an important gap in our understanding of *jyotiṣa* in Java. We can be quite certain that the text was used by Javanese calendar-makers-cum-astrologers for the inscriptions

[28]Gomperts 2001.

in the period AD 1000-1500. I previously stated that they afterwards added the *muhūrta* hours in the later copies of Old Javanese inscriptions AD 840–933. In the light of the text of the *Muhūrtalakṣaṇa*, the implicit references to it in Old Javanese inscriptions and its relation to the early medieval Sanskrit text *Ātmajyotiṣa*, the chronology remains the same. A Javanese author probably composed the Sanskrit text of the *Muhūrtalakṣaṇa* in East Java at the end of the tenth century or the beginning of the eleventh century AD.[29] However, it is possible that the Sanskrit *ślokas* in *Muhūrtalakṣaṇa* 1.4 were composed at a later date. The final redaction of the Old Javanese adaptation perhaps might date from the fourteenth-sixteenth centuries AD.

In my previous publication, I concluded that there were errors in the *lagna*-s because their times did not correspond to the *muhūrta*-s in the inscriptions.[30] The gnomonic scheme in the *Ātmajyotiṣa* seemed to me too crude for Java. The text of the *Muhūrtalakṣaṇa* and al-Bīrūnī's explanation shows that the gnomon could be operated in Java. Therefore, my conclusion is that there are computational errors in the *muhūrta*, not in *lagna*. Moreover, the divinatory function of the *Muhūrtalakṣaṇa* must have been important.

From Appendix 2, we can conclude that the *lagna*-s fall within time frames of 4^h-12^h and 17^h-21^h. All this reflects the active moments of the daily rhythm of life in ancient Java as it still exists in non-electrified and non-air conditioned villages in the island. Moreover, 80 per cent of the 21 inscriptions refer to the time between just before sunrise and noon.

[29]Gomperts 2001:116-117.
[30]Gomperts 2001.

Appendix 1: Text and Translation of the Muhūrtalakṣaṇa

Two manuscripts of the *Muhūrtalakṣaṇa* were available to me, a palm-leaf *lontar* from the Lombok Collection (ms. LOr 5233, p. 1, front side to p. 4, front side) and a romanized text from Bali (ms. LOr 10058) that lacks diacritical details. In the Lombok *lontar* (ms. LOr 5233, p. 4, rear side to p. 6, front side), the Old Javanese texts of *Muhūrtalakṣaṇa* 1.5 and 2.1-15 are integrated per *muhūrta* hour and repeated in almost identical wording. Therefore, this part has been omitted. However, variant readings appear in the edition below. Although, in the footnotes I have made a few comments, I have not edited the Javano-Sanskrit text.

I have attempted to edit and translate the Old Javanese text as closely as possible to its original punctuation. In the unedited Sanskrit text, the original punctuation reappears as metrical marks for the *śloka* metre. For the transcription of Old Javanese, Sanskrit orthography has been adopted. Sanskrit *ṅ* and *v* denote the Javanese *ng* and *w* respectively. The final *-ḥ* has been reserved for Sanskrit which is rendered as *-h* for Old Javanese words. The distinction between *ñ* and *ny* is according to its original orthography.

I have used the following conventions:

(...)	comment
[...]	addition
...	correction
O.J	Old Javanese
Skt.	Sanskrit

O.J. *nihan tiṅkahiṅ muhūrtta mvaṅ lakṣananya, kavruhanā tkap saṅ mahāpuruṣa. ndya ta nihan, vyaktinya. pitāmaha para deva* ...[31]

'The arrangement of the *muhūrta* and their characteristics ought to be known according to the great man. They are as follows... . The ancestor of all gods... .'

1.1. Skt. .... | *guru lokapitāmahaṃ* | *brahmaloke sukasaṇaḥ* | *kasyapaḥ pariprcchanti* ||[32]

O.J. *saṅ hyaṅ brahma sira turun iṅ loka; sira maṅaran pitamaha; pinarĕk sira de*[33] *bhagavān kasyapa; sira tumakvan deyaniṅ muhūrtta ri bhaṭāra brahma.*

'Lord Brahma descended from heaven. He was called the ancestor. He was approached by the Reverend Kāśyapa. He asked Lord Brahma to explain the *muhūrta*.'

1.2. Skt. *mahaṅke muhūrttasya manyataḥ ity ettet pracyantye* |

nāmaḥ svahā kasyapasya | *mahātmane nāmaḥ svahā* ||[34]

O.J. *saṅ hyaṅ brahma sira carittan, vilaṅiṅ muhūrtta. 'nimittanira' bhagavān kasyapa tumanya ri*[35] *bhaṭāra brahma.*

'Lord Brahma told about the division [of diurnal time] into *muhūrta*-s. The Reverend Kāśyapa asked Lord Brahma: 'What is the reason for it'?'

---

[31]LOr 5233: *pitāmaha māra deva.* LOr 10058: *pitamaha para deva.* The text seems corrupt here. In the manuscripts, it is the first foot of the Sanskrit *śloka* (1.1.a). However, it does not make sense as Sanskrit.

[32]LOr 10058:...*parimrcyanti* ||.
The three last feet are identical to Skt. *Ātmajyotiṣa* 1.1.b-d:
atha brahmaṇaṃ svayaṃbhuṃ | *guruṃ lokapitamahaṃ* | *brahmaloke sukhāsīnaṃ* | *kāśyapaḥ pariprcchati* ||.

[33]LOr 10058: *pinarĕk denira*

[34]LOr 10058:*ṅke muhurta samakyatah* | *iti yetat pracyante namah* | *kasyapasya mahatmane nama svaha* ||.

[35]LOr 10058: *tumanya ya ri.*

1.3. Skt. *uvāccha bhaṭara brahmaṁ |saṅśayaṁ samuda-krttaṁ manicchа pradaraktakam |muhūrttanam banamattaḥ ||*[36]

O.J. *maṅucap saṅ hyaṅ brahma: 'makahetu kahilaṅaniṅ saṅśaya, agave kahlĕtaniṅ*[37] *muhūrtta, mvaṅ namanya'.*

'Lord Brahma answered: 'In order to cause the disappearance of unfavourable [moments, diurnal time] is divided into different *muhūrta*-s with their [respective] names'.'

1.4. Skt. *rodra śvettañ ca maitrañ ca|arabhā<ṭ>añ ca savitri||*

verājya viśvavasuñ ca|abici-rohaṇa-smṛtaḥ||
bolañ ca vijayās thaṭā| nairiti-varuṇa-smṛtaḥ||
somyañ ca tata bhāgañ ca| muhūrtta-parikirttitaḥ||[38]

O.J. *nihan pratekaniṅ namānya: rodra, ṣvaitta, maitra, arabā <ṭ>a, savitri, vairājya, viśvavasu, abici, rohaṇa. bāla, vijaya, nairiti, vāruṇa, somya, bhāga. yeki inajarakna namaniṅ muhūrtta. nihan deniṅ amalakṣaṇākĕn udayādhi makanimitta, tinampakan ikaṅ chāya, paścimāmulat.*[39]

'The sequence of their names is: *Rodra, Śvaitta, Maitra, Arabāṭa, Savitri, Vairājya, Viśvavasu, Abici, Rohaṇa, Bāla, Vi-*

---

[36]LOr 10058: ... *paranica pradaraktam|....*

[37]LOr 10058: *agave hĕlĕtaniṅ.*

[38]LOr 10058: ... *arabavas... visvasus... abyaci rovana... balas ca somyas... bagas...* . In the two Skt. *Śloka*-s, the co-ordinative particle *ca* appears seven times. Moreover, Skt. *smṛta* is repeated in the next line. It would point to the style of someone who was not proficient in composing Sanskrit in the *śloka* metre. Therefore, I would qualify the fragment as Javano-Sanskrit.

[39]LOr 5233: *arabäva.* LOr 10058: *nihan pratekanya: rodra... arabava... visvava... rovana... inajarakĕn udayanadi... tinampakaṅ ikaṅ taya... mula.* Both the Sankrit and the Old Javanese texts of the *Muhūrtalakṣana* 1.4 omit the astronomical statement that the gnomon has a height of twelve digits. Cf. Skt. *Ātmajyotiṣa* 1.5.cd: *dvadaśaṅgulaṃ utsedhaṃ|tasya chaya pramāṇataḥ||*. 'The height [of the gnomon] is twelve digits. Of which, according to the measure, there are shadows.'

jaya, *Nairiti*, *Vāruṇa*, *Somya* and *Bhāga*. These are the names of the *muhūrta*-s that ought to be known. They are to be characterized by [observing] the rising of the Sun and so forth. The digits of its shadow [should] be traced [which, at sunrise,] appears westwards.'

1.5. Skt. *ṣalavatya tulāñ chāye|muhūrtta rodram ucyatte||*
ṣaṣṭi śvetta samūkyatte|metra vai dvādaśaṅgulaḥ||
ṣadbhiḥ arabhā<ṭ>a proktaḥ| savitri tata pañcabhiḥ||
verājya catur rojyaiyaḥ| triniḥ viśvavaśus thatha||
abhici ceva madhyahnai| yatra saya praṇaśyatiḥ||
pradhmaka tuṅgulañ chāyeḥ| muhūrtta rohaṇa smṛtaḥ||
catūrbhis tu valoñ choyaḥ| pañcabhi vījayas thatha|
ṣadbhis tya neritij cheyaḥ| varūṇa-dvadaśaṅgulaḥ||
ṣaṣti somya samakyatiḥ| bhāga ṣaṇavatis chaye||[40]

O.J. *nihan paḍarttanya, yyesūk vijil sūryya mārĕp aṅulvan.*[41] *yan 96 tampak pañjaṅiṅ chāya, rodra muhūrtta ṅa. yan 60 tampak, śvetta-muhūrtta ṅa. yan 12 tampak, maitra-muhūrtta ṅa. yan 60 tampak, arabhā<t>a-muhūrtta ṅa. yan 5 tampak, savitri-muhūrtta ṅa. yan 4 tampak, verājya-muhūrtta ṅa. yan; 3 tampak, viśvavasu-muhūrtta ṅa. yan madhyāhna, abici-muhūrtta.*

---

[40] LOr 10058: *sabih arabava...yatra yaya pranasyataḥ|| pradmuka... sanavati sthita||*.
Cf. Skt. *Ātmajyotiṣa* 1.6-1.10:
navatiṣataṃgulāṃś caiva| pratīcīṃ tāṃ prakālayet| purastāt sandhivelāyāṃ| muhūrto raudra ucyate||
śvetaḥ ṣaṣṭiḥ samākhyāto| maitro vai dvādaśāṅgulaḥ| ṣaṭsu sārabhaṭo jñeyaḥ| sāvitraḥ pañcasu smṛtaḥ||
caturṣu caivaṃ vairājas| triṣu viśvāvasus tathā| madhyāhne abhijin nāma| yasmiñ chaya pratiṣṭhita||
prācīṃ vai gāminīṃ chāyāṃ| rauhiṇas triṣu vartate| balaś caturṣu vikhyāto| vijayaḥ pañcasu smṛtaḥ||
nairṛtas tu ṣaḍaṅgulyo| varuṇo dvadaśaṅgulaḥ| saumyaḥ ṣaṣṭiḥ samakhyato| bhagas tu paramas tathā||.

[41] LOr 10058: line is missing.

yan vantĕn kulvan ikaṅ sūryya, chāya mahyūn maṅetan deniṅ anampaki vavayaṅan.[42] *yan pramūkha luhuriṅ sūryya, abici-muhūrtta ṅa. yan 3 tampak, iki luhuriṅ sūryya, rohana-muhurtta ṅa. yan 4 tampak, bāla-muhūrtta ṅa. yan 5 tampak, vijaya-muhūrtta ṅa. yan 6 tampak, nairiti-muhūrtta ṅa. yan 12 tampak, varūṇa-muhūrtta ṅa. yan 60 tampak, somya-muhūrtta ṅa. yan 96 tampak, bhāga-muhūrtta ṅa.*[43]

'The explanation is that the Sun rises [in the east] and heads westwards. For 96 digits of shadow length, the *muhūrta* is *Rodra.* For 60 digits, the *muhūrta* is *Śvetta.* For 12 digits, the *muhūrta is Maitra.* For 6 digits, the *muhūrta* is *Arabāṭa.* For 5 digits, the *muhūrta* is *Savitri.* For 4 digits, the *muhūrta* is *Verājya.* For 3 digits, the *muhūrta* is *Viśvavasu.* At noon, the *muhūrta* is *Abici.* When the Sun is in the west, [its] shadow proceeds eastwards as observed by tracing the digits of the shadow [of the gnomon]. When the Sun culminates, the *muhūrta* is *Abici.* For 3 digits of the Sun's altitude, *Rohaṇa* is the *muhūrta.* For 4 digits, the *muhūrta* is *Bāla.* For 5 digits, the *muhūrta* is *Vijaya.* For 6 digits, the *muhūrta* is *Nairiti.* For 12 digits, the *muhūrta* is *Varūṇa.* For 60 digits, the *muhūrta* is *Somya.* For 96 digits, the *muhūrta* is *Bhaga.*'

O.J. *kunaṅ lakṣaṇanya nihan.*
The [divinatory] characteristics [of the *muhūrta*-s] are as follows:'

2.1. Skt. *rodra rodrani kārmmaṇām̆ | ṛreṣasu parodānām̆ ||*
śatru pakṣa vinaṣāṇām̆ | tasmi kālo prajayatte || [44]

O.J. *kunaṅ svakāryya hāri*[45] *kālaniṅ rodra-muhūrtta, ksana*

[42]LOr 10058: *mahyun maṅetan deniṅ anampak.*

[43]The *Muhūrtalakṣaṇa* omits to say that the cycle of the 15 *muhūrta* hours were also used at night, from sunset until sunrise (cf. *Ātmajyotiṣa* 1.1.11).

[44]LOR 10058: ... *karamani | rese rasa... | satya... pujayetva |.*

[45]Note that, in the O.J. text of the *Muhūrtalakṣaṇa*, the topic-comment

aglĕṅ,[46] *andona musuh, kājarnya, agave kahilaṅaniṅ musuh.*

'During the time of the *muhūrta* hour *Rodra*, one's own actions are favourable for moments of anger. One can march against enemies. It should be said that [one could] cause the disappearance of enemies.'

2.2. Skt. *aṣṭi-śikṣaśva-śikṣañ ca| vidya-sastra samudvitĕn|*
śvaita bhāśamayet dhaṇaṁ| tabhāyanantada kṛṣi|| [47]

O.J. *kunaṅ svakāryya*[48] *hari kālaniṅ śveta-muhūrta, aṣṭi-śikṣa, aśva-śikṣa, kabhyāṣahaniṅ*[49] *vidyasastra, kahuṅguhaniṅ deva-sthana, mintara laku-laku, mitan asasavah.*[50]

---

structure with O.J. particle *ta* is absent. Instead, the O.J. *ari*, *arih*, *hari* and *harih* may have been used as an emphatic particle as appearing in the O.J. Javanese texts *Kiduṅ Harṣa-Vijaya, Tantri Kāmandaka, Koravāśrama, Tantu Paṅgĕlaran, Tantri Dĕmuṅ* and *Tantri Kaḍiri*. All these texts date from the 14th-16th centuries AD. Moreover, in the *Kiduṅ Harṣa-Vijaya*, the O.J. *ari* could also be a term of address (Zoetmulder 1982, 1:126, *ari* IV, *arih* I). In the context of the *Muhūrtalakṣaṇa*, it also would make sense because the O.J. *kārya* often has the meaning of the Skt. future passive participle 'to be made, done, practised, performed, practicable, feasible or proper to be done'. The frequent use of the O.J. areal suffix *-a* further emphasizes a notion of optionality. Furthermore, Zoetmulder (1982, 1:594-595, *harih*) translates O.J. *harih, arih, hari* and *ari* as 'to soothe' where, in my view, Mardiwarsito's (1990:75, 212) additional interpretation in Modern Indonesian also is appropriate: 'menyenangkan hati, menghibur'. Throughout the O.J. text of the *Muhūrtalakṣaṇa*, therefore, I have translated the constituent O.J. *kunang svakārya hāri...* as 'one's own actions are favourable for, when, towards...'.

[46]LOr 5233: *saka glĕṅ* synonymously is 'at a time of anger'. Is Skt. *kṣaṇa*→ O.J. *ksana* used a synonym for *muhūrta* (cf. Zoetlmulder 1982 , 1:1154, *muhūrta*)? Although O.J. *ksana* as Skt. *kṣaṇa*, 'killing', is not in the corresponding Sanskrit text, could O.J. *ksana agĕlĕṅ* refer to Skt. *kṣaṇa-dīpta*, 'blasted by injury/destruction', that in Varāhamihira's *Bṛhatsaṃhitā* 86.15 is an omen at a *muhurta* that belongs to a dreadful and fierce *nakṣatra*, 'lunar asterism' (cf. Bhat 1993, 2:763)?

[47]LOr 10058: ... *samudvintĕn| sveta nasapayet sanam| tadayanan...* .

[48]LOr 5233: *karyya*. LOr 10058: *svakarya*.

[49]LOr 10058: *kabyasaniṅ*.

[50]LOr 5233: *mitan aśaśavah*. LOr: 10058: *mintara sasavah*. Skt. *kṛṣi*,

'During the time of the *muhūrta* hour *Śveta*, one's actions are favourable for training elephants, training horses, studying texts on knowledge, [making] a place for the gods, going away on a trip, and taking leave to work in wet rice-fields.

2.3. Skt. *maitre maitreni kuryyāṇām̆ | maṅgalan ipa karāyet | akārāviś vidaś ca | bhāndapañ ca dhaṇaniś ca ||*[51]

O.J. *kunaṅ svakāryya hāri kālaniṅ maitra-muhūrtta, akāryya amitra,*[52] *śubha-divaśa-kāryya,*[53] *kavilaṅaniṅ bhuṣana, gavehan-iṅ dhaṇa.*

'During the time of the *muhūrta* hour *Maitra*, one's own actions are favourable for matters relating to [the deity] Mitra (or: friends), activities for auspicious days, counting one's pieces of jewellery and making donations.'

2.4. Skt. *areñ ca rehateśrame | deśaṅ ca bhaharaniś ca | sāndi-medañ ca katavyam̆ | sareṣañ ca hire dhanam̆ ||*[54]

O.J. *kunaṅ svakāryya hāri kālaniṅ arabā<ṭ>a-muhūrtta,*[55] *kraya-vikraya, ameta uṅgvan, akāryya asāndi-bheddha, mvaṅ upaya, aṅucapa dhaṇa.*

'ploughing, cultivation of the land', also appears in *Ātmajyotiṣa* 2.2.b. It is synonymous to O.J. *sasavah*, 'to work in wet rice-fields'.

[51]LOr 10058: ... *kuryani* | ... *akaras ca vidas ca* | *ninda vacanananis ca* ||.

[52]LOr 10058: *akarya amitra* is missing.

[53]Such Skt. → O.J. *śubha-divasa-kārya*, 'activities for auspicious days', apparently were Skt. *maṅgala*, 'benedictive ceremonies'. In another bilingual Sanskrit-Old Javanese text, the *jyotiṣa* aspects of auspicious days are expounded: *iti śubha-vāra-divaśa-vidya-śāstra*, 'this is a text on the knowledge of auspicious days [of the seven-day week]'. The text appears on the three final pages of Lombok *lontar* ms. LOr 5233, p. 6, back side until p. 7, back side.

[54]LOr 10058: ... *rebavesrame* | *desan cana ari nisca* | *sandi-beda ca kartavyam* | ... *tare danam* ||. In the *śloka*, the co-ordinative Skt. particle *ca* appears five times. It would seem, therefore, Javano-Sanskrit.

[55]LOr 5233: *arabāva*. LOr 10058: *arabava*.

'During the time of the *muhūrta* hour *Arabāṭa*, one's own actions are favourable when selling and buying, looking for a place (or position), negotiating alliances and sowing dissension with stratagems and [one] could discuss money.'

2.5. Skt. *śvarambe vavitri praṇāṁ* | *amitrena tu karayet* | *śulākane sunayane* |[56] *sarvva-mantram praṣasyatte* ||[57]

O.J. *kunaṅ svakāryya hāri kālaniṅ savitri-muhūrtta, aṅucap-ucapa, svakāryya lavan saṅ dvija, mvaṅ kahucapaniṅ sarvva-mantra kunaṅ, muvah akāryya apriya-vacana.*

Regarding one's own actions during the time of the *muhūrta* hour *Savitri*, it should be talked about that oneself [could] perform a religious ritual together with the twice-born (that is a *brāhmaṇa*) and recite all kinds of *mantra*-s. Moreover, [one] should express friendly words.'

2.6. Skt. *vairājyana triyanaś ca* | *sārvva-rambesu karayet* | *poṣṭika kṣatriyanañ ca* | *muhūrttasu praṣasyatte* ||[58]

O.J. *kunaṅ svakāryya hari kālaniṅ vairajya-muhūrtta, agoṣṭ-[h]i ālāvan saṅ kṣatriya, kocapaniṅ*[59] *sārvva-kāryya, mvaṅ kahucapaniṅ poṣṭika-mantra.*

During the time of the *muhūrta* hour *Vairajya*, one's own actions are favourable for gathering with noble-men and, it is said, all kinds of activities. Moreover, [one should] recite *mantra* for prosperity.'

[56] The *Atmajyotiṣa* 2.5.d refers to Skt. *cūḍa*, 'tonsure ceremony', and Skt. *upanayana*, 'investiture with the sacred thread': Skt. .../ *cuḍopanayananı ca* ||. In the Sanskrit *śloka* 2.5.c, I also would read Skt. *cūla*, 'tonsure ceremony', and Skt. *upanayana*.

[57] LOr 10058: ... *beya suci prani* | *avitrena*... | ... *mantra prapasyate* ||.

[58] LOr 10058: *verajya trisayanas ca* | ... *sa triyanas ca* |... .

[59] LOr 10058: *satriya kopayaniṅ*.

2.7. Skt. *viśvavaśuś ca sārvvaśan | bhruha karmmani karayet |*
sārvva-rambesu viśyaṇām̆ | gṛha-vastra yanāni ccha ||[60]

O.J. *kunaṅ svakāryya hāri kālaniṅ viśvavaśū-muhūrtta, kapahayvaniṅ alis,*[61] *ka-ucapaniṅ sarvva-kāryya veśya, akāryya agṛha,*[62] *mvaṅ vastra, alalampaha.*[63]

'During the time of the *muhūrta* hour *Viśvavaśu*, one's own actions are favourable for embellishing the eye-brows. It is said [that it also is favourable to] all kinds of agricultural matters, activities regarding houses, garments and travels.'

2.8. Skt. *sārvva kāryya hisidyanti | nityat madhyanti deṣṭite |*
saveśaṅ cova varṇanā |[64] *abicite praṣasyate ||*

O.J. *kunaṅ svakāryya hari kālaniṅ abici-muhūrtta,*[65] *sārvva-kāryya siddha kājarnya,*[66] *ri kalaniṅ madhyahna.*

'During the time of the *muhūrta* hour *Abici*, one's own actions are favourable for all kinds of activities. It is said that [all will be] successful during the time of noon.'

---

[60] LOr 10058: *...bru karmani karalayet | ... rambes...grahan.*

[61] O.J. alis is synonymous to Skt. *bhrū*, 'eyebrow'.

[62] In Van der Tuuk's dictionary (1912, 4:486-487), there is a recent Balinese text on *muhūrta* divination regarding houses. At the end of text, we read: O.J. *iti muhūrtta gṛha, viddhi kayatnakna de saṅ amaṅuna gṛha.* 'This is on the *muhūrta* divination regarding houses. [Its] knowledge must be carefully considered by those who intend to construct houses.'

[63] LOr 10058: ... *visvava... karyaniṅ vesya... alalapaha.*

[64] LOr 10058: ... *madyandi...* |... *savesan ceva varnani* |...
The corrected foot Skt. *sarveṣāṃ caiva varṇānām* | appears almost identically in Skt. *Ātmajyotiṣa* 2.8.c: *sarveṣām eva varṇānām* | 'of them all, indeed, of [the four] castes'.

[65] Skt. text reads *Abicit* instead of O.J. *Abici.* The correct spelling *Abhijit* appears in the O.J. text *Ādipàrva* where Kuntī gave birth to Yudhiṣṭhira at noon during *Abhijit-muhurta* (Zoetmulder 1982, 1:3; cf. Skt. *Mahābhārata*, Critical Edition 1.7.114.4).

[66] LOr 10058 *kajar denya.*

2.9. Skt. *rohaṇe rohaṇa dṛkṣaṁ | vahu salambanam itam | sthavaraṇi catūrtthītam | muhūrttesu praśasyate ||* [67]

O.J. *kunaṅ svakāryya hari kālaniṅ rohaṇa-muhūrtta, ananma variṅin, kahajar akveh paṅnya, mvaṅ sakalviraniṅ tinanĕm, vṛddhi.*[68]

'During the time of the *muhūrta* hour *Rohaṇa*, one's own actions are favourable for planting *variṅin* trees. It is said [that they will have] many aerial roots. Moreover, every kind of [plant] which is sown [shall] ripen.'

2.10. Skt. *tale tuṅ ca bālo-vyakṣaṁ | sthavaye bāla vaddhanāṁ |*
bālosa yojayed[69] *atra | patra vṛkṣa bālani ccha ||*[70]

O.J. *kunaṅ svakāryya hari kālaniṅ bāla-muhūrtta, aveha uṅgvaniṅ bāla-pradhaṇa, mvaṅ asuṅa dana riṅ vadva, ṅuniveh umarikṣa hulahniṅ vadva, kamnaknaṅ catur-upaya.*[71]

'During the time of the *muhūrta* hour *Bāla*, one's own actions are favourable for appointing the chief of an army. Moreover, [one could] present gifts to the troops. Certainly, [one should] carefully inspect the conduct of the troops and should apply the four stratagems'.[72]

---

[67] LOr 10058: *rovane rovane... atam | svasvaranı...* .

[68] LOr 10058: ... *rovana...* . O.J. *kahajar* is missing.
Read: Skt. 2.9.ac, Skt. *vṛkṣa*, 'tree', *bahu*, 'many', *lambana*, 'hanging down', *sthāvara*, '(belonging to the) vegetable (world)' and *tvarita*, 'quick' which correspond in translation to O.J. *variṅin, akveh, paṅ, tanĕm, vṛddhi* respectively.

[69] For the same *muhurta Bala*, the *Ātmajyotiṣa* 2.11.b also employs the Skt. verbal form *yojayet*.

[70] LOr 10058: *taletu ca balodyasamtapayet bala varganam | ... cayo...*

[71] LOr 10058: *uṅgahaniṅ... guna riṅ vadva... sulahniṅ vadva kakĕna...* .

[72] The fragment deviates from the wording in the Skt. foot 2.10.d. The four strategems (Skt.. *caturupāya*) are: *sāma*, 'negotiation', *dāna*, 'bribery', *bheda*,

2.11. Skt. *vijaya śrināyet syen| dvija*[73] *reti prasaṣṭavān|*
śatru karmma dhaṇaś caiva| śatru arttha nirvvatante||[74]

O.J. *kunaṅ svakāryya hari kālaniṅ vijāya-muhūrtta, maṅkata nukuha musuh, aṅde kajayan, mvaṅ saprasaṣṭa, ṅūniveh kahilaṅa-niṅ śatru.*

'During the time of the *muhūrta* hour *Vijāya*, one's own actions are favourable for marching against and waging war on enemies. [One should] predestine victory and proclaim it. One shall succeed in the destruction of enemies.'

2.12. Skt. *nairite praśayañ coran| lubdakañ ceva pañcoyet|*
pāpa-karmmani yat-kiñcit| śvam vametani karayet||[75]

O.J. *kunaṅ svakāryya hari kālaniṅ neriti-muhūrtta, aṅulahakna corah, lumkas abuburu.*[76] *akāryya apāpa kiñcit-kiñcit.*

'During the time of the *muhūrta* hour *Neriti*, one's own actions are favourable for engaging with thieves. [One could] start hunting. [One] could do [something] vicious [or] whatever.'[77]

2.13. Skt. *varūṇe tu vape dvijām| padmāni rajatani ca|*
vapi-kupañ ca kurvitam| ladbakāñ ceva prasayet||[78]

O.J. *kunaṅ svakāryya hari kālaniṅ varūṇa-muhūrtta, agoṣṭ[h]i*[79] *alāvan saṅ dvijā, asuṅa kambaṅ lan salaka, muvah*

'sowing dissension' and *daṇḍa*, 'open assault' (Zoetmulder 1982, 1:316).

[73]The Skt. *dvija*, 'twice-born,' does not appear in the Old Javanese text.

[74]LOr 10058: ...` *syan|* ... *nivaktakte||*.

[75]LOr 10058: *nairitiye... ceran|* ... *pancayet|* ... *svam ametami...*

[76]LOr 10058: *aṅulahna corah, lumkasakĕna buburu.*

[77]I have translated the O.J. words in agreement with the Skt. foot 2.12.c: *pāpa-karmānī yat-kiṃcit/* 'vicious acts or whatever'. In *Ātmajyotiṣa* 2.1, 2.3 and 3.4., the Skt. construction *yac ca... kiṃcit* appears three times.

[78]LOr 10058: ... *nica|* ... *kurvitam|*. LOr 5233: ...*nidha|* ... *tūrvitam|*.

[79]LOr 10058: *agusti.*

agave <kūpa>,[80] *maṅkata abuburū.*[81]

'During the time of the *muhūrta* hour *Varūṇa*, one's own actions are favourable for gathering with the twice-born (that is a *brāhmaṇa*). [One] could offer flowers and silver. Moreover, [one could] dig a well and set out hunting.'

2.14. Skt. *somya somyani karmmani| maṅgalani ca karāyet|*
vastrani gandha-malyani| cula baruaṇaṁ eva ca||[82]

O.J. *kunaṅ svakāryya hāri kālaniṅ somya-muhūrtta, agave ya priya-vacana, manohara. aṅūyakna sapta-svara,*[83] *acaruha vastra,*[84] *gandha-malya, aspa-spa, kaglaraniṅ bhāraṇi.*[85]

'During the time of the *muhūrta* hour *Somya*, one's own actions are favourable for making friendly speeches and being charming. [One] could perform music. [One] could make an offering of garments, fragrances and garlands. [One] could burn incense [and] lay out [one's] ornaments.

2.15. Skt. *bhāgya dupārideka ca| sobhāgya karttikkatini|*

---

[80]Both LOr 5233 and LOr 10058 read *kupaṅ*, 'coin'. However, Skt. *vāpi* and *kūpa* are 'a pond' and 'a well' respectively. Moreover, the deity Varuṇa is associated with the waters (Monier-Williams 1899:921).

[81]O.J. *abuburū* would correspond to Skt. *lubdhaka*, 'hunter'. However, it would seem to me an erroneous interpretation of Skt. *labdhaka*, 'obtained, got'.

[82]LOr 10058: ... *maṅkalanı... sandamalyani*| ... .

[83]Skt. *maṅgala*, 'benidictive ceremony,' corresponds with Sanskrit-derived concept O.J. *saptasvara*, 'seven tones,' that refers to Indian classical music as expounded in early Sanskrit texts on musical theory. In Java. a *maṅgala* often involved music (cf. Zoetmulder 1982, 1:1109-1110).

[84]LOr 10058: *acaru vavastra*. Should we read LOr: 5233: *acaru avastra*? In the context of Skt. *saumya*, 'relating to Soma', Skt. → O.J. *caru*, 'oblation (of rice, barley and pulse) boiled with butter and milk for presentation to the gods' is appropriate.

[85]O.J. *asĕpa-asĕpa*. *kagĕlar* corresponds to Skt. *cula*, 'the tonsure ceremony'. For Skt. *barunaṁ* and O.J. *bhārani*, I would read Skt. *ābharaṇa*→ O.J. *bharana*, 'ornament. decoration (jewels and so forth)'.

satya kanyā pato bhakti| kālyani subhāga dvittā||[86]

O.J. *kunan svakāryya hāri kālanin bhāga-muhūrtta, <andāni> kasobhāgya,*[87] *ri kālanin stri*[88] *kinasut, pati-bhakti kahajar muvah, rahayu*[89] *rivan subhāga.*

'During the time of the *muhūrta* hour *Bhāga*, one's own actions are favourable for arranging happiness during the time of intimate encounters with women, [and those who are] devoted to their husbands. Moreover, it is said [that it will be] beautiful and fortunate.'

O.J. *iti muhūrtta-lakṣaṇa samaptā.*

'This is the end of the *Muhūrtalakṣaṇa.*'

---

[86] LOr 10058: ... *cuparineka... giṇi|* ... .

[87] O.J. *sobhagya* LOr 5233: *andani kasobhagya*; *andani sobhagya.* LOr 10058: *andani subagya.* The connotation of O.J. *sobhāgya* refers to Skt. *saubhāgya* 'happiness' as 'conjugal felicity'.

[88] LOr 10058: O.J. *vastra.* In translation, Skt. *satya*, 'faithful', and Skt. *kanyā*, 'girl', correspond to O.J. *stri*, 'woman, wife'.

[89] O.J. *rahayu*, 'beautiful', is synonymous to Skt. *kalyāṇa.*

APPENDIX 2: TIMES OF LAGNA AND MUHŪRTA

No.	Inscription (see Damais 1955 and Boechari 1985)	*Śaka*	*Māsa*	*Tithi*	Day	Converted Date AD
1	later copy, O.J. Copper Plates of Kuṭi, Joho area, near Sidoarjo (A.12)	762	1 *Śrāvaṇa*	15	Sun	18 Jul 840
2	later copy, O.J. Copper Plate of Kaladi, Penanggungan area (A.88, E.71)	831	12 *Āṣāḍa*	8	Tue	27 Jun 909
3	later copy, O.J. Copper Plates of Waharu II (A.108)	851	11 *Jyeṣṭa*	13	Sun	24 May 929
4	later copy, O.J. Copper Plate of Waharu IV from Lamongan-Gresik (A.116, E.20)	853	1 *Śrāvaṇa*	25	[Fri]	12 Aug 931
5	later copy, O.J. Copper Plates of Sumbut from Sidoarjo (A.118)	855	3 *Aśuji*	11	Wed	02 Oct 933
6	O.J. Copper Plates of Tērēp I from Penanggungan area (A.139)	954	4 *Karttika*	15	Sat	21 Oct 1032
7	O.J. Stone of Sumēngka (A.144)	98[1]	9 *C[ai]t[r]a*	15	Wed	31 Mar 1059
8	O.J. Copper Plates of Mūla Malurung from Kediri area (E.90)	1177	5 *Mārgaśira*	15	Wed	15 Dec 1255
9	O.J. Copper Plate from Pakis Wetan village, Tegalrejo, Yogya area (A.172)	1188	7 *Māgha*	13	Tue	08 Feb 1267
10	O.J. Copper Plates of Sarwadharma from Penampihan, Mount Willis area (A.173)	1191	4 *Kārttika*	5	Thu	31 Oct 1269
11	mid-14th century inscription in Skt. in stone statue of King Kṛtanāgara as Mahākṣobhya, from Trowulan (A.174)	1211	3 *Aśuji*	5	Wed	21 Sep 1289
12	O.J. Stone Statue of Goddess Cāmuṇḍā from Candi Singosari (A.175)	1214	9 *Caitra*	29	Thu	17 Apr 1292
13	O.J. Copper Plates of Kudadu (A.177)	1216	2 *Bhadrawāda*	20	Sat	11 Sep 1294
14	O.J. Copper Plates of Sukamērta from Penanggungan area (A.178)	1218	4 *Kārttika*	2	Mon	29 Oct 1296
15	O.J. Copper Plates of Balawi, probably from Trowulan (A.179)	1227	10 *Waiśāka*	30	Mon	24 May 1305
16	O.J. Copper Plates of Tuhañaru from Sidoteko village, Mojokerto area (A.180, E.25)	1245	5 *Mārgaśira*	15	Tue	13 Dec 1323
17	O.J. Stone of Palungan (A.183)	1252	2 *Bhadrawāda*	30	Thu	13 Sep 1330
18	O.J. Inscription of Gajah Mada in Stone Statue of Marīci from Candi Jago area (A.187)	1273	10 *Weśāka*	1	Wed	27 Apr 1351
19	O.J. Copper Plate of Canggu from Trowulan (A.188)	1280	1 *Śravaṇa*	1	Sat	07 Jul 1358
20	O.J. Copper Plates of Her Abang II (D.65)	130[5]	7 *Māgha*	5	Thu	28 Jan 1384
21	O.J. Copper Plates of Pamintihan from Sendang Sedati village, Bojonegoro area (A.209)	1395	10 *Waiśāka*	18	Fri	14 May 1473

IN OLD JAVANESE INSCRIPTIONS

Rāśi as *Lagna*	Zodiac Sign	*Muhūrta*	Time of Zodiac Sign in *Lagna*	Mean *Muhūrta* Time	Gnomonic *Muhūrta* Time	Differences between Midpoints of *Lagna* and Mean *Muhūrta* Times
Kumbha	10 Aqr	15 *Bago*	18h 14m - 20h 16m	17h 12m - 18h 00m	17h 19m	+1h 39m
[Ka]nya	5 Vir	2 *Sveta*	09h 57m - 11h 40m	06h 48h - 07h 36m	06h 58h	+3h 37m
Mithuna	2 Gem	6 *Vairoja*	06h 10m - 08h 20m	10h 00m - 10h 48m	09h 58m	-3h 09m
Siṅha	4 Leo	2 *Śveta*	05h 06m - 06h 57m	06h 48m - 07h 36m	06h 52m	-1h 10m
Kanyā	5 Vir	12 *Nerih*	03h 50m - 05h 33m	02h 48m - 03h 36m	01h 52m	+1h 30m
Mrcchika	7 Sco	2 *Śveta*	06h 10m - 08h 07m	06h 48m - 07h 36m	06h 39m	-0h 03m
Mithuna	2 Gem	2 *Śveta*	09h 41m - 11h 52m	06h 48m - 07h 36m	06h 47m	+3h 35m
Karkkaṭa	3 Cnc	7 *Viśvabasu*	19h 00m - 21h 02m	22h 48m - 23h 36m	22h 23m	-3h 11m
Kumbha	10 Aqr	13 *Baruṇa*	04h 53m - 06h 53m	03h 36m - 04h 24m	03h 12m	+1h 53m
Mrccika	7 Sco	6 *Vairajya*	05h 39m - 07h 38m	10h 00m - 10h 48m	10h 19m	-3h 45m
Tulā	6 Lib	14 *Somya*	06h 24m - 08h 10m	04h 24m - 05h 12m	05h 16m	+2h 29m
[M]eśa	0 Ari	6 *Vairājya*	04h 39m - 06h 38m	10h 00m - 10h 48m	10h 04m	-4h 45m
Kanyā	5 Vir	6 *Verajya*	05h 18m - 07h 00m	10h 00m - 10h 48m	10h 21m	-4h 15m
Mrcchika	7 Sco	6 *Vairājya*	05h 47m - 07h 46m	10h 00m - 10h 48m	10h 00m	-3h 37m
Vṛṣabhā	1 Tau	5 *Sāvitri*	04h 16m - 06h 23m	09h 12m - 10h 00m	09h 44m	-4h 16 m
Mituna	2 Gem	11 *Vijaya*	17h 01m - 19h 11m	14h 00m - 14h 48m	14h 10m	+3h 43m
Kanya	5 Vir	5 *Savitri*	05h 11m - 06h 54m	09h 12m - 10h 00m	10h 07m	-3h 33m
Vṛṣabha	1 Tau	2 *Śveta*	06h 06m - 08h 13m	06h 48m - 07h 36m	06h 53m	-0h 02m
Karkkaṭa	3 Cnc	1 *Rodra*	05h 37m - 07h 38m	06h 00m - 06h 48m	06h 41m	+0h 14m
Meṣa	0 Ari	10 *Bala*	09h 38m - 11h 37m	13h 12m - 14h 00m	13h 39m	-2h 58m
Dhanū	8 Sgr	1 *Rodra*	18h 43m - 20h 52m	18h 00m - 18h 48m	18h 41m	+1h 24m

BIBIOGRAPHY

Manuscripts

Old Javanese-Sanskrit:

- *Muhūrtalakṣaṇa* and *Śubhavāradivaśavidyaśāstra*, University of Leiden Library, ms. LOr 5233, *lontar* Lombok Collection, Balinese script, 8 palm leaves, undated.
- *Muhūrtalakṣaṇa*, University of Leiden Library, ms. LOr 10058, romanized version of Kirtya *lontar* 1984 by I Gusti Nyoman Ngurah Prongot, three single-sided typescript pages, Buleleng, 10th of March 1941.

Dutch:

- *The Grĕsik Records* (Dutch title: *De Statistieken van Grissee*) by jhr. A.D. Cornets de Groot sr., KITLV (Koninklijk Instituut voor Taal-, Land- en Volkenkunde), Leiden, ms. H 379, paper, AD 1820-1822. The Dutch text without drawings has been published as an article (see Cornets de Groot 1852).

Published Works

Abhyankar, Kāśīnāth Vāsudev (ed.)
1951 *Jaiminīyam Upadeśasūtram* (*The Upadeśa Sūtra of Jaimini*). Ahmedabad: Gujarāt Vidyāsabhā.

Bhat, M. Ramakrishna (ed., tr.)
1992-1993 *Varāhamihira's Bṛhatsaṃhitā with English Translation, Exhaustive Notes and Literary Comments.* 2nd ed., reprint. New Delhi: Motilal Banarsidass.

Billard, Roger
1971 *L'astronomie indienne.* Publications de l'Ecole Française de l'Extrême-Orient 83. Paris: Maissoneuve.

Boechari (ed.)

1985-1986 *Prasasti Koleksi Museum Nasional.* Vol. 1. Jakarta: Proyek Pengembangan Museum Nasional.

Burgess, Ebenezer (tr.)

1860 *The Sūrya Siddhānta: A Text-book of Hindu Astronomy.* 1989 reprint. Delhi: Motilal Banarsidass.

Casparis, Johannes Gijsbertus de

1978 *Indonesian Chronology.* Handbuch der Orientalistik, Dritte Abteilung, Erster Band, Lieferung 1. Leiden: Brill.

Cornets de Groot, A.D.

1852 Bijdragen tot de kennis van de zeden en gewoonten der Javanen. *Tijdschrift voor Nederlandsch Indië* 14:257-280, 346-432.

Damais, Louis-Charles

1955 'Etudes d'épigraphie indonésienne, vol. IV: Discussion de dates des Inscriptions' in *Bulletin d'Ecole Française d'Extrême Orient* 47:7-290.

Datta, Bhagavad

1924 *Ātharvaṇa Jyotiṣam or the Vedāṅga Jyotiṣa of the Atharva Veda edited for the First Time.* Lahore: Moti Lal Banarsi Dass and the Punjab Sanskrit Book Depot.

Eade, John Chris and Lars Gislén

2000 *Early Javanese Inscriptions: A New Dating Method.* Handbook of Oriental Studies. Section 3 Southeast Asia, 10. Leiden: Brill.

Fisher, N.I.

1993 *Statistical Analysis of Circular Data.* Cambridge: Cambrigde University Press.

Gomperts, Amrit

2001 'Sanskrit Jyotiṣa Terms and Indian Astronomy in Old Javanese Inscriptions' in *Fruits of Inspiration: Studies in Honour of Prof. J. G. de Casparis.* Edited by Marijke

J. Klokke and Karel R. van Kooij, pp. 93-134. Groningen: Forsten.

Kane, Pandurang Vaman

1958 *History of Dharmaśāstra (Ancient and Mediaeval Religious and Civil Law in India)*, vol. V, pt. 1. Poona: Bhandarkar Oriental Research Institute.

Mardiwarsito, L.

1990 *Kamus Jawa Kuna-Indonesia.* 3rd ed.. Ende, Flores: Nusa Indah.

Monier-Williams, Monier

1899 *A Sanskrit-English Dictionary.* Oxford: Clarendon Press.

Neugebauer, Otto and David Pingree (ed. & tr.)

1970-1971 *The Pañcasiddhāntikā of Varāhamihira.* 2 parts. Det Kongelige Danske Videnskabernes Selskab Historisk-Filosofiske Skrifter 6, 1, 1-2. Copenhagen: Munksgaard.

Panse, Murlidhar Gajanan (ed.)

1957 *Jyotiṣaratnamālā of Śrīpati Bhaṭṭa: A Marathi Ṭīkā on his own Sanskrit Work.* Poona: Deccan College.

Pingree, David

1981 *Jyotiḥśāstra: Astral and Mathematical Literature.* A History of Indian Literature, vol. VI, fasc. 4. Edited by Jan Gonda. Wiesbaden: Harrassowitz.

Poucha, Pavel

1948 'La Jyotiṣratnamālā ou guirlande de joyaux d'astrologie de Śrīpatibhaṭṭa' in *Archiv Orientální, Journal of the Czechoslovak Oriental Institute* 16:277- 309.

Robson, Stuart O.

1995 *Deśawarṇana (Nāgarakĕrtāgama) by Mpu Prapañca.* Verhandelingen van het Koninklijk Instituut voor Taal-, Land- en Volkenkunde 169. Leiden: KITLV.

Raghavan, V.

1966 *New Catalogus Catalogorum: An Alphabetical Register of Sanskrit and Allied Works and Authors.* Vol. 2 (Ā-U). Madras: University of Madras.

Sachau, Edward C.
1910 *Aberuni's India: An Account of the Religion, Philosophy, Literature, Geography, Chronology, Astronomy, Customs, Laws and Astrology of India about AD 1030.* 1983 reprint in one volume. Delhi: Munshiram Manoharlal

Santoso, Soewito (ed., tr.)
1986 *Krĕṣṇāyana: The Krĕṣṇa Legend in Indonesia.* New Delhi: International Academy of India Culture.

Sharma, Ram Swarup *et al.*
1966 *Brāhma-sphuṭa-siddhānta with Vāsanā, Vijñāna and Hindi Commentaries.*
Vol. 1, New Delhi: Indian Institute of Astronomical and Sanskrit Research.

Türstig, Hans-Georg
1980 *Jyotiṣa: das System der Indischen Astrologie.* Wiesbaden: Steiner.

Tuuk, Herman Neubronner van der
1897-1912 *Kawi-Balineesch-Nederlandsch woordenboek.* 4 vols. Batavia: Landsdrukkerij.

Zoetmulder, Piet J., with the collaboration of Stuart O. Robson
1982 *Old Javanese-English Dictionary.* Koninklijk Instituut voor Taal-, Land- en Volkenkunde. 2 vols. The Hague: Nijhoff.

Nāḍī Divination and Indian Astrology

MARTIN GANSTEN

Astrology (*jyotiṣa* or *jyotiḥ-śāstra*) is the most prestigious and encompassing form of Indian divination. Other divinatory arts, such as auspices (*śakuna-śāstra*), chiromancy and physiognomy (*sāmudrika-śāstra*), oneiromancy (*svapna-śāstra*), geomancy (*vāstuśāstra*) and pneumomancy (*svarodaya-śāstra*), are often subsumed under the heading of astrology and regarded as its auxiliary branches (*śākhā*).

The pride of place which is thus given to astrology is presumably due at least in part to its 'scientific' character. By this I mean not only its complexity and systematic nature, but above all its claims to objectivity; for divinatory arts vary in their degree of dependence on the diviner. The planetary positions at a person's birth may be calculated any number of times by different astrologers, with more or less identical results. A personal ability on the part of the astrologer to apply the various rules of interpretation is, admittedly, called for, but this is predominantly seen as an intellectual skill, rather than a mystical or magical one, and the rules as such are extraneous to the astrologer.

The divinatory art known as *nāḍī* reading is generally described as a form of astrology, although this designation does not apply in an equally strict sense to all branches of the art. Its power of fascination lies precisely in the supreme objectivity that it claims to achieve. In *nāḍī* reading, the role of the diviner is minimized: he is merely the mouthpiece of ancient sages or divinities who are believed to have set down in writing the details of the client's life long before the birth of either reader or client. Predictions for a client's future and answers to his or her questions are supposedly read out from pre-existent, physical texts (generally in the form of palm-leaf manuscripts).[1] These texts are not considered subject to the symbolic interpretation of the diviner, as is the case in bibliomancy (where texts of a basically non-divinatory nature, such as sacred scriptures, are used for oracular purposes).[2] On the contrary, a *nāḍī* reading is ideally so specific as to be applicable to one client only; indeed, many *nāḍī* readers claim that their texts supply not only the name of the person consulting the text, but even the names of his or her parents, spouse, and so forth.

The term *nāḍī* itself (also *nāḍi*, Tamil *nāṭi*) is probably derived from the Tamil verb *nāṭu* 'to enquire after, examine, look at', and all texts containing the term in its astrological sense, even when composed in Sanskrit, appear to originate in the Dravidian language area. Today, two fairly distinct forms of *nāḍī* divination can be observed in South India. The more common variety is based on a form of thumb reading, although the readings as such still maintain an astrological structure, and the texts used are generally composed in Tamil. The less common variety appears actually to be based on astrological considerations, utilizing the client's birth horoscope, and its texts are composed in Sanskrit.

---

[1] A 'grey area' would seem to be the so-called *jīva-* ('living') *nāḍīs*, believed to be inhabited by a deity or *ṛṣi* (sage) who at the time of reading supposedly manifests the text on an otherwise blank page.

[2] For a description of Hindu bibliomantic practices, see Kane 1977: 811f.

It is with these Sanskrit *nāḍīs* and their relation to Indian astrology generally that I am concerned here, and in particular, with three texts: the *Gurunāḍī*, *Aṃśanāḍī*, and *Dhruvanāḍī*.[3]

The authorship and transmission of these three texts are unknown, but the text-internal evidence points to an origin in or near the Kerala area, and the horoscopes discussed in the texts can be dated to a period from the late seventeenth to the mid-nineteenth century. The three texts display many similarities with regard to form as well as content, and a high degree of intertextuality. Many verses found in these works also occur in a text known as *Candranāḍī*, *Candrakalānāḍī*, *Keralanāḍī*, or *Devakerala*. All three texts are written in simple, often ungrammatical Sanskrit, and the style is highly formulaic and repetitive.

The precise relations between these works remain to be established, but the term *devakerala* seems properly to refer to a certain body of astrological teachings rather than to a single text. The *Aṃśanāḍī*, *Gurunāḍī* and *Candrakalānāḍī* all frequently describe their predictions as *pratyakṣaṃ devakeralam*, 'the *devakerala* evident to perception'. The term finds its explanation in a legend of origination which states that the knowledge was originally revealed by Bṛhaspati, the priest-preceptor of the gods, to 'a certain brahmin named Acyuta in the district of Kerala',[4] a state noted for its unique contributions to astrology.

Astrology, Fate, and Karman

In order to understand the *nāḍī* texts, we must first examine some fundamental, if often only implied, principles of Indian

[3]The copies of these texts used are Devanāgarī transcripts made from Grantha originals, the *Gurunāḍī*, the *Aṃśanāḍī* and the *Dhruvanāḍī*.

[4]This legend occurs at the very beginning of the *Gurunāḍī*.

astrology generally. Astrology is primarily a descriptive, secondarily a prescriptive art. In its descriptive aspect, it attempts to analyze and interpret the qualities inherent in a given moment of time, such as a birth or the asking of a question: indeed, *kālajña* 'knower of time' is a common Sanskrit word for 'astrologer'. In the astrological view of things, the development and destined end of anything is inherent in the beginning, like a full-grown tree in a seed. Once the qualities of a particular point in time have been understood, therefore, the future of anything begun at that moment - such as the unfolding of a human life or the answer to a question - may be predicted.

In its prescriptive aspect, astrology advises on how to make the best use of time by undertaking or refraining from particular actions. but also on how to mitigate the ill-effects of evil periods by acts of *śānti*: propitiation or pacification. This dual role of astrology obviously presupposes both an element of determinism or predictability and a certain measure of freedom to act on the part of the individual. If the future were absolutely undetermined, there could be no question of predicting it, and astrology, like all forms of divination, would lose its *raison d'être*. If, on the other hand, the future were absolutely predetermined, there could be no question of advising one or the other course of action, or of mitigating an evil fate. Insofar as the promotion of human happiness is considered the proper concern of any branch of knowledge, astrology would therefore be meaningless; and indeed the art has been criticized on such grounds.[5]

---

[5]The fatalist argument is rehearsed and refuted by the seventeenth century astrologer Balabhadra in his *Hōraratna*, introductory chapter, verse 35 (my translation, reading *duḥkhe na* for *duḥkhena*):
avaśyaṃbhāvibhāvānāṃ pratīkāro bhaved yadi |
tada duḥkhe na badhyeran nalaramayudhiṣṭhirāḥ ||
... *tathā ca jyotiṣasmṛtyāveditajātakādiphalanirūpaṇasya vaiyarthyaṃ bhāsata iti cen naivaṃ karmaṇāṃ hi vaicitryaṃ kānicid dṛḍhamūlāni kānicic*

In classical Indian thought, however, the coexistence (in varying proportions) of fate and free will is generally taken for granted, and both are subsumed under the concept of action or *karman*. What we experience as fate (*daiva*) in this lifetime is simply the result of our own effort (*puruṣakāra*) performed out of free will in previous lifetimes. The fruition of past acts is thus inextricably linked to the performance of present acts, and all concrete life events are formed by a combination of the two. This view is made explicit in a number of traditional metaphors: as a cart will not move on a single wheel, or fire not be produced from a single kindling-stick, so fate and human effort are both necessary for the production of an event.

Given the scope allowed for the interplay of fate and free will, and therefore for prediction as well as prescription, *karman* thus offers an excellent theoretical model to support the practice of astrology; and from the earliest Sanskrit astrological texts on, the art is indeed interwoven with the concept of *karman*.

In the words of Mīnarāja, writing in the early fourth century, 'even as a lamp [reveals] objects in utter darkness, this science reveals the edict [i.e., fate] which, carrying the impact of previous action, was inscribed on [man's] forehead by the Creator.'[6]

---

chithilamūlāni.
'[Objection:] If states that will inevitably occur could be counteracted, then Nala, Rāma, and Yudhiṣṭhira would not have been confined to misery. [...] [Reply:] And if [you say] that this shows the futility of the delineation of results by birth horoscopy, etc., as laid down in astrological texts, [then we say:] not so, for actions are manifold, some being firm-rooted (*dṛḍha-mūla*) and others, loose-rooted (*śithila-mula*).'

[6]Mīnarāja, *Vṛddhayavanajātaka* 1.3:
yā pūrvakarmaprabhavasya dhātrī dhātrā lalāṭe likhitā praśastiḥ |
taṃ śastram etat prakaṭaṃ vidhatte dipo yatha vastu ghane 'ndhakare ||
The image of karmically determined destiny as written by God on a person's forehead is still widespread.

Śānti, the act of propitiating or pacifying an angry or malevolent deity, is discussed in both astrological and non-astrological works. It may be seen as atonement (*prāyaścitta*) in reverse: by undertaking atonement for a known offence (whether of omission or commission), the performer hopes to avoid or mitigate any future retribution. The practice of *prāyaścitta* therefore presupposes an awareness of sin committed, for which retribution is expected. This practice generally comprises such acts as recitations of sacred texts, physical austerities, oblations, fasting, and donations.[7] The performance of *śānti*, while taking basically the same forms, is meant to avert an existing or imminent misfortune, which in accordance with *karman* theory is believed to result from some unknown sin previously committed. Thus, while the rationale of *prāyaścitta* is the anticipation of a future effect (suffering) from a past or present cause (sin), the individual undertaking *śānti* deduces the existence of a prior cause from the observation of a present or impending effect.

In astrology, this anticipation of misfortune is based on the astrological chart. The particular forms of *śānti* to be chosen, including the deity or deities to whom ritual worship is directed, are likewise astrologically determined. Frequently, the recipients of propitiatory worship are the planetary deities themselves; but various texts also give lists of correlations between the planets and the greater Hindu pantheon, so that horoscopic afflictions due to any planet may be counteracted by worship of the corresponding major deity. In a similar vein, donating valuables which by symbolic correspondences fall under the jurisdiction of a given planet may alleviate the affliction.

---

[7] *Gautamadharmasūtra* 19.11: *tasya niṣkrayaṇāni japas tapo homa upavāso dānam.*

The elevation of the planets to the status of deities receiving propitiatory worship does raise the question of whether they are seen as mere signs, like dreams, facial features, or the movements of birds and beasts in other divinatory systems, or as active causes of the effects they signify in the horoscope. For practical purposes, however, the question is of little importance: even God, who 'writes the destiny of men on their foreheads', does so only in accordance with their previous actions or *karman*.

Nāḍī Astrology: Patterns of Destiny

Unlike mainstream Sanskrit astrological works, which are, as a rule, concerned exclusively with universal principles, the *nāḍī* texts consist almost entirely of the delineation of individual horoscopes. The readings vary in regard to length and amount of detail; but most conform to a standardized pattern or structure, and almost every reading begins with the unique feature which has given *nāḍī* astrology its name: the *nāḍī* into which the native of the horoscope was born.

A *nāḍī* in this sense is also called an *aṃśa* or 'part'. It is a division of each zodiacal sign into 150 parts, each bearing a particular name. The texts do not state how these parts are calculated; obviously such knowledge is presupposed in the reader.[8] Birth in a given *aṃśa* is explicitly linked to certain basic destiny patterns, particularly, but not exclusively, relating to the circumstances of birth and early life. These patterns are further

[8]I am not aware of any contemporary *nāḍī* reader who claims to make use of the *aṃśas*, but modern Hindu astrologers have speculated on the nature of these divisions. While some assume them to be equal 1/150 parts of a zodiacal sign, each part comprising 0°12′ of arc (Santhanam 1992: v ff.), others have argued that they represent a 'consolidation' of the classical *ṣoḍaśavargas* or sixteen divisions of a sign, which, if superimposed upon each other, create a matrix of 150 parts varying in arc from 0°01′40″ to 0°30′00″ (Bhagat 1990: 1 ff.).

modified according to whether birth is in the 'former half' or 'latter half' of an *aṃśa*: for instance, if the early demise of a parent is indicated, the former half of the *aṃśa* may be fatal to the father, while the latter would be so to the mother; etc. Within each *aṃśa* there is also a division known as *kāla* 'time', which is generally related to the native's caste or religious community.

After stating these details, the reading typically goes on to describe the horoscopic placements, superimposing the common considerations of astrology on the fixed destiny pattern of the *aṃśa*. The place of birth is described: whether in a small or large village or a town; near a river, the sea, or a forest; in the vicinity of a temple of Śiva or Viṣṇu; in the ancestral home of the mother or father; etc. The direction of the street (east-west or north-south) and that faced by the house are often stated, as is the intensity of labour pains, and possible danger to mother or child.

Another topic almost invariably brought up at the beginning of a reading is the number of brothers and, secondarily, sisters: whether elder or younger, long-lived or not. The financial and professional status of brothers, and marital status of sisters, are typically discussed, and the trouble of childlessness is occasionally mentioned.

In detailing the ascendant or rising sign, the *nāḍīs* often mention three different times for which the chart may be cast. The first is the moment of birth, at which the infant leaves the body of the squatting mother and 'falls on to the ground' (*bhūpatana*); but there is also the moment when the head first becomes visible in the birth canal (*śirodarśana*), as well as the moment of impregnation (*ādhāna*). However, these latter two are rarely used for interpretative purposes.

The structure of the delineation is partly thematic, partly

chronological, often commencing with a description of the father, the happiness the native will derive from him, and his time of death. A similar but briefer and even more stereotyped description of the mother then follows, typically emphasizing her devotion to her husband, her dutiful efforts to secure the increase of the family, and her liberal dispensing of food. Longer readings may include similar sketches of the native's brothers and sisters before moving on to his (or, very occasionally, her) own life.

In contrast to modern 'astro-psychological' consultations, the *nāḍīs* tend rather to slur over the native's childhood, merely stating — in standard phrasing and without fear of contradiction — that in spite of various childhood illnesses, he happily reached adulthood. The narrations of adult life are more detailed and individualized, though similar in focus: marriage and childbirth, income and livelihood, status and profession are topics of universal interest. The astrological argumentation presented is generally quite superficial, and there is no sharp dividing line between results related to *aṃśa* and to planetary positions.

As in mainstream Hindu astrology, important life events are timed using astrological time-cycles (*daśā*) as well as the 'transits' (*gocara*) or continuous movements of the planets in relation to their natal placements. This latter technique is rather more emphasized in the *nāḍī* texts than in standard works, with particular attention paid to the slow-moving Saturn and Jupiter for evil and good events, respectively. Again, the reasoning presented is often simple, not to say simplistic.

The results of time-cycles are also related to the birth *aṃśa*, and the sequence of these periods, along with the transits of Saturn and Jupiter, provide the chronological framework of the narrative. This narrative ends with the prognostication of the native's death, typically to the very day, the only event other than birth to be stated with such precision. This date is based on a supposed 'maximum longevity' (*paramāyuṣ*) which may, however, be cut short by 'untimely death' (*apamṛtyu*) at certain critical times. Such and other misfortunes should be averted by the performance of *śānti*, propitiation, which is a frequently recurring subject in the *nāḍī* texts.

The objects of such propitiatory worship may be the afflicting planets themselves or deities of the greater Hindu pantheon, but may also include the brahmins (who are 'gods on earth') and deceased ancestors, particularly when their displeasure is thought to cause childlessness. Among the planets, the dreaded Saturn is the one most often propitiated. The methods of *śānti* comprise various practices such as ritual worship (*pūjā*), recitation of *mantras* or sacred texts (*japa*), fasting, pilgrimage and sacred baths, and, above all, donations.

In striking contrast to standard texts, the *nāḍīs* occasionally prescribe donations to the astrologer himself, alone or in conjunction with worship of the planetary deities. The astrologer of the *nāḍī* texts thus functions as a two-way representative of the planets: firstly, in acting as their mouthpiece by delineating the results of *karman* made manifest through planetary positions; and secondly, in accepting, on behalf of the planets, worship meant to remedy undesirable results.

This doctrine of *karman* and its corollary rebirth, which as seen above presents a middle way between fatalism and indeterminism, is upheld explicitly as well as implicitly, and a sense of continuity between lifetimes is sometimes very concretely expressed, as when an illness in the present lifetime is said to have begun in the previous one. In discussing rebirth, the *nāḍīs* also occasionally touch upon soteriological aspects by predicting final liberation within a certain number of lifetimes. More often, however, it is merely asserted that the native will 'attain a good world' after death. Only very rarely is someone said to be destined for a less pleasant location.[9]

Conclusion

Like medicine, astrology is concerned with diagnosis, prognosis, and prescription. The object diagnosed is the particular point in space-time at which anything begins, e.g., the birth of a human being. From the qualities inherent in this point the latent promise of events to come may be read; the projection of such events in time constitutes the prognosis. Finally, prescription relates to the counteraction of undesirable future events by ritual means (*śānti*), or to the commencement of undertakings at auspicious times. This division of the art, allowing for a high degree of predictability as well as for a certain measure of individual freedom, makes it excellently suited for accomodation in a worldview dominated by the concept of *karman*. Teachings on *karman* thus serve as a means of legitimizing astrology, and once this connection is made, the practice of astrological divination will in its turn serve to uphold the authority of the *karman* theory.

The concept of fixed life patterns inherent in minute divisions of the zodiac itself seems to be, practically speaking, unique to *nāḍī* astrology. A similar idea, the *myriogenesis* doctrine, is outlined by the fourth century Roman astrologer Firmicus Maternus

---

[9]E.g., in a reading for a *śūdra* given in the *Aṃśanaḍi*:
vyayeśe kaluṣāṃśasthe vyaye pāpayutekṣite |
dehānte narakaṃ yāti gurunāḍīṣu vistaret ||
'When the ruler of the twelfth house is in *kaluṣāṃśa*, and the twelfth house is joined [and] aspected by malefics, at the end of the body he goes to hell. One should refer to the *Gurunāḍī* for details.'

in his *Mathesis*;[10] but to my knowledge, no horoscope interpretations actually purporting to be based on this doctrine have been recorded.

Apart from its uniqueness as a divinatory approach, the *nāḍī* or *aṃśa* doctrine has implications of definite interest for the study of Hindu views on human freedom and the operations of *karman.* As every human being is necessarily born into some particular *aṃśa*, the number of which is limited, and as each *aṃśa* corresponds to a basic destiny or event pattern, it follows that the number of possible human *curricula vitae* is likewise limited. There are only so many basic plots, as it were, and although the plot inherent in each *aṃśa* may vary in detail, the number of possible variations is still finite. We thus see in this doctrine the perhaps greatest deviation of *nāḍī* authors from mainstream Hindu orthodoxy: a view of *karman* and rebirth not as an infinitely variable flux, but rather in the nature of a flow chart in which movement, though voluntary, takes place from one predefined square to the next. It is not the view of the religious moralist, emphasizing the dimension of free will and the possibility of moral choice, but rather a view suited to the concerns of a diviner, intent on 'decoding impersonal patterns of reality'[11] by means of 'predictable, ordable processes'.[12]

---

[10] Maternus 1975.

[11] Zuesse 1987: 375. Zuesse is speaking of what he terms 'wisdom divination', as opposed to intuitive or possession divination.

[12] Cf. Smith 1991: 283: 'Like science, divination is concerned with natural phenomena and predictable, ordable processes; but like religion, it relies heavily on faith and presupposes some sort of personal connection with the constantly unfolding but mysterious patterns of cosmic change.'

Bibliography

Primary Texts

Aṃśanāḍī
MS, Oriental Research Institute, Mysore.

Balabhadra, *Horāratna*
Hora Ratnam, text and transl. R. Santhanam, New Delhi 1995.

Dhruvanāḍī
MS, Government Oriental Manuscripts Library, Chennai.

Gautamadharmasūtra
The Institutes of Gautama, ed. A. F. Stenzler, London 1876.

Gurunāḍī
MS, Oriental Research Institute, Mysore.

Mīnarāja, *Vṛddhayavanajātaka*
Mīnarājaviracitaṃ, ed. D. Pingree, Baroda 1976.

Secondary Literature

Bhagat, S. K.
1990 *Golden Key to Unfold Nadi Granthas*, Bombay.

Kane, P. V.
1977 *History of Dharmaśāstra*, vol. V, part II, Poona.

Maternus, Firmicus
1975 *Matheseos Libri VIII*, published as *Ancient Astrology: Theory and Practice*, tr. J. R. Bram, New Jersey.

Santhanam, R.
1992 *Deva Keralam (Chandra Kala Nadi)*, ed. & tr. R. Sathanam, Book 1, New Delhi.

Smith, R. J.
1991 *Fortune-Tellers and Philosophers: Divination in Traditional Chinese Society*, Boulder & Chicago.

Zuesse, E. M.
1987 'Divination' in M. Eliade (ed.): *Encyclopedia of Religion*, vol. 4, New York.

Beliefs, Aspirations and Accomplishments of the Medieval Indian Alchemist as depicted in the Rasopaniṣad

VIJAYA J. DESHPANDE

This article briefly investigates the following through an eleventh century Sanskrit work the *Rasopaniṣad*,[1] which is representative of alchemical culture of the time.

1. Thought processes and aspirations of the medieval Indian alchemist that formed the basis of the distinctive Indian alchemical theory,
2. Contents of medieval alchemical texts in general and special features of the *Rasopaniṣad*,
3. Problems encountered in the study of this Sanskrit work,
4. Unusual chemical insights of the alchemist that appear to be ahead of his time, and lastly,

[1]Considering the historical references and also the contents, an approximate date of eleventh century AD is ascribed to the *Rasopaniṣad*. The *Gorakṣasaṃhita* mentions it in one of its chapters, which is a thirteenth century work since it was compiled following a directive of king Siṃhana who ruled in the early thirteenth century AD.

5. Accomplishments of the alchemist in the long course of the medieval alchemical practice.

Beliefs and Aspirations of the Medieval Alchemist

It is an everyday experience that gold retains its pure state at normal atmospheric conditions and remains unaffected by heat, moisture and common acids and bases. Therefore the ancients considered it as imperishable and the purest and noblest of all metals.

The notion that gold could confer its imperishability upon things that came in contact with it resulted in the practice of taking it internally in the form of potions. This also explains the introduction of gold and its compounds in medicinal preparations. These ideas of rejuvenation, longevity and immortality that became the basis of physiological alchemy can be traced to earlier Vedic notions related to *Soma* juice that conferred immortality.[2] One finds references to brass and other kinds of gold-like alloys in Kauṭilya's *Arthaśāstra.*[3] A synonym for gold is given as *rasa-viddha* (pierced/transformed by mercury) in this text, suggesting the practice of metallurgical alchemy.[4]

The alchemist looked upon gold as the purest of all metals and the base metals as its impure forms. He believed that impure metals could be converted to pure state by means of certain processes. Therefore he considered transmuting base metals into gold as purifying them and bringing them to an imperishable state, and this belief was behind the practice of metallurgical

---

[2] *Soma* or *Somavallı*. Indian authors identify it as *Sarcostemma Acidum* Voigt, family Asclepiadaceae.

[3] Kauṭilya, *Arthaśāstra*, 2.12.23: *lohādhyakṣas tāmra-sīsa-trapu-vaikṛntakārakuṭa-vṛtta-kaṃsatāla-lohakarmantān kārayet.*

[4] Ibid, 2.13.3: *jāmbūnadaṃ śātakumbhaṃ hāṭakaṃ vaiṇavaṃ śṛṅgi-śuktijaṃ jātarūpaṃ rasaviddham ākarodgataṃ ca suvarṇam.*

alchemy. Simultaneously another notion developed that the human body could achieve imperishability just as the baser metals do by means of specially made elixirs. Thus cultivating the human body to make it indestructible, also called physiological alchemy, became an integral part of the alchemist's activities. The two processes were considered as parallel. The following verse clearly depicts the belief.

> *kathayāmi na sandehas tat tvayā paripṛcchatām* ||
> *valīpalitanāśaṃ ca tathā kālasya dhvaṃsanam* |
> *yathā lohe tathā dehe kṣamate nātra saṃśayaḥ* ||[5]
>
> I shall certainly tell you whatever is asked by you, i.e. the remedies for warding off wrinkles and gray hair, and also to stop ageing. [These preparations] undoubtedly can bring it about on the metals as well as on the human body.

In fact, gold-making was looked upon as a test to check the efficacy of an elixir before taking it internally. If an elixir proved successful in transmutation of metals, it was believed to be effective through internal administration.

Alchemy and Society

Alchemical notions became deep-rooted in contemporary society. There were very few who actually indulged in this practice, but the philosophy was well known, in the sense that it was being discussed by laypersons as well, as seen in popular literature, e.g. the *Vāsavadattā*[6] and other novels. Alchemy was also taught

[5] Nāgārjuna, *Rasaratnākara*, p. 317. See also Wujastyk 1984.
[6] Subandhu, *Vāsavadattā*, p. 177: *pāradapiṇḍa iva kāladhātuvādinaḥ*.

in Nalanda University as a part of the curriculum around the seventh century AD.[7]

We come across evidence of alchemical practice in texts written during the late medieval period in Sanskrit and other regional languages.[8] In fact, the rise of alchemy at that time (tenth to sixteenth century AD) could probably be collectively attributed to the following facts. Firstly, flourishing chemical activity of the period preceding it discovered numerous methods of making gold-like alloys and amalgams.[9] This suggested to the alchemists the possibility of synthesizing gold. Secondly, contacts with China increased and, either through these or independently, alchemical ideas entered Buddhist literature.[10] Thirdly, Tāntric cults were on the rise and alchemical notions were part of their philosophy, and by about the sixth-seventh century AD Tāntric beliefs and practices started getting reflected in Āyurvedic texts. Vāgbhaṭa the Elder in his *Aṣṭāṅgasaṃgraha* used mercury for the first time in medicines that were to be taken internally. Caraka does not mention mercury, whereas Suśruta uses it only as an ingredient in eye ointments.

Who wrote the Alchemical Works?

Āyurvedic practitioners were learned people who had read the ancient texts. They would prescribe medicines to patients on that basis. Furthermore, they would also prepare the medicines themselves, from scratch, as we now say. Mercury along with other metals and inorganic compounds were needed in pure form for that purpose. The medical practitioners separated metals in the form of essences from their respective ores. In all probability,

[7] Mukherji 1931: 139.
[8] Roy 1980.
[9] Deshpande 1996a.
[10] Deshpande 1987.

they themselves carried out metallurgical operations like extraction and purification of metals, alloy-making etc., or supervised them. This was a merger of hands and brain that happened at this time. In all, a vast accumulation of chemical observations and a firm belief in the possibility of synthesizing gold from baser metals possibly attracted learned people to the field of alchemy. This is seen in western countries as well. Although practitioners of alchemy were people from all walks of life, the texts must have been the creation of learned people, and Āyurvedic practitioners could be the first choice.

In this way, Indian chemistry broke fresh ground during the alchemical period. Alchemical experiments were on a small scale since they involved the use of very pure substances including precious metals. The alchemists tried to explain the observed phenomena with the help of the then established alchemical theory. They designed new methods to give improved products. The most distinguishing feature of this period was the fact that descriptions of the experiments were written down fully. Though alchemical products were rarely preserved, the theory and practice was very well discussed in these texts and important aspects of medieval chemistry may be studied through them. Numerous texts were written during the tenth to sixteenth century AD, such as the *Rasārṇava*, *Rasakāmadhenu*, *Rasārṇavakalpa*, *Rasaratnasamuccaya*, *Rasopaniṣad*, and many more.

The Rasopaniṣad

The *Rasopaniṣad* is one of the largest Sanskrit treatises written on alchemy. It contains some 2500 verses in eighteen chapters. It stands apart from other alchemical texts like the *Rasārṇava*. Among the alchemical treatises which appeared in the eleventh-twelfth century AD, the *Rasārṇava* is the most extensive and widely referred to. It is a large work consisting of over 2600 verses. This work systematically deals with all aspects of alchemical practice in its eighteen chapters. The first four chapters are devoted to the philosophy of mercury and the rituals performed by the practitioner, selection and initiation of disciples, apparatus, fires and further characteristic tests of a number of substances which are employed. Then come medicinal plants, salts, acids, bases, metals, minerals, methods for their extraction, purification, dissolution in solvents etc. Chapters eleven to fifteen are devoted to mercury, its fixation, its physical states and cultivation processes. Metallurgical alchemy forms the sixteenth and seventeenth chapters, whereas physiological alchemy is discussed in the last eighteenth chapter. In short, the *Rasārṇava* gives the fundamentals of medieval Indian alchemy.

The *Rasopaniṣad*, on the other hand, does not provide primary information on the subject, like the description of the apparatus or the eighteen *saṃskāras* or treatments of mercury, but records details of alchemical experiments instead. All eighteen chapters deal largely with metallurgical alchemy. Chapters are divided according to the chief chemical substance or the reaction discussed in it, e.g. chapter 8: *Golakavidhāna*, chapter 10: *Nāgasaṅkramaṇa*, chapter 11: *Tārotkarṣavidhāna*, chapter 13: *Vaṅgastambhana-śodhana* etc. This work is full of procedures and alchemist's comments as well. It vividly depicts efforts made by the alchemist at systematic documentation of his countless experiments and for that reason can be called a chemist's manual instead. E.g. the author cautions the reader on many occasions about the following:

1. Not to touch a product which is likely to be poisonous (*Rasopaniṣad* 2.12).
2. The reaction could produce smoke and exploding sound (Ibid, 15.98).

3. The product will burn the hand on touching (Ibid, 3.24).

The Alchemical Language

Every field of study as it expands develops its own language. Medieval Indian alchemy was no exception. Indian alchemy developed its peculiar expressions for various reagents and chemical phenomena as well. In fact, these terms were coined to make the description short and more expressive but, after centuries of disuse, the very terminology became an obstacle to study. In fact, obstacles have a dual character. The usual ones that arise in the case of ancient texts, e.g. copying errors, missing words, use of obscure synonyms are found in this text too. Identification of plants poses an altogether different and huge problem in itself, since there are over six hundred plants introduced in this work.

Particular problems are related to the typical alchemical terminology. Therefore, merely knowing the rules of grammar is not enough to take in all that is implicated. Terms that appear to be unrelated fall into place once the process is understood. A particular operation by virtue of which mercury loses its volatile nature was termed as 'cutting wings' (*pakṣacchedana*)[11] and the reagent as *pakṣacchedakara* or *aṅkuśa*.[12] If a golden alloy did not contain gold as a constituent it was called *nirbīja*.[13] Substances that helped in the extraction of a metal from its ore or impure state were called 'friends' (*mitra*) because they give its natural and pure form or life back. Five such reagents which act as reducing agents were called *pañcamitra*, and the process as *pañcamitra-saṃskāra*. On the other hand, those oxidizing agents when roasted with a metal converted it into its calx, i.e. killed them or made them lose their 'life' were supposed to be

[11] *Rasopaniṣad* 7.1
[12] Ibid, 16.17
[13] Ibid, 18.282

their enemies and the process was called *māraṇa*[14] or 'killing'. *Mūkamūṣā*[15] (one who cannot speak or one with mouth closed) is a closed crucible, as is an *andhamūṣā*.[16] *Kūrpa*[17] was the furnace or crucible charge. Alcoholic liquors had peculiar names that indicated their application in alchemy, e.g. *drāvaṇī, rañjanī, sarvacāriṇīsurā*[18] etc. Ores of metals with high or low melting points were called *dīrghadrāvi* and *laghudrāvi*[19] respectively. These ores needed strong and prolonged heating. Moreover, borax and other organic matter were to be added to remove the traces of oxides of metals to make them low melting and homogeneous. Certain substances, like borax, carbonates of soda and potash, molasses and plants like *dhātakī* and *guggula* that were useful in this respect, were called *dvandvaja* where *dvandva*[20] means an alloy.[21] It is difficult to find the significance of all these terms from any teacher or in any dictionary or *kośa*, and nothing less than an in-depth study of the subject is a necessary prerequisite to understand them. Yet one is always left with a few unidentified terms for substances, processes and plants.

Alchemical Practice and Literature as a Database

Alchemical processes usually consisted of diluting the noble metals with baser ones, syntheses of gold or silver-like alloys or amalgams from baser metals alone — amalgams of tin, lead, copper are silver-colored whereas that of silver is golden— and mak-

[14]Ibid, 16.178

[15]Ibid, 4.59

[16]Ibid, 14.44

[17]Ibid, 11.12

[18]Ibid, 15.238-251

[19]Ibid, 18.538

[20]Ibid, 16.68.

[21] *Rasārṇava* 8-37: *dhātakī-guggulu-guḍa-sarjaka-ṭaṅkaṇaiḥ| strīstanya-peśitaiḥ sarvaṃ dvandvajaṃ tu rasāyane||*

ing the surface of the base metal golden or silvery by using various techniques. The base metals used were copper, tin, iron, lead or alloys like bronze and brass.[22] Once it was assumed that gold was the purest of all metals and that other base metals could be converted into it by means of certain processes, it was the right process that the alchemist was seeking, and that is why there was repeated experimentation which helped to accumulate considerable chemical data.

In fact, alchemy could be compared to modern chemical experimentation to some degree. Alchemy had specific goals that were based on the knowledge and beliefs of the day. Its practice meant, just as in any other chemical experiment, bringing about reactions, usually involving more than one step, under controlled conditions of purity, composition, temperature, and apparatus. Each step involved combining a number of ingredients in a specific proportion, and it was aimed at a specific end product. It involved pyro-techniques, since other modes of energy supply were unknown in the ancient and medieval period.

Alchemists' goal of transmuting base metals into gold has been proved to be unattainable by modern atomic theory. Although the whole enterprise never yielded what they were looking for, it formed a database for further experimentation in chemistry and metallurgy. Alloys with varying percentage compositions were synthesized. The alchemists observed variation in physical properties due to variation in the composition or the chemical process adopted. Control over temperature was achieved by using various furnaces and fuels. A suitable apparatus was also designed to serve specific functions. Discoveries of mineral acids and gunpowder were probably the most sensational of medieval discoveries that originated in alchemical practice.

---

[22] Deshpande 1984; see also Deshpande 1994.

Poisonous water, moon water and mountain waters that are mentioned in medieval *Rasāyana* texts were mixtures of mineral acids. They were used in alchemical operations. The *Rasārṇava* gives a method of separation of sulfuric acid as essence of alum. Alum is washed in *kāñjika*, 'sour rice gruel,' and mixed with *kṣārāmla*, 'ferrous sulfate,' and heated to get the essence. Also the *Rasaratnasamuccaya* gives a process with green vitriol. The *vidas* described in these texts probably contained mixture of acids. Later medical texts give the preparation of *mahādrāvaka* and *śaṅkhadrāvaka* using alum, green vitriol, Sal ammoniac and saltpeter etc. They could be mixtures of acids like nitro-muriatic acid, sulfuric acid, hydrochloric acid, etc.

Ideas regarding mineral acids began to appear in Arab and western alchemy and medicine by the end of the thirteenth century AD. Nitric acid was made by distilling nitrate with alum and ferrous sulfate. Aqua regia was thus made if salt or ammonium chloride was also added. Sulfuric and hydrochloric acids came by the sixteenth-seventeenth century. Daṇḍin in the sixth century mentions fireworks in his *Daśakumāracarita*, suggesting the use of saltpeter (*yogacūrṇa*).[23] The *Shiyao erya* by Mei Biao refers to a visit of an Indian Buddhist monk to China in 664 and about his knowledge of various poisonous waters and of saltpeter, its extraction, and applications such as a flux in smelting and also in transmutation of metals. The above-mentioned monk also knew about the flame test for examining samples of saltpeter. Chinese records have helped in confirmation of the fact that some mineral acids and saltpeter were used in India before the seventh century.[24]

[23]Daṇḍin, *Daśakumāracarita*, p. 77: *phaṇimukha-kākalī-sandaṃśaka-puruṣaśirṣaka-yogacūrṇa-yogavartikā-mānasūtra-karkaṭaka-rajjudīpa-bhājana-bhramara-karaṇḍaka-prabhṛty-anekopakaraṇa-yuktaḥ.*

[24]Needham 1974: 111.

The *Rasopaniṣad* amply portrays extensive experimentation of the medieval alchemist and also his noteworthy achievements. The *Rasopaniṣad* narrates synthesis of an explosive mixture[25] in one of its chapters. Alcoholic liquors were used as reagents in alchemy,[26] and there is a clear indication of the knowledge of antimony as a separate metal.[27]

A twelfth century text, the *Rasendracūḍāmaṇi*, gives the method for separating antimony, or *varanāga*, from its compound antimony sulphide or stibnite by means of iron. Dioscorides[28] probably knew about it in the second century, but it was Agricola[29] who finally gave the recipe in the sixteenth century.

Some Unique Observations that demonstrate Profound Study of the Author of the Rasopaniṣad

1. Tin Metallurgy

A chapter on tin in the *Rasopaniṣad* describing the use of tin in gold and silver making also reveals the following facts which were known to the alchemist, apart from the physical and chemical properties of tin, and basic or acidic nature of specific plant products etc.[30]

1. It was known that borax[31] could act as a flux and the alchemist used it to remove the impurities in the form of dross.
2. Pure crystalline tin resembles silver and when a little silver

[25] *Rasopaniṣad* 16.171.
[26] Ibid, 15.238-251.
[27] Ibid, 18.461
[28] See Gunther 1968.
[29] Agricola 1950: 428.
[30] Deshpande 1992.
[31] Borax-Sodium Borate or $Na_2 B_4 O_7.10 H2O$. Flux is a substance used in smelting of metal ores that combines with impurities that can then be removed as a flowing mass of slag.

is added to it, the color improves. (It is possibly due to the inhibition of Beta-tin to Alpha-tin transformation.)

3. Tin combines with copper and gold to produce an emerald colored green alloy.

4. While synthesizing the alloys of noble metals, the noble metal is added during the second melting to get homogeneous alloys and to reduce the unnecessary loss of the noble metal.

5. Arsenic compounds are to be avoided in tin metallurgy because even traces of arsenic make tin brittle.

2. Knowledge of Crucibles and Crucible Linings

The alchemist not only knew uses of distinctive crucibles to carry out specific chemical processes, but knew about the appropriate crucible linings[32] to be used as well. Each different crucible lining served one of the following purposes, e.g. to securely close joints and cracks, reduce porosity of the crucible, to reduce absorption of molten metals, to provide a non-absorbent surface, to provide reducing or oxidizing atmospheres as required in the crucible reaction, to facilitate formation of homogeneous alloys by producing a reducing atmosphere to eliminate oxides that would otherwise make the alloy heterogeneous.[33]

Though the reactions carried out in the crucible were on a small scale, they may have similarities with those carried out in a furnace at that time. Their study could lead to the solution of some unsolved problems of medieval metallurgy.

---

[32] *Muṣa* and *muṣalepa* at *Rasopaniṣad* 2.27, 2.29, 2.34, 2.36, 4.59, 4.104-5, 14.40 etc.

[33] Deshpande 1996b.

3. Identification of Ores

In the eighteenth chapter of the *Rasopaniṣad* a novel method for identification of ores of gold, silver, copper, tin and lead is described.

A small portion of the ore is mixed with various substances like plant juices, and that of *Āmalakī*[34] fruit to make a paste. It is then smeared on a copper sheet. The sheet then acquires specific color depending upon the metal contained in the ore. The color could be explained on the basis of the principle of displacement of a metal from the solution of its salt by the other metal which is more electronegative in character and has the tendency to pass into solution.[35]

If the ore contained gold or silver, the copper sheet acquired those respective colors. Both silver and gold, being lower in the series, are replaced from the solution of their respective salts by copper and get deposited on the plate. In the case of copper ore, the sheet became dark possibly due to compound formation. Similarly no displacement occurs when the ore is that of tin or lead.[36]

---

[34] *Āmalaka, Phyllanthus Emblica* Lin.

[35] Electrochemical Series

Metal		Std electrode potential in Volts at 25 degrees C.
Iron	Fe	−0.440
Tin	Sn	−0.136
Lead	Pb	−0.126
Hydrogen	H_2	0.000
Copper	Cu	+0.337
Mercury	Hg	+0.854
Silver	Ag	+0.899
Gold	Au	+1.500

[36] *Rasopaniṣad* 18.456-458.

4. Collecting Pure Metal using Displacement Method

This phenomenon is described in the eighteenth chapter of the *Rasopaniṣad*: *tāreṇojjīvayet hemaṃ tāmraṃ nāgena jīvati*,[37] i.e. 'enliven gold by using silver and enliven copper by using lead.' These reactions can again be explained on the basis of the electrochemical series. They were known in the case of copper-iron pair. The Chinese used to get pure copper on a large scale by this method. It was known in western countries also but probably only for the copper-iron pair.

Concluding Remarks

Alchemy never realized its goal. As we know, no true gold was ever made by an alchemist and, ironically, the alchemical potions sometimes led to premature deaths due to indiscriminate intake of poisonous material, as in the case of some Chinese emperors of the Tang dynasty, viz. Xian zong (AD 806-820), Mu zong (821-824), Jing zong (825-826), Wu zong (841-846), and Xuan zong (847-859).[38] The alchemical myth faded with every failure and slowly alchemy became practically obsolete. As a result, not many know what the alchemical practice was like, how it developed historically and what it actually involved.

Was it just a foolish endeavor that led to nothing but waste of time, money and precious lives? Did anything useful come out of it over the very long period it existed? We know that a great visionary like Newton (1642-1727) indulged in it and left voluminous alchemical notes in his manuscripts.

Was alchemy a forerunner of chemistry or an inhibitor or a hurdle in its progress? Achievements of alchemy are the accumulation of vast chemical data on metals, minerals and chemical

---

[37] Ibid, 18.29-30

[38] Ho & Needham 1959.

processes. Its greatest contribution may be that it helped in redefining the concept of 'element' by seventeenth century chemists. Robert Boyle (1627-1691), the father of modern chemistry, was a secret but unsuccessful alchemist, who indicated that he undoubtedly considered gold as an element, when he wrote his famous definition in his *The Sceptical Chymist*:

> I now mean by Elements certain Primitive and Simple, or perfectly unmingled bodies, or of which those called perfectly mingled bodies are immediately compounded and into which they are ultimately resolved. — I know no fact that would prove that gold, for instance, might not as well be called an element as anything else.[39]

Why does one open up the subject of alchemy or other proto-sciences if they are no more useful or meaningful after the emergence of modern science? Apart from preservation of the cultural history of a particular area, these studies can provide answers to a number of historical problems. Medieval chemical-metallurgical techniques that have continually intrigued scholars could be reconstructed through a study of medieval alchemical texts.

Non-development of modern science in eastern civilizations has been a long-standing problem in history of science. It is necessary to understand the development in the period immediately preceding the events that led to the grand finale. Proto-scientific literature would provide a database from which one could draw reliable inferences. Detailed study of the majority of them will reveal the true nature of the role of medieval practices in the development of sciences like chemistry and metallurgy. When all the pieces of the jigsaw fall in place, we will have the complete picture.

---

[39] See Boas 1958; Stillman 1924.

BIBLIOGRAPHY

Primary Texts

Daṇḍin, *Daśakumāracarita*
of Daṇḍin, ed. M. R. Kale, Bombay 1917.

Kauṭilya, *Arthaśāstra*
The Kauṭilīya Arthaśāstra ed. R. P. Kangle, Bombay 1969.

Nāgārjuna, *Rasaratnākara*
ed. P. Ray, in: idem, *History of Chemistry in Ancient and Medieval India*, Indian Chemical Society, Calcutta 1956.

Rasakāmadhenu
ed. Jadavji Trikumji Acharya, Subodhini Printing Press, Bombay 1925.

Rasārṇava
ed. P. C. Ray & Haris Chandra Kaviratna, Bibliotheca Indica 174, Asiatic Society, Calcutta 1990.

Rasārṇavakalpa
ed & tr. Mira Roy & B. V. Subbarayappa, Indian National Science Academy, New Delhi 1976.

Rasopaniṣad
ed. K. Sambasiva Sastri, Trivandrum 1928 (Trivandrum Sanskrit Series 92).

Subandhu, *Vāsavadattā*
Mahākavi Subandhu-viracitā Vāsavadattā, Banares 1954.

Vāgbhaṭa, *Rasaratnasamuccaya*
of Vāgbhaṭa, ed. Vinayak Apte, Poona 1890 (Anandasrama Sanskrit Series 19).

Secondary Literature

Agricola, Georgius
1950 *De Re Metallica*, tr. Herbert Clark Hoover & Lou Henry Hoover, Dover Publications, New York 1950.

Boas, Marie

1958 *Robert Boyle and Seventeenth Century Chemistry*, Cambridge University Press, Cambridge.

Deshpande, Vijaya

1984 'Transmutation of Base Metals into Gold as described in the Text *Rasārṇavakalpa* and its Comparison with parallel Chinese Methods,' *Indian Journal of History of Science*, 19 (1984) 186-192.

1987 'Medieval Transmission of Alchemical and Chemical Ideas between India and China,' *Indian Journal of History of Science*, 22 (1987) 15-28.

1992 '*Vaṅgastambhanaśodhanam*: A Chapter on Metallurgy of Tin in Sanskrit Alchemical Text *Rasopaniṣad*,' *Indian Journal of History of Science*, 27 (1992) 121-131.

1994 '*Śulbārākālikācchedaḥ:* Medieval Methods for Cleansing Metal Surfaces and Removing Tarnishes,' *Indian Journal of History of Science*, 29 (1994) 315-328.

1996a 'History of Chemistry and Alchemy in India from Prehistoric to Pre-modern Times' in: *Science, Philosophy and Culture: Multidisciplinary Explorations*, vol. I, ed. D. P. Chattopadhyaya & Ravinder Kumar, Project of History of Indian Science, Philosophy and Culture in association with Indian Council of Philosophical Research, New Delhi 1996, pp. 264-323.

1996b '*Mūṣāvijñāna* or the Ancient Science of Crucibles,' *Indian Journal of History of Science*, 31 (1996) 359-373.

Gunther, R. T. (ed),

1968 *The Greek Herbal of Dioscorides,* Hafner Publishing Company, London and New York.

Ho, P. Y. & J. Needham

1959 'Elixir poisoning in Medieval China,' *Janus*, 48 (1959) 221-251.

Mukherji, P. K.

1931 *Indian Literature in China and Far East*, Prabasi Press, Calcutta.

Needham, Joseph
1974 *Science and Civilization in China*, vol. 5, part II, Cambridge University Press, Cambridge.

Roy, Mira
1980 'Some aspects of Sanskrit texts dealing with chemical, iatro-chemical and biological ideas,' *Proceedings, International Sanskrit Conference,* III (I).

Stillman, J. M.
1924 *The Story of Early Chemistry*, D. Appleton & Co., New York, London.

Wujastyk, Dominik
1984 'An alchemical Ghost: the Rasaratnākara by Nāgārjuna,' *Ambix*, 31.2 (1984) 70-83.

Ratnaśāstra in Kauṭilya's Arthaśāstra

GYULA WOJTILLA

Ratnaśāstra means both 'science of gems' or simply gemmology, and a 'textbook of gemmology'. It covers a great deal of experimental knowledge; therefore it is also called *ratnaparīkṣā*, 'examination of gems'. This knowledge benefits people engaged in the gem business and those interested in the study of the stones themselves. Professionals belonging to the first group are the jewellers who know the essence of gems (*ratnatattvavid*)[1] and who are buying and selling gems. They are regarded as craftsmen (*śilpin*).[2] This kind of expertise is one of the sixty-four skills (*kalā*) called *maṇirāgākarajñāna*, 'knowledge of the colour and the places of occurrence of gems'.[3]

It is generally agreed that Kauṭilya's *Arthaśāstra* (= KA)[4] is the oldest text which makes allusions to the origin of this science and contains a coherent treatment of *ratnaparīkṣā*.[5] We learn

---

[1] *Bṛhatkathaślokasaṃgraha*, 18.371.

[2] *Mṛcchakaṭika*, p. 239.

[3] *Kāmasūtra*, I.3.15.

[4] I use *The Kauṭilīya Arthaśāstra*, ed. by R. P. Kangle, Bombay, 1969². The *sigla* of the manuscripts and commentaries are taken from this edition.

[5] Cf. Wojtilla 1980.

from KA VII.12.23 that conch-shells, diamonds, rubies, pearls and gold 'are more plentiful on the southern route' than on the northern one. As S. R. Sarma aptly says, the *Shilappadikāram* ('The Ankle Bracelet') provides rich information about gem markets in South India where this science might have developed.[6] It is a pity that the chronological framework of this development is hazy: *Shilappadikāram* has variously been dated to the third-fourth centuries or to the fifth-sixth centuries CE.[7] KA II.1.28 is a minor *ratnaparīkṣā* and forms part of Book II which precedes the age of the compilation of the KA, i.e. the middle of the second century CE.[8] The Greek and Latin accounts point to the first century CE: Pliny the Elder highlights the values of the Indian diamond and enumerates almost all the significant precious and semi-precious stones of India;[9] the *Periplus Maris Erythraei* of an unknown author definitely speaks of diamonds and sapphires from the southern part of India.[10] Curiously, the only place where a considerable number of pendants, rings, necklaces and bracelets were found is Sirkap, Taxila, datable to the first century BCE -first century CE.[11] It is surprising that neither the KA nor its commentaries refer to earlier authorities on gemmology. It may indirectly indicate that at that time no such works had existed. The extant comprehensive textbooks on the subject are indeed from the medieval times.

In the present paper I am going to make a scrutiny of KA II.11.28-41. My approach is basically that of a philologist; however, I occasionally take into account the results of modern sci-

[6]Sarma 1984: 14.
[7]Bytsihina & Dubianski 1987: 40.
[8]Trautmann 1971: 174, 183.
[9]Wojtilla 1973: 223.
[10]*Periplus* 56.
[11]Ghosh 1989: 222.

ence.[12]

KA II.11.28-41 under investigation form part of the chapter called *kośapraveśyaratnaparīkṣā*, in Kangle's translation 'Examination of precious articles to be received into the treasury.'[13] This work has to be carried out by an officer called *kośādhyakṣa*, 'superintendent of the treasury.' Like many other *adhyakṣas*, he is supposed to possess a wide range of expert knowledge. KA II.11.116-117 goes into details about it: 'Of precious articles other than these, he should be conversant (*jānīyāt*) with the amount, price, characteristics, class and appearance, their storing, manufacture of new ones and repair of old ones, secret treatment, tools, their use according to place and time, and remedies against things destructive (to them).' It is not by accident that the KA uses *jānīyāt* instead of *vidyāt*. It may suggest that he must have certain knowledge of gems, but in special cases has to consult somebody who really knows (*vetti*) gems. As KA II.11.1 puts it, while receiving precious stones etc., he presides over the bureaux of experts.[14] Similarly the superintendent of agriculture is assisted by experts (*tajjñasakha*: KA II.24.1). It is a pity that the names of the experts in the science of precious stones are missing in the KA. We learn from medieval sources like the *Agastimata* (61-75) and the *Rayaṇaparikkhā* (106-109) that the designation of such an expert was *maṇḍalika*.[15]

Let us start with a brief survey of the structure of the paragraph. Passage 28 gives the places of occurence of gems. Pas-

[12]In this connection I am greatly indebted to my old friend Dr Imre Orsovai, formerly of Eötvös Loránd University, Budapest, for reading my translation and making very valuable comments on certain passages from the geological point of view. Unless I quote statements from specialist literature, modern comments are his.

[13]Kangle 1972.

[14]Following Sorabji 1914:17, I read here *tajjñāta* for *tajjāta*.

[15]Finot 1896: 77-139; Sarma 1984: 72.

sages 29-32 contain a list of gems. The KA does not seem to make a difference between the precious stones (*mahāratna*) such as ruby (*saugandhika* or *padmarāga*) and sapphire (*indranīla*) and the semi-precious stones (*uparatna*) such as pure rock crystal (*śuddhasphaṭika*). The position of beryl (*vaidūrya*) is controversial: Indian tradition holds it as a semi-precious stone,[16] while modern gemmology maintains that certain shades of beryl resembling the grass green emerald can exceptionally reach the standard of precious stones.

It is striking that diamond and emerald (*marakata*) are missing in the list of the *mahāratnas*: more precisely, diamond has been dealt with later in passages 37-41. At first sight this appears quite unusual because the description of the *mahāratnas* normally begins with diamond in the classical *ratnaśāstras* such as the *Ratnaparīkṣa* of Buddhabhaṭṭa, the *Agastimata*, the *Bṛhatsaṃhitā* of Varāhamihira, or Ṭhakkura Pherū's *Rayaṇaparikkhā*. This circumstance can be explained by various reasons. Breloer is of the opinion that the paragraph could be a fragment of a lost *vārttāśāstra*, 'textbook of economy,' where gems and diamonds are separately treated.[17] This suggestion could well be true because all commentators follow this arrangement of the text. The lack of emerald can perhaps be explained by practical reasons: there is no report of any emerald mine in ancient India.[18] Its grass green variety can easily be confused with beryl.

Passage 32 which describes *śuddhasphaṭika* 'pure [transparent] rock crystal' is not without problem. Manuscripts D, G and M omit the words *śuddhasphaṭiko mūlātavarṇaḥ*. Kangle admits that they 'are from the commentators, but seem to be

[16]Finot 1896: xvi.
[17]Breloer 1934: 293.
[18]Biswas 1994: 146.

genuine'. Nevertheless, I find the word *mūlātavarṇa* rather suspicious. Kangle understands it as the flower of the *mūlātī* plant. Unfortunately this plant is still enigmatic: R. Schmidt identifies it with *dadhimūlam*, a name attestable in *Yaśastilaka*, but he does not give its meaning.[19] I think that the explanation of *mūlāta* offered by the commentaries Cb and Cp namely 'curds with the upper layer removed' is somewhat fanciful. Rock crystal or quartz may have the quality of precious stones if it is clear as water, transparent and looks like white glass. If the KA uses the attribute *śuddha* intentionally here it could mean that the passage speaks of rock crystal in the above-mentioned sense.

Passages 33-34 are appropriate to the *ratnaśāstras* proper: we are given a list of qualities (*guṇa*) and flaws (*doṣa*) of the above-mentioned gems. The interpretation of *durviddha*, translated as 'badly bored' by Kangle and 'schlecht durchbohrt' by Meyer,[20] conceals technical problems. The Russian translation is more careful: 'plohaya obrabotka,' i.e. 'bad workmanship'.[21] The term is a *hapax legomenon* and stands only in the commentary Cs, while the commentaries Cj and Cp keep silent. It is hard to conceive technically that boring of gems might have been done in the age of the composition of the KA. On the other hand, drilling certain semi-precious stones such as carnelian or agate has been known since the age of the Harappa culture.[22] We learn from the *Rayaṇaparikkhā* 36 that the tools for boring or cutting gems must be made of diamond.[23] Such instruments are listed in the *Agastyasaṃhitā* dated to before 1334/5 CE.[24] It is noteworthy that in the *ratnaśāstras* we find the negative attribute *bhinna*

[19] Somadevasūri, *Yaśastilakacampu* I.406.3; cf. Schmidt 1991: 202.
[20] Meyer 1926: 109.
[21] Kal'yanov 1959: 83.
[22] Ghosh 1989: 217.
[23] Sarma 1984: 51.
[24] *Agastyasaṃhitā*; cf. Sarma 1990; see also Rau 1982.

'broken' in the place of *durviddha*.[25] Although manuscripts give the reading *durviddha* I suspect here a later interpolation.

Passage 35 also gives food for thought. As we shall see, the readings of the manuscripts and the commentaries considerably differ at places. The commentary Cp suggests that the passage deals with those gems which are neither the best nor the most inferior, i.e. items between the precious and semi-precious stones and the artificial ones. It is a pity that this explanation is not supported by any evidence from the extant *ratnaśāstras*: these names are totally missing there. Perhaps this passage is a gloss, but this too is not certain.

Passage 36 is quite in order: it has to do with the falsification of gems which is normally treated in *ratnaśāstras* under the heading *vijāti*, 'simulants and spurious gems'. The KA does not dwell upon this subject, but the methods of imitating precious stones by colouring crystals were known around the first century CE; at least Pliny the Elder referred to it.[26] The *Divyāvadāna*, conventionally dated to the third century CE, uses the term exactly in the same sense (*kācamaṇayo ratnasadṛśāḥ*).[27] The term *kācamaṇi* is explained by the commentary Cj as an object that imitates the splendour of the colour of a precious stone.

Passages 37-41 are fully devoted to the diamond. This treatment is systematic: mines (*ākara*), colours (*varṇa*), qualities (*guṇa*) and flaws (*dośa*) are discussed here.

Now let us look at the slightly revised text together with an English translation and brief notes. Here I generally follow Kangle's excellent translation and explanatory notes. I offer a new rendering only at places where the modified text makes it

[25] Finot 1896: xliii, xxxix.
[26] Pliny, *Natural History*, 37.5.20, p.130.
[27] *Divyāvadāna*, p. 438, lines 17-18.

necessary, or where I hold Kangle's interpretation to be not quite satisfactory.

KA II.11.28: *maṇiḥ kauṭo māleyakaḥ pārasamudrakaś ca*, 'Gems are from *Koṭi*, from *Mālā*, and from beyond the sea.' The identification of these geographical names is highly uncertain; the commentators identify *Kauṭa* with Mount *Kūṭa*, or *Koṭi* between Malaya and the sea; M. G. S. Narayanan takes it for modern *Dhanuṣkoṭi* at the tip of the Peninsula; *Mālā* may be a part of Malaya also called *Karṇīvana*; in spite of the fact that some commentaries think of mount *Rohaṇa* in Sri Lanka, the name *Pārasamudraka* denotes more likely all those countries which have to be contacted across the Eastern sea.[28]

29: *saugandhikaḥ padmarāgo 'navadyarāgaḥ pārijātapuṣpako bālasūryakaḥ*. 'The ruby (*saugandhika*) is of the colour of the red lotus, of faultless colour, of the (colour of) the flower of the coral tree, (and) of the (colour of the) morning sun.' Following the commentary Cp and the *Mānasollāsa* 2.475-6, Kangle takes *saugandhika* as a generic name for ruby. The *Agastimata* 174 regards *saugandhika, kuruvinda* and *padmarāga* as three separate species of ruby. On the other hand, *Bṛhatsaṃhitā* 82.1 takes *saugandhika* as sulphur from which ruby (*padmarāga*) originates. The *Ratnaparīkṣā* 114 has the same idea.[29] Unfortunately this derivation does not stand the test of modern science. *Anavadyarāga* is saffron colour according to the commentary Cn, and Meyer conjecturally takes the word as 'red'. At any rate saffron colour does not suit the colour of ruby. *Bālasūryaka* may be the transparent, clear ruby of the kind found in Burma.[30] Altogether the passage remains problematic.

---

[28] Narayanan 1993: 23.
[29] Buddhabhaṭṭa, *Ratnaparīkṣā*, pp. 1-58.
[30] Murthy 1990: 18.

30: *vaiḍūrya utpalavarṇaḥ śirīṣapuṣpaka udakavarṇo vaṃśarāgaḥ śukapatravarṇaḥ puṣyarāgo gomūtrako gomedakaḥ.* Kangle: 'The beryl, of the colour of the blue lotus, of the *śirīṣa*-flower, of the colour of water, of the colour of (green) bamboo, of the colour of the parrot's wing, yellow-coloured, of the colour of cow's urine (and) of cow's fat.' This interpretation appears sound but we must admit that *vaiḍūrya* may also denote other gems, for instance the cat's eye.[31]

31: *indranīlo nīlāvalīyaḥ kalāyapuṣpako mahānīlo jāmbavābho jīmūtaprabho nandakaḥ sravanmadhyaḥ.* On the basis of the manuscripts G and M, the commentaries Cb and Cs and following Dātāra,[32] I prefer *jāmbavābho* to Kangle's *jambvābho*: 'The sapphire, with blue lines, like the *kalāya*-flower, deep blue, having the lustre of the *jambū* fruit, having the lustre of the dark cloud, the 'delighter' (and) the 'streaming interior.' In the light of modern gemmology this description is inexact and superficial: what is not blue cannot be a sapphire.

32: *śuddhasphaṭiko mūlātavarṇaḥ śītavṛṣṭiḥ sūryakāntaś ca iti maṇayaḥ.* This reading is not quite beyond question because the manuscripts D, G and M omit *śuddhasphaṭiko mūlātavarṇaḥ.* It is based on the commentary Cp the reading of which, according to Kangle, seems 'to be genuine.' 'The pure rock crystal, of the colour of *mūlāta*-flower, shedding a cool shower and the sunstone. These are the gems.' Kangle's translation is not unambiguous; moreover in his notes he raises the possibility that these are independent names of gems. The name *śītavṛṣṭi* can be taken as a synonym of *candrakānta*, 'moonstone'. At least the *Yuktikalpataru* states that *candrakānta*, and *sūryakānta* are two kinds of *sphaṭika*.[33] The problem is that the name 'moonstone'

[31] Sarma 1984: 67.

[32] Kauṭilya, *Arthaśāstra*(b).

[33] Bhojarāja, *Yuktikalpataru*, p. 137, verse 6; cf. Gangadharan & Ra-

is a commercial category and not a proper gemmological name. It is also likely that the passage deals with rock crystal and its varieties (the commentary Cs and Meyer).

33: *ṣaḍaśraś caturaśro vṛtto tīvrarāgaḥ saṃsthānavān acchaḥ snigdho gurur arciṣmān antargataprabhaḥ prabhānulepī ceti maṇiguṇāḥ.* Kangle: 'Hexagonal, square or round, of a flashing colour, having a suitable form, clear, smooth, heavy, lustrous, with lustre inside and imparting lustre — these are the excellences of gems.' It is uncertain whether these qualities refer to the natural condition of the stones or to them after cutting. In terms of modern gemmology the attribute 'heavy' which suggests heaviness is not regarded as a special quality of gems.

34: *mandarāgaprabhaḥ saśarkaraḥ puṣpacchidraḥ khaṇḍo durviddho lekhākīrṇa iti doṣāḥ.* Kangle: 'With a dull colour and lustre, with grains, with a hole in the bloom, broken, badly bored,' (and) covered with scratches — these are blemishes.' The attribute *durviddha*, 'badly bored' is, however, problematic.

35: *vimalakaḥ sasyako 'ñjanamūlakaḥ pittakaḥ sulabhako lohitako 'mṛtāṃśuka jyotīrasako maileyako 'hicchatrakaḥ kūrpaḥ pratikūrpaḥ sugandhikūrpaḥ kṣīrapakaḥ śukticūrṇakaḥ śilāpravālakaḥ pulakaḥ śukrapulaka ity antarajātayaḥ.* On the basis of the manuscripts G and M, the commentary Cn and following Dātāra, I prefer *lohitaka* to Kangle's *lohitākṣa.* Following the manuscripts G and M, the commentary Cn and the reading of Dātāra, I prefer *amṛtāṃśuka* to *mṛgāśmaka* taken by Kangle from the commentary Cs. On the basis of the manuscripts G and M, the commentaries Cb and Cp and the reading of Dātāra, I prefer *śukrapulaka* to *śuklapulaka.* Following the manscripts G and M, the commentary Cp and the reading of Dātāra, I prefer *maileyaka*

---

jasekaran 1990: 136.

to *māleyaka.* On the basis of the manuscript G_1, the commentary Cs and the reading of Dātāra, I prefer *kṣīrapaka* to *kṣīravaka.* As Kangle justly puts it, 'most of these names have no doubt reference to colour' and two names (*ahicchatraka* i.e. the modern Rāmnagar in Bareilly district, U.P., and *maileyaka*) point to the places of occurrence. As a matter of fact, mere colour does not characterise gems. It is also not clear whether this list has any connection with the above descriptions of gems. I find two names where the possible rendering may denote gems; *śilāpravālaka* and *pulaka* can independently be 'astroite' and 'garnet'; however, they rather refer to characteristics in the given context. The tentative translation is as follows: 'Spotless, blue, dark-blue, of the colour of cow's bile, white, copper(-coloured), always radiating, of flood of light, vermilion-coloured (*maileyaka*), of a faint red colour (*ahicchatraka*), with sand-grains inside, looking like beeswax, of the colour of *mudga*-bean, milk-coloured, resembling the powder of pearl shell, coral-coloured (*śilāpravālaka*), with a black interior (*pulaka*) and with a white interior — these are the intermediate kinds.'

36: *śeṣāh kācamaṇayaḥ.* 'The rest are glass jewels.' These are not simulants or spurious gems because the production of artificial gems was unknown in ancient India and also the outside world.

37: *sabhārāṣṭrakaṃ tajjamārāṣṭrakaṃ kāstīrarāṣṭraṃ śrīkaṭanakaṃ maṇimantakam indravānakaṃ ca vajram.* Kangle: 'Diamonds come from *Sabhārāṣṭra*, from *Tajjamārāṣṭra*, from *Kāstīrarāṣṭra*, from (Mt.) *Śrīkatanaka*, from (Mt.) *Maṇimanta* and from *Indravāna.*' At the present stage of research we cannot identify these localities with known diamond producing areas in medieval or modern India. The identifications proposed by the commentators are mostly whimsical.

38: *khaniḥ srotaḥ prakīrṇakaṃ ca yonayaḥ.* Kangle: 'The mine, the stream and miscellaneous are the sources.' It is remarkable that the KA uses here the word *yoni* 'source' i.e. 'place of occurrence', 'finding place', which is not the proper technical term. It is curious because KA II.12 records the proper term, namely *ākara*, used in the Sanskrit textbooks on gemmology. Apart from this, it is a competent passage by any modern standard.

39: *mārjārākṣakaṃ śirīṣapuṣpakaṃ gomūtrakaṃ gomedakaṃ śuddhasphaṭikaṃ mūlātīvarṇaṃ maṇivarṇānām anyatamavarṇam iti vajravarṇāḥ.* Following Kangle, I render it with slight modifications thus: 'Like the cat's eye, the *śirīṣa*-flower, cow's urine, cow's fat, pure crystal, (or) of the colour of curds with the upper layer removed and of the colour of any one of the gems -- these are the colours of diamonds.' The cat's eye mentioned here is likely to be chrysoberyl which can abundantly be found at Morawak-Korale and in Saffragana district, in the alluvial deposits of river Ratkanga and in the vicinity of Matara in Sri Lanka.

40: *sthūlam gurū prahārasahaṃ samakoṭikaṃ bhājanalekhi tarku-bhrāmi bhrājiṣṇu ca praśastam.* Kangle: '(A diamond that is) big, heavy, capable of bearing blows, with symmetrical points, (capable of) scratching a vessel, revolving like a spindle and brilliantly shining is excellent.' The manuscripts G and M offer a problematic reading and, as Sorabji remarks, the commentary Cp is also hopelessly corrupt here. Kangle's rendering seems to be satisfactory. The attribute, 'bearing blows', is due to an universal superstition that diamond cannot be crushed with a hammer and is accordingly unscientific. The two most important optical features of diamond are the high index of refraction of light, the strong shine and dispersion of light. The white light appears to emerge from it as blue, yellow and red rays.

41: *naṣṭakoṇam niraśri pārśvāpavṛttam cāpraśastam.* Kangle: 'That with points lost, without edges and defective on one side is bad.' This statement is well in line with the standpoint of modern science.

Summing up what has been said, I want to highlight the following findings.

1. The text is highly problematic at places and this can only partially be cured on the basis of the commentaries. In contradiction to Kangle, I rely more on the basic manuscripts of the text.

2. The edition of these passages is very loose and its contents may represent a text between *vārttāśāstra* and *ratnaśāstra.*

3. It can be regarded as the first *ratnaśāstra* where scientific theory is strongly intermingled with commercial expertise. This circumstance explains its modern statements and also the terminological inconsistencies.

4. Although the KA has not preserved names of authorities on the subject, it clearly indicates the existence of gemmology by its time as well as the geographical limits of the birth of this science, i.e. South India.

5. Future tasks are many: textual studies, semantical and technical research in Greek, Latin and Tamil sources, and meticulous study of the archaeological evidence.

BIBLIOGRAPHY

Primary Texts

Agastimata
ed. & tr. L. Finot, *Les lapidaires indiens*, Paris 1896, pp. 77-139.

Agastyasaṃhitā
Agastyaproktā Agastyasaṃhitā, ed. by Kṛṣṇaprasāda Bhaṭṭarāī, Kathmandu 1962/63.

Bhojarāja, *Yuktikalpataru*
ed. by Isvara Chandra Sāstrī, Calcutta 1917.

Buddhabhaṭṭa, *Ratnaparīkṣā*
ed. & tr. L. Finot, *Les lapidaires indiens*, Paris 1896, pp. 1-58.

Budhasvāmin, *Bṛhatkathāślokasaṃgraha*,
ed. by P. K. Agrawala, Varanasi 1977.

Divyāvadāna
ed. by P. L. Vaidya, Darbhanga 1959.

Kauṭilya, *Arthaśāstra*
(a) *Kauṭilīya Arthaśāstra*, ed. by R. P. Kangle, Bombay 1969[2]
(b) *Kauṭilīyam Arthaśāstram of Ācārya Visṇugupta*, ed. by V. S. Dātāra, Varanasi 1991.

Somadeva Sūri, *Yaśastilakacampū*
ed. by Śivadatta, Kāśināth Pāṇḍurang Parab and Vāsudeva Laxmaṇ Śāstrī Paṇaśīkar, Bombay 1903-1916.

Someśvara, *Mānasollāsa*
ed. by G. K. Shrigondekar, Baroda 1925-1931.

Śūdraka, *Mṛcchakaṭika*
ed. by Rāmānuja Ojhā, Varanasi 1974[3].

Varāhamihira, *Bṛhatsaṃhitā*
tr. by M. Ramakrishna Bhat, Delhi 1986-1987[2].

Vātsyāyana, *Kāmasūtra*
ed. by G. D. Shastri, Benares 1929.

Secondary Literature

Biswas, A. K.
1994 'Vaidūrya, Marakata and Other Beryl Family Gem Minerals: Etymology and Traditions in Ancient India,' *Indian Journal of History of Science*, 29.2 (1994) 139-54.

Breloer, B.
1934 *Staatsverwaltung im alten Indien. Kauṭalīya Studien III*, Erster Band: Finanzverwaltung und Wirtschaftsführung, Leipzig.

Bytsihina L. V. & A. M. Dubianski
1987 *Tamils'kaya literatura*, Moskva.

Finot, Loius
1896 *Les Lapidaires Indiennes* (Bibliothèque de l'école des hautes études, publicée sous les auspices du ministère de l'instruction publique, sciences philologiques et historiques, cent-onzième fascicule), Paris 1896.

Gangadharan, N. & K. C. Rajasekaran
1990 'Lapidary Section of Bhoja's Yuktikalpataru. An Assessment' in: *History of Science and Technology in India*, ed. by G. Kuppuram & K. Kumudamani, vol. VI, Delhi 1990, pp. 125-139.

Ghosh, A. (ed)
1989 *An Encyclopaedia of Indian Archaeology*, vol. 1, New Delhi.

Kal'yanov, V. I. (ed)
1959 *Arthashastra ili nauka politiki, perevod s sanskrita*, Moskva-Leningrad.

Kangle, R. P.
1972 *The Kauṭilīya Arthaśāstra*, Part II: An English Translation with Critical and Explanatory Notes. Bombay 1972[2]

Meyer, J. J.
1926 *Das altindische Buch vom Welt- und Staatsleben. Das Arthaśāstra des Kauṭilya. Aus dem Sanskrit übersetzt und mit Einleitung und Anmerkungen versehen.* Leipzig.

Murthy, S. R. N.
1990 *Gemmological Studies in Sanskrit Texts*, vol. I, Bangalore.

Narayanan, M. G. S.
1993 'Product-Associated Place-Names in the Arthasastra' (sic!), *Studies in Indian Place Names,* 14, pp. 21-25

Pliny, *Natural History*
in: J. W. Mc Crindle, *Ancient India as described in Classical Literature*, Westminster 1901.

Rau, Wilhelm
1982 *Die Brennlinse im alten Indien*, Mainz/Wiesbaden.

Sarma, S. R.
1990 'Historical Notices on Gem Cutting in India,' *History of Science and Technology in India*, Vol. VI, ed. by G. Kuppuram & K. Kumudamani, New Delhi, 1990, pp. 141-158 (146-51).

Sarma, Sreeramula Rajeswara
1984 *Ṭhakkura Pherū's Rayaṇaparikkhā. A Medieval Prakrit Text on Gemmology*, Aligarh.

Schmidt, R.
1991 *Nachträge zum Sanskrit Wörterbuch in kürzerer Fassung von Otto Böhtlingk*, First Indian Edition, Delhi.

Sorabji, I. J.
1914 *Some Notes on the Adhyakṣa-Pracāra*, Allahabad.

Trautmann, T. R.
1971 *Kauṭilya and the Arthaśāstra. A Statistical Investigation of the Authorship and Evolution of the Text*, Leiden.

Wojtilla, Gyula.
1973 'Indian Precious Stones in the Ancient East and West,' *Acta Orientalia Hung*, 28.2 (1973) 211-224.
1980 'Contribution to the Sanskrit Sources of the Knowledge of Precious Stones,' *Bhāratī-bhānam [Light of Indology] [Being Dr K. V. Sarma Felicitation Volume]*, ed. by S. Bhaskaran Nair, Hoshiarpur 1980, pp. 396-402.

The Body of the Musician
The Embryology and Anatomy in Indian Musicology

MAKOTO KITADA

The Sanskrit musicological text from the thirteenth century, the *Saṅgītaratnākara* (= SR), 'the Ocean of Music', written by Śārṅgadeva is considered to be one of the most important texts on this subject.[1] It deals with musical theoretical topics like intervals (*śruti, svara*), scales (*grāma*), modes (*jāti*) etc., and also contains many compositions with their notations. But the contents of the second chapter of the first section, entitled *Piṇḍotpatti Prakaraṇa*, 'the Chapter of the Arising of the Embryo,' is rather peculiar. The first half of this chapter deals with Āyurvedic embryology and anatomy, and the second half deals with *cakra*-s and *nāḍī*-s, or the respiratory tubes, in accordance with Haṭhayoga. I studied this chapter for my dissertation,[2] where I formulated two questions: Why are these topics dealt with in a musicological text? Of what origin is the Ayurvedic theory of embryology and anatomy?

I would like to address the second question first. As the result

[1]Sastri 1992: ix.
[2]Kitada 2006. See also Kitada 2003.

of my comparative study of classical medical texts and purāṇas which deal with embryology and anatomy, I found that the medical theory of the SR is closest to Vāgbhaṭa's *Aṣṭāṅgasaṃgraha*, although there are also many differences. It seems that the medical theory was handed down in the family of the author Śārṅgadeva. His was a family of medical doctors, originally from Kashmir but settled later in the kingdom of Yādavas in the Deccan.[3] Therefore, his theories must come from a medical tradition either of Kashmir or of the Deccan, a tradition closely connected to that of Vāgbhaṭa, but nevertheless independent from it.

Actually I found a parallel text, the *Śivagītā*, which is a purāṇic text.[4] Most of the embryological and anatomical verses in the *Śivagītā* are identical, word for word, to those in the SR. But this fact does not mean that the SR is indebted to the *Śivagītā*. The SR contains theories which are parallel to the classical medical texts like the *Aṣṭāṅgasaṃgraha*, but which are not contained in the *Śivagītā*. Meanwhile, some of the medical theories contained in the *Śivagītā* are more archaic than those in the SR. For instance, the SR contains a statement on the state in the first month of embryonic development in accordance with the classical medical texts, mentioning *ghana, peśī* and *arbuda* according to the embryo's three sexes,[5] while the *Śivagītā* contains a totally different system of embryonic development, mentioning *budbuda, kalala, peśī, ghana* and *piṇḍa* as the states in the first and second month without any association to the embryo's sex, which is not a classical medical theory, but a theory in accordance with the *purāṇas*. Therefore, it seems more logical to assume a third text which the SR and the *Śivagītā* are both indebted to.

---

[3]Kitada 2006: xiii-xiv.

[4]On the *Śivagīta*, cf. Vallauri 1942. On the embryological verses contained in the *Śivagītā*, cf. Comba 1981.

[5]I.e., male, female and the third sex.

This third text is supposed to be a treatise on medical science unknown to our days.

Now to the first, more difficult, question: why are topics like Āyurveda and Haṭhayoga dealt with in a musicological treatise? The reason for Haṭhayoga being dealt with is not difficult to find. The author Śārṅgadeva associates music with *anāhata nāda*, the subtle sound perceived only by Yogins. But the reason why embryology and anatomy are dealt with is not so easy to answer. I could assume the following:

Many non-medical texts like purāṇas also contain verses on embryology and anatomy. In such texts, these topics usually occur in relation to *saṃnyāsins* or ascetics. Ascetics investigate the wandering of the soul, including the birth of the human body, and describe the process of birth as the origin of pain and suffering.[6] Thus the code of law, *Yājñavalkyasmṛti*, contains embryology and anatomy in its chapter on ascetics (*yatidharma-prakaraṇa*).[7] Intriguingly, in this text, in the verses immediately after the verses on embryology and anatomy, the Haṭhayogic theory of respiratory tubes and the playing of music are mentioned. According to this statement, secular music, i.e. singing of songs from the *Nāṭyaśāstra* and playing the *vīṇā* or lute, are praised as a substitute means to attain *mokṣa* or liberation.[8]

I assume that the SR is based on the *Yājñavalkyasmṛti*, namely the tradition of ascetics. As a matter of fact, the author Śārṅgadeva, in concluding the chapter *Piṇḍotpatti*, states that music is a means to attain liberation, a substitute for the

[6] Hara 1980.

[7] Cf. Yamashita 2001/2003.

[8] *Yājñavalkyasmṛti* 3.115:
vīṇā-vādana-tattvajñaḥ śruti-jāti-viśāradaḥ |
tālajñaś cāprayāsena mokṣamārgaṃ niyacchati ||

Haṭhayogic meditation.[9]

But his way of associating music with Haṭhayoga is not very convincing. As previously remarked, Śārṅgadeva's verses on embryology and anatomy are identical to the *Śivagītā*'s. Surely Śārṅgadeva quoted these verses from the medical treatise inherited from his ancestors. On the other hand, I found out that the verses on the *nāḍī*-s or respiratory tubes of Haṭhayoga are parallel to the *Yogayājñavalkya*, the Haṭhayogic text ascribed to the ancient sage. Unfortunately I could not identify the source of the verses on the *cakra*-s: the SR mentions 10 *cakra*-s, i.e. 3 *cakra*-s added to the well-known 7-*cakra* system. But I am convinced that these verses are also a quotation from another text.[10]

---

[9]SR 1.2.163cd-168:
evaṃvidhe tu dehe 'smin mala-sañcaya-saṃvṛte||163cd||
prasādayanti dhīmanto bhuktiṃ muktim upāyataḥ|
tatra syāt saguṇād dhyānād bhuktir muktis tu nirguṇāt||164||
dhyānam ekāgra-cittaika-sādhyaṃ na sukaraṃ nṛṇām|
tasmād atra sukhopāyaṃ śrīman-nādam anāhatam||165||
gurūpadiṣṭa-mārgeṇa munayaḥ samupāsate|
so 'pi rakti-vihīnatvān na manorañjako nṛṇām||166||
tasmād āhata-nādasya śrutyādi-dvārato 'khilam|
geyaṃ vitanvato loka-rañjanaṃ bhavabhañjanam||167||
utpattiṃ abhidhāsyāmas tathā śrutyādi hetutām||168ab|| (This verse, while concluding the *Piṇḍotpattiprakaraṇa*, opens the next chapter.)

[10]Concerning this topic, I would like to call attention to the following fact. In SR 1.2.119, Śārṅgadeva mentions another work of his own, the *Ādhyātmaviveka*. The English translator, R. K. Shringy (Shringy 1999: Introduction, xiv) states that this text is no more available to us. Intriguingly Avalon 1924 presents the same 10-*cakra* system, based on the description in the SR. But besides the SR, he refers to another text entitled *Ādhyātmaviveka*! The respective descriptions of the *cakra*-s which Avalon quotes from this '*Ādhyatmaviveka*' are very similar to those in the SR.

Therefore I would like to suggest that Avalon is possibly mentioning here the identical *Ādhyātmaviveka*, i.e. the work composed by Śārṅgadeva. However, we have to remain cautious with regard to this matter, for the book mentioned in SR 1.2.119 seems to be a treatise on anatomy, while the one mentioned by Avalon is obviously a treatise on *cakra*-theory.

Śārṅgadeva took these three parts from three separate sources and joined them together, without providing logical connections between one another. The text makes an awkward impression: one part is abruptly interrupted and the next is suddenly started, and the gap between them remains explicitly perceptible.

Therefore I am very skeptical as to what degree these statements on *cakra*-s and respiratory tubes reflect the reality of the musical practice of that time. One could certainly speculate that the music described in the SR was utilized for the Haṭhayoga practices of meditating on the *cakra*-s and controlling the respiratory tubes. But the text, being a mere patchwork of fragments which originally had nothing to do with one another, provides neither proof nor concrete information. In my opinion, the author Śārṅgadeva probably only quoted the verses on *cakra*-s and respiratory tubes to legitimize the practice of secular music.

Anyway the *cakra*-theory does not occur further in the other parts of the book. The chapter following the *Piṇḍotpattiprakaraṇa*, which describes the process of producing the intervals and the octave, does not contain any single word belonging to the *cakra*-theory. The commentaries (*Kalānidhi* and *Sudhākara*), which explain the concise expression of the original text in more detail, do not mention the *cakra*-s either.[11]

R. K. Shringy, who translated the SR into English, mentions a very useful text for elucidating the character of the *Piṇḍotpattiprakaraṇa*, namely Śāradātanaya's *Bhāvaprakāśana* ('the Manifestation of Aesthetic Mental States') which is a dramaturgical

[11] However, it is also true that practice does not anticipate a consistent system of theory. A musician might describe his musical practice by more than one system which could differ from one another. E.g. a musician might describe his personal experience of voicing by using the vocabulary of the *cakra*-theory, while he might rely on another theoretical system to explain the origin of intervals and octave.

text containing a chapter on music. This chapter on music, in the opening verses, deals with embryology and anatomy in relation to music. The author, Śāradātanaya, was almost a contemporary of Śārṅgadeva. Therefore the two authors might supplement each other reciprocally.

Shringy believes that Śāradātanaya supports Śārṅgadeva's argument on the relationship between music and *cakra*-s.[12] In this context I may quote Shringy's statement: 'He (= Śāradātanaya) relates the seven tones to seven different places located in the body [...] These places roughly correspond to the psychophysical centres (= *cakra*-s). It can, therefore, be concluded that the line of thought linking musical sound (*āhata nāda*) to the yogic experience of *anāhata nāda* already existed in his time.'[13]

I examined the verses of the *Bhāvaprakāśana* in question. What Shringy states seems to be true up to a certain degree, but the matter is actually a little more complicated. The verses do not directly deal with the *cakras*, but with a different theory.[14]

The theory presented in the *Bhāvaprakāśana* is pseudo-Āyurvedic. According to this theory, which looks like an Āyurvedic one, the seven musical tones originate in the seven *dhātu*-s, or the seven elements of the human body, namely the well-known seven links of the metabolic chain according to

[12] SR (b), p. 393ff., Appendix II.

[13] Ibid, p. 102.

[14] The *Bhāvaprakāśana* actually presents two different theories. One of them (pp. 184-186) is, however, not relevant to my discussion here. It is stated that the seven musical tones arise in various areas in the human body, namely the throat, the root of the palate (*tālu-mūla*), the lips, the middle of the head, and the teeth; these areas are connected to each other with the *nāḍī*-s or respiratory tubes. A similar, but slightly different theory is dealt with by the *Sudhākara* commentary on SR 1.3.24ab-25 (SR(a), pp.102-103). There, the areas of sound manifestation are: the nose, throat, chest, palate, tongue, teeth, navel, head (*śīrṣa*), and heart.

Āyurveda. These seven elements are skin, blood, flesh, fat, bone, marrow, and semen.[15] The *Bhāvaprakāśana* intriguingly states that the *dhamanī*-s, or vessels, nourishing the seven *dhātu*-s are situated in certain areas of the human body. The four vessels nourishing semen are in the 'bulb' (*kanda*) of the base area; the three nourishing marrow are in the navel; the two nourishing bones are in the heart; the four vessels for fat are in the throat; the four for flesh are in the root of the palate; the three for blood are in the head; and the two for skin are in the middle of the brows. The seven musical tones, which originate in the seven *dhātus*, therefore arise in the seven areas of the body, namely the base area (*ādhāra*), the navel, heart, throat, the root of the palate, the head, and the middle of the brows successively. Actually, this theory deviates from the classical medical theory of Āyurveda. The numbers of the vessels (4, 3, 2, 4, 4, 3, 2) have no equivalents in the classical medical theory. These numbers are in reality derived from the musicological theory: the octave contains 22 microtones, and the respective intervals between the seven musical tones are 4, 3, 2, 4, 4, 3, 2 microtones successively.[16]

After this statement, the *Bhāvaprakāśana* mentions the lotus of the heart and the hollow in the heart which is called '*dahara*'. This statement concerning the heart is not Āyurvedic, but Haṭhayogic in origin. So this musicological school presented in the *Bhāvaprakāśana* seems to try to integrate the Āyurvedic theory of the seven *dhātu*-s with the Haṭhayogic theory of the heart-lotus. In other words, this school has a theory which has similarities to Āyurveda and Haṭhayoga, but is, at the same time, independent of the two.

---

[15]According to the classical medical theory, the first link of this chain is usually nutritious fluid. But musicological works mention skin as the first; cf. Das 2003:547.

[16]On the so-called *Saḍja-grāma*, cf. Gomperts 2000: esp. p. 575.

Concerning this, one question springs to mind: whether these seven areas of the human body in which the seven *dhātu*-s and the seven musical tones arise could be identified with the seven *cakra*-s. These areas, namely the base area (*ādhāra*), the navel, heart, throat, the root of the palate, the head, and the middle of the brows, seem to correspond closely to the *cakra*-s, as Shringy has already noted. But they are not called '*cakra*' at all in this text. The question is whether it is appropriate to consider this theory, which is contained in the *Bhāvaprakāśana*, to be identical to the *cakra*–theory in the SR.

Actually there is another text which mentions *dhātu*-s and *cakra*-s in relation to music, namely Mataṅgā's *Bṛhaddeśī*, which is a musicological text of an earlier date than the SR and is quoted in the *Sudhākara* commentary on the SR (1.3.56-59; (a), p.120, ll.6-10). The *Bṛhaddeśī* (*anuccheda* 29) contains the statement that the seven musical tones are derived from the seven *dhātu*-s of the human body too. In the same paragraph, the *Bṛhaddeśī* states that the seven musical notes are also related to the seven *cakra*-s and seven continents! This passage suggests that the musical tones, *dhātu*-s and *cakra*-s are somehow associated with one another. But this statement is too fragmentary to provide any substantial facts which would help answer the question posed.

BIBLIOGRAPHY

Primary Texts

Mataṅga, *Bṛhaddeśī*

of Śrī Mataṅga Muni, ed. Prem Lata Sharma & Anil Bihari Beohar, Indira Gandhi National Centre for the Arts, New Delhi & Motilal Banarsidass, Delhi 1992 (Kalāmūlaśāstra Series 8).

Śāradātanaya, *Bhāvaprakāśana*
ed. Yadugiri Yatiraja Swami of Melkot & K. S. Ramaswami Sastri Siromani, Oriental Institute, Baroda 1930 (Gaekwad's Oriental Series 45).

Śārṅgadeva, *Saṅgītaratnākara* (=SR)
(a) *Saṅgītaratnākara of Śārṅgadeva with the Kalānidhi of Kallinātha and the Sudhākara of Siṃhabhūpāla*, vol. 1, adhyāya 1, ed. S. Subrahmanya Sastri, revised by S. Sarada, The Adyar Library and Research Centre, Madras 1992 (The Adyar Library Series 30).
(b) *Saṅgītaratnākara of Śārṅgadeva,* Sanskrit and English Translation with Comments and Notes by R. K. Shringy & . Prem Lata Sharma, vol. 1, chapter 1, Munshiram Manoharlal Publishers, New Delhi 1999.

Yogayājñavalkya
The Yogayājñavalkya, ed. K. Sāmbaśiva Śāstrī, Government Press, Trivandrum 1938 (Trivandrum Sanskrit Series 134; Śrī Citrodayamañjarī 23).

Yājñavalkyasmṛti
with *Vīramitrodaya* Commentary of Mitramiśra and *Mitākṣara* Commentary of Vijñāneśvara, ed. Narayana Shastri Khiste & Jagannatha Shastri Hoshinga, Chowkhamba Sanskrit Series Office, Varanasi 1997 (Chowkhamba Sanskrit Series 62).

Secondary Literature

Avalon, Arthur
1924 *The Serpent Power, being the Shat-chakra-nirūpana and Pāduka-panchaka.* Two Works on Laya Yoga, translated from the Sanskrit, with Introduction and Commentary, second revised edition, Ganesh & Co., Madras.

Comba, Antonella

1981 'Un capitolo della Śivagītā sulla medicina Ayurvedica.' Torino: Accademia delle Scienze, 1981. Memorie dell'Accademia delle Scienze di Torino, Serie V, 5.1981, II. Classe di Scienze Morali, Storiche e Filologiche, pp. 173-223.

Das, Rahul Peter

2003 *The Origin of the Life of a Human Being, Conception and the Female according to Ancient Indian Medical and Sexological Literature*, Motilal Banarsidas, Delhi 2003 (Indian & Medical Tradition, ed. Dominik Wujastyk & Kenneth G. Zysk, vol. 6).

Gomperts, Amrit

2000 'Indian Music, the Epics and Bards in Ancient Java,' *Vorträge des Internationalen Musikarchäologischen Kolloquiums des Deutschen Archäologen Instituts. Studien zur Musikarchäologie III: Archäologie für Klangerzeugung und Tonordnung; Musikarchäologie in der Ägäis und Anatolien,* ed. Ellen Hickmann, Anne D. Kilmer and Ricardo Eichmann. Rahden: Leidorf 2000, pp. 573-596.

Hara, Minoru

1980 'A Note on the Buddha's Birth Story' in: *Indienisme et Bouddhisme (Mélanges offerts à Mgr Étienne Lamotte)*, Louvain-La-Neuve 1980, pp.143-157.

Kitada, Makoto

2003 'Embryology, Asceticism and Music: *Yājñyavalkya-smṛti* and *Saṅgītaratnākara*,' *Traditional South Asian Medicine,* 7 (2003) 111-113.

2006 *The Body of the Musician. An Annotated Study of Śārṅgadeva's Saṅgītaratnākara,* PhD Dissertation, Martin-Luther University, Halle-Wittenberg.

Sastri, S. Subrahmanya

1992 *Saṅgītaratnākara of Śārṅgadeva with the Kalānidhi of Kallinātha and the Sudhākara of Siṃhabhūpāla*, vol. 1, adhyāya 1, ed. S. Subrahmanya Sastri, revised by S. Sarada, The Adyar Library and Research Centre, Madras 1992 (The Adyar Library Series 30).

Shringy, R. K.

1999 *Saṅgītaratnākara of Śārṅgadeva*, Sanskrit and English Translation with Comments and Notes by R. K. Shringy & Prem Lata Sharma, vol. 1, chapter 1, Munshiram Manoharlal Publishers, New Delhi 1999.

Vallauri, Mario

1942 'La <<Śivagītā>>.' Torino: R. Accademia delle Scienze, 1942. Memorie della R. Accademia delle Scienze di Torino. Serie II, Tomo 70, Parte II: Classe di Scienze morali, storiche e filologiche. N. 9. 1942.

Yamashita, Tsutomu

2001/2003 'On the Nature of the Medical Passages in the Yājñavalkyasmṛti', *ZINBVN*, Kyoto, 36.2 (2001/2003) 87-129.

The Art and Science of Perfumery in the Nāgarasarvasva

JAMES MCHUGH

Introduction

India is the source of an enormous number of exceptional aromatic substances, from tropical woods to Himalayan roots and fresh flowers. From a quite early period, trade contacts with Southeast Asia and the Middle East further enriched the aromatic material possibilities available to an affluent citizen, or to a member of a royal court. In a society where the pursuit of sensuous pleasure was a religiously sanctioned goal in life, and where the technology of pleasure was also applied to the worship of the divine, the art and science of perfumery became very sophisticated. Indeed, I would argue that this is an important, though almost entirely overlooked cultural, aesthetic, and technological achievement of South Asian civilization.[1]

References to beautiful smells abound in Sanskrit literature, but here I would like to examine a somewhat neglected genre

[1] Nevertheless, there have been some excellent studies of the aromatic history of South Asia, in particular the work of P. K. Gode (Gode 1961) and also the introduction by Ramkrishna T. Vyas to his edition of the *Gandhasāra* (Vyas 1989).

of text: technical texts describing the blending of perfumes, *gandhaśāstra*, or *gandhayukti*, as it is more commonly known. Rather than survey these texts in general, I shall focus on a single case: the short chapter on perfumery in the *Nāgarasarvasva*, the 'Complete Man About Town', a medieval Buddhist text on erotics by a certain Padmaśrī.[2]

The most detailed discussion of this text in English is by Siegfried Lienhard,[3] who also discusses the manuscript history and the identity and name of Padmaśrī. There also exists a short and interesting commentary on the text by the Nepali king Jagajjyotirmalla of Bhatgaon (1617-1633 CE). The text is for the most part in a standard *śāstric* style, though Padmaśrī does use a variety of metres: the opening verse I will discuss below is in *pṛthvī* metre, and the verses on perfumery in *jāti* metres, *gīti* and *āryā*. I have not taken this line of enquiry any further, but it is something to bear in mind when looking at this text in future. Professor Babulal Shukla Shastri in his Hindi introduction to one recent edition notes that the probable date of the text is around the final decades of the ninth century to the first half of the tenth century.[4] This is also the date Zysk gives.[5] Lienhard gives a latest possible date of the first half of the fourteenth century.[6]

As I mentioned already, it appears that Padmaśrī was a Buddhist. There are several factors that suggest this; the opening verse, for example, praises the Bodhisattva Mañjuśrī:

> Recalling whom for just a moment, the lover may
> instantly obtain the desired, captivating, and lustful

[2] I use the edition *Nāgarasarvasva* (b) and cite from this edition; I have also consulted *Nāgarasarvasva* (a).

[3] Lienhard 1979.

[4] *Nāgarasarvasva* (b), Introduction, pp. xii-xiii.

[5] Zysk 2002: 8.

[6] Lienhard 1979: 98.

beloved, to him I constantly pay homage: of flashing beauty, and ruddy with very bright fragrant unguents, with flower-arrows, the Noble Mañjuśrī. [7]

As Catherine Benton discusses in her recent book on Kāmadeva,[8] the Bodhisattva Mañjuśrī is frequently identified with Kāmadeva, especially the form of Mañjuśrī known as Vajrānaṅga. Lienhard also notes that Mañjuśrī is identified with both Kāmadeva and Sarasvatī.[9] In the very final chapter we see more evidence that the author was a Buddhist: for Padmaśrī here describes a ritual to obtain a son, and mentions that one should feed monks, as well as worship the Buddhist goddess Tārā.[10] Alternative instructions for Brahmins are even provided.[11] Lienhard suggests that our author may have been a married Nepalese Vajrācārya, presumably respectably permitted to write about erotic matters.[12] Whether or not this be the case, I think it is important that we view this sensual and erotic text not as an anomaly within the Buddhist world view, but rather as challenging some of our contemporary views about the lived reality of Buddhism in medieval India. If, for example, we turn to contemporary India we see in the Jain community that ascetic religious ideals can comfortably co-exist with various worldly values amongst the lay.[13]

---

[7] *Nāgarasarvasva* (b), p. 1:
muhūrtam api yaṃ smarann abhimatāṃ manohāriṇīṃ
labheta madavihvalāṃ jhaṭiti kāminīṃ kāmukaḥ |
tam ullasitaḍambaraṃ surucirāṅgarāgāruṇaṃ
namāmi sumanaḥśaraṃ satatam āryamañjuśriyam ||

[8] Benton 2006: 174-181.

[9] Lienhard 1979: 98.

[10] *Nāgarasarvasva* (b), 38.2-3, p. 119.

[11] Ibid., 38.10, p. 121.

[12] Lienhard 1979: 99.

[13] As Cort 2001 has so excellently demonstrated.

I wish to focus here on one chapter of the *Nāgarasarvasva*, that on perfumery, but I will first provide a brief introduction to the text as a whole. As with the *Kāmasūtra* of Vātsyāyana, the text begins with a discussion and defense of the *trivarga*, particularly with reference to the goal of *kāma* (ch. 1). Then the author moves on to the material aspect of the world of *kāma*, providing a description of how the lover should adorn his body, as well as how he should furnish his dwelling (ch. 2). Following this, Padmaśrī discusses in detail a couple of valuable commodities that play an important role in sensuous matters. In one rather short chapter he relates the essentials of the examination and virtues of gemstones (ch. 3). Thereafter he discusses perfumes, by which term I mean aromatic preparations in general, not just liquid fragrances (ch. 4). Indeed, the European perfumes of today, based on alcohol and concentrated natural and synthetic aromatic substances, bear very little resemblance to what Padmaśrī discusses here.

Following these chapters is a very interesting section, seven brief chapters in all, discussing secret lovers' signals (*saṅketa*), including verbal signals (ch. 5), bodily signals (ch. 6), what appear to be special signal-parcels (*poṭalī*) (ch. 7), signals using clothes (ch. 8), *tāmbūla* (ch. 9), garlands (ch. 10), all concluded by some comments on the general importance of understanding these signals (ch. 11). Next follows a chapter on various methods to treat the sexual organs, seduce people etc.(ch. 12); erotic enticing gestures (*hāva*) of women (ch. 13); the types of lovers (hare, bull, horse etc.) (ch. 14); on protecting one's own women (ch. 15); the different age ranges of women, and their different applications in love (ch. 16); a chapter on correspondences between the body parts of women and the lunar cycle (ch. 17); two chapters, showing tantric influence, about sex and bodily channels (*nāḍīs*) (chs. 18-19); there then follows a discussion of the sexual practices of women from different regions (ch. 20). The rest of the text deals with the various practices and positions of lovemaking: kissing, scratching, biting, embraces etc. The final chapter describes the rite to obtain a son mentioned earlier.

As for the perfumery chapter, it is quite short, nineteen verses in all, and describes a variety of preparations. After introducing the topic, Padmaśrī himself lists the contents of the short chapter, which consists of a number of aromatic formulae for the hair (*keśapaṭavāsa*), armpits (*kākṣikavāsa*), dwelling (*gṛhavāsa*), mouth (*mukhavāsa*), water (*jalavāsa*), betel-nut (*pūgaphala*), bathing-powder (*snānīya*), for a perfume called *catuḥsama* (consisting, according the commentator, of one part musk, two parts camphor, four parts saffron and sixteen parts sandalwood),[14] massage-unguent (*udvartana*), powder (*cūrṇa*), incense-sticks (*dhūpavarti*), and lamp-wicks (*dīpavarti*).

Padmaśrī's introduction itself is quite informative. and worth quoting in full:

> Various artful perfumes are celebrated as eminent inflamers of lust. The best lover should be carefully instructed at the start from perfume texts. Having collected the essential part of the perfume texts, which are difficult to understand for those who are not clever, [and] which are by Lokeśvara etc., I set

[14] Hemacandra also mentions this preparation in his *Abhidhānacintāmaṇi*. Perhaps this was a popular formula in the centuries around the turn of the second millennium of the common era. In Hemacandra's version, the ingredients differ, camphor being replaced by aloeswood. Thus it consists of sandalwood, aloeswood, musk, and saffron: *candanagarukasturīkuṅkumais tu catuḥsamam*, cf. Hemacandra, *Abhidhānacintāmaṇi*, verse 639, p. 117. The *Śabdakalpadruma* entry on this term discusses the '*sama*' in this name, concluding that it could imply either that the ingredients are added in *equal* quantity, or that the ingredients are all used *together* in the preparation. Rādhākāntadeva 1886: 2.423.

[it] forth with very well known words.[15]

The reference to the named author of a *gandhaśāstra* text is interesting. From earlier periods, we do not have any complete texts devoted exclusively to *gandhaśāstra*, though interestingly there has survived one verse from a work on perfumery by a certain Īśvara, in Bhaṭṭotpala's mid-tenth century[16] commentary, the *Saṃhitāvivṛti*, on the chapter on perfumery in the *Bṛhatsaṃhitā* of Varāhamihira. Bhaṭṭotpala relates that the text of Īśvara was called the *Gandhayukti*, and the quotation that survives, defining two technical terms in perfumery, is composed in Prākrit.[17] It is possible that the Lokeśvara mentioned in the *Nāgarasarvasva* might be the same person as this Īśvara.

As we can see, the chapter introduction makes very clear that there is a direct connection between *kāma* and perfumery; that the right smells, carefully blended, can inflame lust in lovers. Therefore a command of the techniques of perfumery is a powerful tool in the hands of the right person. In the *Bṛhatsaṃhitā*, the chapter on perfumery immediately precedes that on the union of a man and a woman and follows the chapter on aphrodisiacs, again placing perfumery in a clearly erotic context. This erotic use of perfume is entirely consistent with the technical/philosophical classifications of smells propounded by almost all schools of thought in India. By the early centuries of the

[15] *Nāgarasarvasva* (b), IV.1-2., p. 14:
nānāvidagdhavāsā mukhyā madanapradīpakāḥ khyātāḥ |
varakāmukaḥ prayatnāc chikṣyetādau sugandhaśāstrebhyaḥ ||
lokeśvarādikebhyo 'puṭamatidurbodhagandhaśāstrebhyaḥ |
saṃgṛhya sārabhāgaṃ pravidhāsye suprasiddhapadaiḥ ||

[16] According to Pingree 1981:270, Bhaṭṭotpala, who lived in Kashmir was active from 966/969 CE. It would appear from the verses at the end that his commentary on Varāhamihira's *Bṛhatsaṃhitā* was composed in the year 967 CE.

[17] Bhaṭṭotpala, *Saṃhitāvivṛti* on *Bṛhatsaṃhitā* 76. 11, p. 948: *uktam īśvareṇa svasyāṃ gandhayuktau.*

first millennium CE these were for the most part unanimous that smells are to be classified as either fragrant and non-fragrant, or desired and not desired.[18] This is quite unlike the objects of the other senses which were not universally classified in hedonic terms. These qualities, fragrant and non-fragrant, were thus established as an unavoidable feature of the experienced world of smell; given that this was the case, the creation of a very beautiful perfume could not fail to please the person smelling it.

This introduction not only connects perfumes to erotics, but Padmaśrī also points out that texts on perfumery are difficult to understand, and he also mentions these texts in the plural. Clearly there existed several sources on this topic, yet these were considered difficult to understand for all but experts. Padmaśrī's introduction is not just typical authorial modesty, for this chapter is indeed shorter and simpler than most other texts on perfumery; nevertheless we shall see that it still contains much that is interesting and difficult.

Formula of the Ratināthakāntā Incense

I think the best way to get a taste, or rather a whiff, of the art and science of Indian perfumery, *gandhaśāstra*, is to examine in detail one formula, discuss the ingredients, the composition, as well as the interesting issue of the *name* of the preparation. I have chosen one quite typical formula, for an incense stick (*dhūpavarti*) called *Ratināthakāntā*, 'Beloved of the God of Love.' In analyzing this formula, we will consider a number of aspects: the technical skill in creating this formula; the origins of the ingredients, in some cases quite exotic to India; other properties of the ingredi-

[18]Cf. for example, Viśvanātha Nyāyapañcānana Bhaṭṭācārya, *Bhāṣāpariccheda*, pp. 101, 102ab: ***saurabhaś cāsaurabhaś ca dvedhā parikīrttitaḥ***, 'It (smell) is proclaimed as twofold: fragrant and unfragrant'.

ents, such as whether they were believed to be heating or cooling, and finally we will reflect on the choice of name of the incense. The formula for *Ratināthakāntā* is as follows:

> The incense stick (*dhūpavarti*) prepared with sequentially increasing parts [of] *nakha, aguru, śilhaka, vālaka, kunduru, śaileya, candana*, and *śyāma*, is 'Beloved of the God of Love'.[19]

As the commentator illustrates, the formula is therefore as follows:

> 1 part *nakha*, 2 parts *aguru*, 3 parts *śilhaka*, 4 parts *vālaka*, 5 parts *kunduru*, 6 parts *śaileya*, 7 parts *candana*, 8 parts *śyāma*.

The term given for the end product is *vartī*, often translated as 'wick'. I do not believe this is a good translation in this case; indeed the term is cognate with the Hindi *battī* in *agarbattī*, and I believe the aromatic prepared here would be an object more on the lines of an incense stick, though perhaps without the central supporting bamboo strip that is almost universal in Indian *agarbattī* today. Rather, it seems this aromatic may have resembled a modern Tibetan incense stick, or a Japanese one: a rolled stick of ground aromatics.

Anyone who has worked on Sanskrit texts in which reference is made to plants and herbs knows very well the difficulties that are often encountered in identifying with certainty the plant or herb in question. In this case some of ingredients have been easy to identify, others less so. One extra factor that is useful in the case of perfumery texts is that, given a number of possible identifications, one at least knows that the ingredient being sought

---

[19] *Nagarasarvasva* (b) IV.17, p. 18:
nakhāguruśilhakavālakakunduruśaileyacandanaśyāmāḥ |
kramavṛddhibhāgaracitā vartī ratināthakānteyam ||17||

should have some relatively notable aromatic property, though as we will see it does not necessarily have to be *fragrant*, even in the context of a perfume recipe. Where I have encountered difficulties, I have used two less well-known resources, particularly apt for the task in hand, with some success. These are two specialist aromatics glossaries or *nighaṇṭus*: one quoted by Bhaṭṭotpala in his commentary on the *Bṛhatsaṃhitā*,[20] and the other given in the medieval perfumery treatise called the *Gandhasāra* by Gaṅgādhara.[21] The latter author not only provides a large number of synonyms, but he also groups the substances according to whether they are leaf, flower, fruit, bark, wood, root, resin, or animal in origin. The *Gandhasāra* provides some information on the examination of these aromatics, which can also be of use.

Nakha

The first ingredient *nakha* is perhaps the most remarkable item. The word means 'claw', or 'fingernail'. The *nighaṇṭu* of the *Gandhasāra* lists *nakha* in the class of animal products, the *jīvavarga*, and gives a number of synonyms including *śukti* (oyster shell), *śapha* (hoof), *nakha* (claw), *khura* (hoof/claw). Bhaṭṭotpala in his commentary on the *Bṛhatsaṃhitā* explains that *nakha* is *śaṅkodbhavaṃ carma*,[22] 'the hide/skin produced from a conch shell.' And indeed this is what *nakha* is: the operculum, the horn-like 'lid' of a marine snail, resembling a large dirty toe-nail or claw. Known in the west as sweet-hoof, or *unguis odoratus,* or the particularly charming French term *blatte de byzance,* 'Byzantine cockroach', this is in fact a highly significant aromatic, and it has long played an important role in

[20]The *nighaṇṭu* occurs at the beginning of Bhaṭṭotpala's commentary on the 76th chapter of Varāhamihira's *Bṛhatsaṃhitā*, see Bhaṭṭotpala, *Saṃhitāvivṛti*, pp. 941-944.

[21]Gaṅgādhara, *Gandhasāra*, pp. 42-51.

[22]Bhaṭṭotpala, *Saṃhitāvivṛti* on *Bṛhatsaṃhitā* 76.8, p. 947.

Indian perfumery, even until the present day.[23] Where musk from the musk deer, ambergris produced in the stomach of the sperm whale when irritated by squid beaks, and civet from the civet cat, are relatively well known animal-derived aromatics, this substance, derived from certain marine snails, has been almost entirely overlooked.[24] It is still relatively easily available in India, and on my last trip there I brought back some samples which are of a variety of shapes and sizes. I have investigated the possible identity of the shell from which they came. The dealers who sold them to me said they come from South India and Sri Lanka, and Professor Kenneth Boss of Harvard University has confirmed that they are from an order of carnivorous marine snails called neogastropods, though it is not generally possible to identify the species from the operculum alone.[25] David Heppell, the late mollusk expert from the National Museum of Scotland in Edinburgh notes in an article on the chank shell industry in modern India that the operculum of the sacred chank/sacred conch is used in preparing incense.[26]

Not only is the origin of this product unusual, but so is the smell. I have been told by perfume and incense makers on many occasions in India that it is necessary to cook the opercula, or fry them in ghee, to remove any fishy smell before they may be used in perfumery. Yet, even after cooking the *nakha*, the smell when burnt is not very pleasant, somewhat like burnt hair or burnt horn. In the summer of 2005, I was in Mysore and discussed the issue with the incense makers at Cycle-Brand Agarbatti and Vasu Agarbatti, where I learnt that *nakha*, used in small quantities in

[23] Groom 1997: 320.

[24] Given the role of the squid in producing ambergris, and the ancient and widespread use of *nakha*, it is interesting to note that mollusks have played a rather significant role in the history of perfumery.

[25] Personal communication, 15 June 2006.

[26] Heppell 2001.

incense, causes the smell of the rest of the burnt ingredients to linger in the air longer, like a *fixative* in liquid perfumes. Indeed it is for their fixative properties, making a perfume last longer, that the other animal derived aromatics, musk, ambergris, civet, and the less well known beaver-derived castoreum, have been particularly valued in contemporary Western perfumery. In this particular composition, it is notable that *nakha* is used the most sparingly of all the ingredients, for it has an unpleasant smell, and so one would not want to include a large amount of it in an incense; yet a small, relatively undetectable amount will help the perfume of the rest of the ingredients to remain in the environment longer.

Aguru

The second ingredient is perhaps better known: *aguru* or aloeswood. There are a number of words in Sanskrit for this culturally very important aromatic wood: *agaru, aguru, kṛmija* (worm-produced), *pravara* (the very best), *rājārha* (worthy of a king), and so on. In the *Arthaśāstra*, following the section on gemstones is the section on precious aromatics. Here a number of varieties of aloeswood are described, in addition to the general qualities of aloeswood:

> Heavy, oily, having charming smell, diffusive, capable of burning, having smoke that does not mass together, even smell, capable of crushing: thus are the qualities of aloeswood.[27]

Aloeswood is the Indian aromatic wood for burning *par excellence*, and thus it is entirely appropriate to include it in an incense recipe. Where sandalwood is often cooling, smeared on the body as a cool moist paste, aloeswood, heavy, dark, and resinous is very often burnt. So central is aloeswood to traditional Indian

[27] Kauṭilya, *Arthaśāstra* 2.11.60, p. 53: ***guru snigdhaṃ peśalagandhi nirhāry agnisaham asaṃplutadhūmaṃ samagandhaṃ vimardasaham ity aguruguṇāḥ.***

incense that the Hindi word for incense stick discussed already, *agarbattī*, means 'aloeswood/agarwood (incense-) roll/stick'. Yet many people in India today have never smelled aloeswood, and few people in Europe and America have either, nor do most people even know what it is any more. *Aguru*, referred to in English as aloeswood, eagle-wood, agallochum, as well as agar-wood, is the wood from several species of tropical hardwood tree found in the forests of Assam, South East Asia, and China.[28] The wood of a healthy tree is unremarkable, light in colour, and has no special smell, but in certain circumstances the tree becomes infected by a fungus, and in response to the fungus, the tree produces a dark-brown aromatic resin that permeates parts of the wood. When such a tree is felled, the valuable, dark-brown/black, heavy, resinous, diseased wood is removed and this is *aguru*.[29] Nowadays the majority of aloeswood produced is taken to the Middle East and Japan where it is also highly valued, and it is far too expensive to put in mass-produced incense sticks in India, which have thus changed quite radically in composition, and no doubt smell, over the last hundred or so years.[30] Whether from overseas

[28] *Aquilaria agallocha*, also *A. malaccensis* and *A. crasna*. See Groom 1997: 6, and also Hansen 2000. Both sources discuss the distribution and formation of aloeswood.

[29] I am very grateful to Professor S. R. Sarma for providing me with the following additional information about this important and fascinating tree, whose bark served as writing material in Assam. Books made up of the *agaru* bark are known to the poet Bāṇa; in his *Harṣacarita* (p. 378) he enumerates *aguru-valkala-kalpita-sañcayāni subhāṣitabhāñji pustakāni* among the gifts brought from Assam. On the method of processing the bark for writing, see Gait 1926: 375: Appendix D: 'Description of Ahom Manuscript Records.' The processed sheets are called *sāncīpāṭ*. A notable manuscript copied and illustrated on *agaru* bark is the *Hastividyārṇava* which was published in a facsimile edition from Gowhati in 1976.

[30] Mr Krishna of the Vasu Agarbatti in Mysore explained that the use of *aguru* in incense sticks had declined over the past century owing to scarcity and high price. The body of many contemporary incense sticks is made from spent sandal chips, or simply charcoal. As far as I am aware there is no attempt to substitute the specific fragrance of *aguru*. Personal communication,

or from Assam, *aguru*, scarce to begin with, would often have to be transported long distances, passing through many hands, and consequently it must have been a very expensive aromatic, worthy of being stored in the treasury described in the *Arthaśāstra*. Another factor to bear in mind when considering the value of perfumes is that some aromatics, particularly sandalwood and aloeswood, retain their aromatic qualities for many years, and could easily be stored in a treasury for very long periods of time, just like gemstones and gold. The same does not, of course, apply to all aromatics, especially flowers. Their high value also accounts for passages in several texts, including the *Arthaśāstra*, that describe their evaluation.

Śilhaka

The next ingredient, *śilhaka*, also called *silhaka*, is an aromatic resin. One of the synonyms of *silha* given in the *nighaṇṭu* quoted by Bhaṭṭotpala is *turuṣkaka* (Turkish), and the *nighaṇṭu* of the *Gandhasāra*, in the section on resins, gives also *yavana* (Ionian/Greek). It seems therefore very likely that this is a fragrant resin imported from the West, most likely some sort of frankincense, as indeed most Sanskrit/English dictionaries agree. Exactly which type of resin it was is debatable as there are several varieties of frankincense/olibanum (not to mention myrrh) growing in South Arabia, Somalia, Ethiopia, as well as the island of Socotra.[31] Indeed it is even possible that the exact referent of the term *śilhaka* was not in every case the same product from the same place.

In the *Amarakośa*[32] and also in Bhaṭṭotpala's *nighaṇṭu*, *vālaka*, (or *vāla*, or *bāla*) is a synonym of *hrībera/hrīvera*. This would appear to be *Pavonia odorata* Willd., a plant with a musky smelling

July 2005.

[31] Groom 1981: 99. This book is to be highly recommended as a first class study of the incense trade in the Middle East.

[32] *Amarakośa, Vanauṣadhivarga* 122, p. 107.

root, also used in the preparation of *hina* attar.[33]

Kunduru

The term *kunduru*, another fragrant resin, raises some complex philological questions. Monier-Williams gives the translation as 'olibanum', i.e. frankincense, yet it seems that this product is distinct from *śilhaka* discussed above. In both the *nighaṇṭu* of the *Gandhasāra,* and in the *Amarakośa* it is discussed separately from *śilhaka/silha.*[34] One synonym of *kunduru* in Amara is *sallakī,* and none of the synonyms suggest that this is a product imported from the West. It would seem that the difference between *śilhaka* and *kunduru* may be that *kunduru* refers to Indian olibanum, from *Boswellia serrata,* called in Hindi *salai,* whereas *śilhaka*, as discussed above, is an imported Arabian resin. Indian olibanum both looks and smells quite different to Arabian frankincense: it is apparently more 'turpentiny' in smell, and softer in texture.[35]

The Sanskrit word *kunduru* is quite interesting. One word for frankincense in Arabic is *kundur,* and similar terms for incense are found in Armenian: *knudruk*, and Middle Persian: *kundarak.*[36] Lane, in his lexicon, connects the Arabic word with Greek *khondros libanōtou*, meaning a **grain** of frankincense.[37] Scheftelowitz on the other hand believes the Indian word is the origin of the Arabic, Armenian and Middle Persian terms.[38] As frankincense was widely traded throughout the ancient world, it is not surprising that cognates of *kunduru* are so widespread. As for the solution to this philological puzzle, that is something that

---

[33] Ambasta 2000: 435

[34] Gaṅgādhara, *Gandhasāra*, p. 48; *Amarakośa, Vanauṣadhivarga* 124, p. 107

[35] Groom 1981: 102.

[36] Scheftelowitz 1926: 282.

[37] Lane 1984: 2. 2633.

[38] Scheftelowitz 1926: 282.

still eludes me, and may well continue to do so.[39]

Nevertheless, as this paper was presented in Edinburgh I would like to make one small digression at this point. For it was the eminent botanist William Roxburgh (1751-1815), trained at Edinburgh University, who first described the Indian frankincense tree, and he named it *Boswellia serrata* after his friend John Boswell (1710-1780), a physician, also of Edinburgh,[40] who was in fact the uncle of James Boswell (1740-1795), the famous biographer of Dr Johnson. Indeed '*Boswellia*' became the name of the entire genus of frankincense trees, including the perhaps more famous Arabian *Boswellia sacra*. And, although it was Roxburgh who described and named the tree, his description was actually reported by Henry Thomas Colebrooke (1765-1837), the famous English indologist in his 1807 paper '*On* Olibanum *or* Frankincense.'[41] So, in the case of *kunduru*, we have a philological puzzle, aromatics, Edinburgh, and early Indology all rolled into one.

Śaileya

Śaileya, according to Monier-Williams, could be bitumen, benzoin resin, or a type of lichen, all of which have a strong smell. Though this is the case, it is important to try to ascertain which of these substances was more likely to be used in this composition. The latter two, benzoin resin and some lichens, still play an important role in perfumery both in India and the West. Amara gives a number of synonyms for *śaileya*: *kālanusāryam, vṛddham, aśmapuṣpam, śītaśivam*.[42] A similar list, minus the exact term *śaileya* is given in the leaf-section of the aromatics *nighaṇṭu* of the *Gandhasāra* (*kālanusāryaṃ vṛddhādrisaṃjñam aśma ca śailajam*).[43] The *nighaṇṭu* quoted by Bhaṭṭotpala gives:

[39] I am grateful to the advice of Professor Stephanie Jamison on this matter.
[40] Quattrocchi 2000: 1. 331.
[41] Colebrooke 1807.
[42] *Amarakośa, Vanauṣadhivarga* 122-123, p. 107.
[43] Gaṅgādhara, *Gandhasāra*, verse 7, p. 42.

giri, girija, śaileya.[44] As both bitumen and lichens do in fact come from the mountains and from Nepal, and often have origins associated with stones, these synonyms do not clarify the situation any further. The one clue seems to be the location of these terms in the leaf-section of the *Gandhasāra,* which leads me to think that it may be some species of aromatic lichen, as this, more than the other candidates, might be classified as a leaf. Yet, as this is an incense recipe, and the proportion of *śaileya* is quite large, it is possible that it could be benzoin, for as a resin it burns very well and also smells very pleasant. Nevertheless, who am I to say there was not a taste for the aroma of bitumen in medieval India? After all, I personally quite like the smell of hot tar. Though, neither of these other options are substances that would be likely to be classed as leaves.

Candana

Candana is, of course, sandalwood, an enormous topic that I cannot even begin to discuss here, though we should note the large, and expensive, proportion used in this incense. Also, it is important to observe that sandalwood was primarily used ground into a cooling paste with water, aloeswood being the burning wood *par excellence*. Also, note the contrast between the warming properties of aloeswood and the well-known cooling nature of sandalwood. Below is the description of sandalwood from the *Arthaśāstra*:

> Light, unctuous, not dry, smearing oil like ghee, of pleasant smell, suitable for the skin, mild, not fading, tolerant of warmth, absorbs great heat, and pleasant to touch — these are the qualities of sandalwood.[45]

---

[44] Bhaṭṭotpala, *Saṃhitāvivṛti*, p. 942.

[45] Kauṭilya, *Arthaśāstra*, 2.11.56, p. 53: *laghu snigdham aśyanaṃ sarpiḥsnehalepi gandhasukhaṃ tvaganusāry anulbam avirāgy anuṣṇasahaṃ dāhagrāhi sukhasparśanam iti candanaguṇāḥ.*

Śyāma

Śyāma, according to the aromatics *nighaṇṭu* that Bhaṭṭotpala quotes, is a synonym of *priyaṅgu*, and this is confirmed by Amara.[46] *Priyaṅgu* is listed, minus the synonym *śyāma*, in the flower section of the *Gandhasāra*, so it would seem that a medieval Indian perfumer might consider *priyaṅgu* to be an ingredient in the form of a flower. *Priyaṅgu* is a difficult plant to identify and is identified with both panic grass, *Setaria italica*, as well as *Aglaia roxburghiana*.[47] As the latter plant has fragrant flowers, it seem most likely that in this case the formula requires the flowers of *Aglaia roxburghiana*, especially given that it appears that the flowers of another species, *Aglaia odorata*, are used in incense manufacture.[48]

Naming an Incense

Finally, I would like to consider the name of this incense, *Ratināthakāntā*; not just the meaning of the name, but the sheer fact that it has a name: a name that is not a bare description, but rather an erotic, evocative, and suggestive name, the sense of which is very difficult to convey fully in English: 'the Beloved of the God of Love' or maybe 'the Beloved of the Husband of [the goddess called] Sexual Pleasure'.[49] What is striking is that we give similar evocative names to perfumes in the West today, names which appeal to the aspirations of the buyer, be they exotic and sensuous: 'Samsara',[50] or cool and modernist: 'No. 5'.

---

[46] *Amarakośa*, op. cit. *Vanauṣadhivarga* 55, p. 92.

[47] Meulenbeld 1974: 578.

[48] Ambasta 2000: 21.

[49] We should also note that the allusion to Kāmadeva in this context contrasts with the reference to Mañjuśrī at the very beginning of the text. This is most likely because our author, as he mentions, has culled these formulae from other perfumery texts. I have not come across any names of perfumes that are explicitly Buddhist.

[50] On many occasions I have heard indologists and scholars of Buddhism mock the name of this successful fragrance produced by Jean-Paul Guerlain of

But, although many things, such as music, paintings, films, poems, and so forth have names/titles in our society, not everything does; this type of suggestive naming is not inevitable: clothes, for instance, even items of Parisian haute couture, are not generally given such names; yet furniture is, for example 'The Buckingham armchair', at least as long as it sits in the showroom, but it generally loses the name as soon as the buyer brings it home. Cars too are given names, and they retain these after they are purchased. One might argue that this is all a matter of marketing, but then it is far from clear that this is the case for these Indian perfumes, often prepared at home or at court. As far as I am aware, paintings in ancient India would only be given a descriptive name, if given a name at all, but perfumes on the contrary are often not simply called 'musk and aloeswood armpit-powder'; instead they were given the sorts of names we give perfumes today, an evocative concept referring to the whole composition, not to its ingredients or practical function.

This name *Ratināthakāntā* is not unique: there are several other such names for fragrant compositions, be they incenses or pastes, liquids, and so forth.[51] In this very same chapter of the *Nāgarasarvasva* we find a perfume for water called *Malayānila*, 'Breeze from the Malaya (mountains)' (verse 10)[52]; an incense stick, with a similar name to that discussed above, called *Rati-*

the French perfumery house Guerlain, with remarks such as: 'Why on earth would anyone want a bottle of *saṃsāra*?' Yet I believe this misses the point, for surely the name 'Samsara' could also be understood to have exciting and exotic associations of sensuality and decadence. Indeed, launched in 1989, it belongs to an era that also produced 'Poison' (Jean Guichard for Dior: 1985), and 'Obsession' (Jean Guichard for Calvin Klein: 1985), fragrances whose names have a similar, somewhat transgressive appeal.

[51] I am not suggesting that all aromatics have names or even the same sort of name. In the *Nāgarasarvasva* we also encounter the composition mentioned above, presumably called after the proportions of the ingredients: *Catuḥsama* (verse 13).

[52] This would of course be a *cooling* breeze because of the sandalwood trees that grow there.

nātha, 'The Husband of Rati' (= Kāmadeva) (verse 16). Another formula is on the one hand evocative, but also partly suggests the desired affect: *Madanodbhavadīpavarti*, 'The Lamp Wick which is the Origin of the God of Love' (verse 18). In this text, the names are all, appropriately, of an erotic nature, suggesting the presence of Kāmadeva or his wife, or the cooling breeze from the southern Malaya mountains, the home of sandalwood, whose coolness brings relief to the fever of sexual desire.

The Incense in Practice

For the occasion of the Thirteenth World Sanskrit Conference I tried to the best of my ability to reproduce this fragrance; the final product, a brown paste, was burnt on charcoal and had a quite pleasant, rather rich and musky aroma. I had to substitute some ingredients, and as we have seen, the identity of some of the ingredients is not certain; consequently the 'Beloved of the God of Love' utterly failed to achieve her arousing mission, and we avoided any unfortunate incidents amongst the attendees of the conference.

Nevertheless, it is interesting to ponder that the ideal Buddhist man-about-town, who had studied *gandhaśāstra*, when asked by his lover 'What is this fragrance that fills your elegant bedroom?' would be able to reply 'The Beloved of the God of Love,' knowing that this lust-inciting incense-stick was carefully formulated to produce a smoke that would linger in the air, and that it was made of costly ingredients, some of the greatest aromatics in the world: marine mollusk parts, diseased forest trees, and resins, brought from as far away as Assam and South Arabia.

Acknowledgements

I would like to thank Professor S. R. Sarma for inviting me to give this talk, and for all his moral and intellectual support. Also, at Harvard, to Professor Anne Monius, Professor Parimal

G. Patil, Professor Michael Witzel, and Professor Larry McCrea. Professor Stephanie Jamison and also Paul Kosmin for advice on the issue of the term *kunduru*, as well as Nick Boylston and Dominic Longo for advice on Arabic. Professor Ken Boss at Harvard was a great source of information on mollusks. Thanks are also due to all the kind people I met at the Cycle-Brand Agarbatti and Vasu Agarbatti in Mysore in summer 2005.

BIBLIOGRAPHY

Primary Texts

Amara, *Amarakośa*

with the Commentary of Maheśvara, enlarged by Raghunath Shastri Talekar, reprinted, Eastern Book Linkers, Delhi 2002.

Bāṇa, *Harṣacarita*

ed. with Śaṅkara's commentary, Varanasi 1958.

Bhaṭṭotpala, *Saṃhitāvivṛti*

in: *The Bṛhat Saṃhitā by Varāhamihira, with the Commentary of Bhaṭṭotpala*, ed. Sudhakara Dvivedi, E.J. Lazarus, Benares 1895-97.

Gaṅgādhara, *Gandhasāra*

Gaṅgādhara's Gandhasāra and an unknown Author's Gandhavāda, with Marathi commentary, ed. Ramkrishna Tuljaram Vyas, Oriental Institute, Vadodara 1989.

Hastividyārṇava

ed. Pratapachandra Chowdhuri, Gowhati 1976.

Hemacandra, *Abhidhānacintāmaṇi*

ed. O. Boehtlingk and C. Rieu, Kaiserliche Akademie der Wissenschaften, St. Petersburg 1847.

Padmaśrī, *Nāgarasarvasva*

(a) ed. Paṇḍit Bhagīrathasvāmī, Śrīveṅkaṭeśvar Pustak Agency, Kalkattā 1929.

(b) Mahamati Padmashri, *Nāgar Sarvaswam* with the commentary by King Jagajjyotirmalla, ed. Babulal Shukla Shastri, Eastern Book Linkers, Delhi 1994.

Kauṭilya, *Arthaśāstra*

The Kauṭilīya Arthaśāstra, ed. R.P. Kangle, University of Bombay, Bombay 1969.

Viśvanātha Nyāyapañcānana Bhaṭṭācārya

Bhāṣāpariccheda, ed. E. Roer, Bibliotheca Indica, vol. 8, Biblio Verlag, Osnabrück 1980.

Secondary Literature

Ambasta, S. P. (ed)

2000 *The Useful Plants of India*, ed. S. P. Ambasta, National Institute of Science Communication, New Delhi.

Benton, Catherine

2006 *God of Desire: Tales of Kāmadeva in Sanskrit Story Literature*, State University of New York Press, Albany.

Colebrooke, Ḥ. T.

1807 'On Olibanum or Frankincense,' *Asiatick Researches* 9, pp. 377-382.

Cort, John E.

2001 *Jains in the World: Religious Values and Ideology in India*, Oxford University Press, Oxford.

Gait, Sir Edward

1926 *A History of Assam*, second revised edition, Thacker, Spink & Co., Calcutta and Simla.

Gode, P. K.

1961 *Studies in Indian Cultural History*, vol. 1, Vishveshvaranand Vedic Research Institute, Hoshiarpur.

Groom, Nigel

1981 *Frankincense and Myrrh: A Study of the Arabian Incense Trade*, Longman, London.

1997 *The New Perfume Handbook*, 2nd ed., Blackie Academic and Professional, London.

Hansen, Eric
2000 'The Hidden History of the Scented Wood,' *Saudi Aramco World*, Nov/December, 2000, pp. 2-13. http://www.saudiaramcoworld.com/

Heppell, David
2001 'The chank shell industry in modern India,' *Princely States Report* 2.2, April 2001 [journal on-line]; available from http://www.princelystates.com/ArchivedFeatures/fa-03-03a.shtml; Internet; accessed 1 June 2006.

Lane, E. W.
1984 *Arabic-English Lexicon*, The Islamic Texts Society, Cambridge.

Lienhard, Siegfried
1979 'Observations Concerning a Buddhist Text on Erotics: The Nāgarasarvasva of Padmaśrī,' *Central Asiatic Journal*, 23.1-2, pp. 96-103.

Meulenbeld, E.
1974 *The Mādhavanidāna and its Chief Commentary*, tr. G. J. Meulenbeld, E. J. Brill, Leiden.

Pingree, David
1981 *Census of the Exact Sciences in Sanskrit*, Series A, vol. 4, American Philosophical Society, Philadelphia.

Quattrocchi, Umberto
2000 *CRC World Dictionary of Plant Names*, CRC Press, Boca Raton.

Rādhākāntadeva
1886 *Śabdakalpadruma*, Baptist Mission Press, Calcutta.

Scheftelowitz, J.
1926 'Indische Kultureinflüsse,' *Zeitschrift für Buddhismus und Verwandte Gebiete*, VII Jahrgang, Heft 3-4, p. 282.

Zysk, Kenneth
2002 *Conjugal Love in India*, Brill, Leiden.

The Contributors

K. RAMASUBRAMANIAN is a traditionally trained Sanskrit scholar who also holds a PhD in Theoretical Physics, besides a bachelors in Engineering and a masters in Sanskrit. His investigations of the classical Indian texts have shed much light on the development of Indian Mathematics and Astronomy during the medieval period, especially the work of the Kerala School during the 15th and 16th centuries. His accomplishments towards the synergy between the tradition and modernity has fetched him the *Maharshi Badarayana Vyas Samman* for the year 2008 awarded by the President of India. Currently he is a faculty member in the Cell for Indian Science and Technology in Sanskrit, Department of Humanities and Social Sciences at IIT Bombay.

He prepared, jointly with M. D. Srinivas and M. S. Sriram, the Explanatory Notes of the celebrated work *Gaṇita-yukti-bhāṣā* (Rationales in Mathematical Astronomy) of Jyeṣṭhadeva (c. 1530) which brings out the seminal contributions of the Kerala School of astronomers and mathematicians in the field of Mathematical Analysis. The *Gaṇita-yukti-bhāṣā* has been published by Hindustan Book Agency, New Delhi, in two volumes, and is being reprinted by Springer. He has also co-edited *500 Years of Tantrasangraha* (Indian Institute of Advanced Study, Shimla, 2002). His work on *Nīlakaṇṭha*'s *Tantrasaṅgraha* will be brought out by Hindustan Book Agency early 2009.

Address: Department of Humanities and Social Sciences, IIT Bombay, Powai, Mumbai 400 076, India. kramas@iitb.ac.in

S BALACHANDRA RAO is Director, Bhavan's Gandhi Centre of Science & Human Values and Hon. Professor at the National Institute of Advanced Studies, Bangalore. He retired as Principal & Professor of Mathematics from National College, Bangalore, after 35 years of service. He is a member of the Research Council of the National Commission for History of Science, Indian National Science Academy, New Delhi. Currently he is working on a research project 'A Critical Study of Indian Astronomical Tables - Sāriṇis, Padakas & Koṣṭakas.'

Besides textbooks of mathematics, his other publications on Indian astronomy and mathematics are:(1) *Indian Mathematics & Astronomy - Some Landmarks* (Revised 3rd edn.), (2) *Indian Astronomy - An Introduction*, (3) *Ancient Indian Astronomy - Planetary Positions & Eclipses*, (4) *Āryabhaṭa I & His Astronomy*, (5) *Bhāskara I & His Astronomy*, (6) *Grahalāghavam of Gaṇeśa Daivajña - English Exposition* (jointly with S. K. Uma), (7) *Karaṇakutūhalam of Bhaskara II - English Translation with Notes* (jointly with S. K. Uma), (8) *Vedāṅga Jyotiṣa of Lagadha* (Kannada translation), (9) *Indian Astronomy - A Primer.*

Address: 2388 Jnana Deep, 13th Main A Block, Rajaji Nagar, II Phase, Bangalore 560 010, India. balachandra_rao@rediffmail.com

KIM PLOFKER is Visiting Assistant Professor in the Department of Mathematics at Union College in Schenectady, New York. She received her PhD from the Department of the History of Mathematics at Brown University under the late David Pingree. Her areas of interest include the history of mathematics and astronomy in India and the medieval Islamic world, and the cross-cultural transmission of scientific models.

Her recent publications include the chapter 'Mathematics in India' in *Mathematics of Egypt, Mesopotamia, China, India, and Islam: A Sourcebook* (ed. Victor J. Katz, Princeton 2007), and 'Euler and Indian Astronomy' in *Leonhard Euler:Life, Work and*

Legacy (ed. R. Bradley and E. Sandifer, Elsevier 2007); her book on the history of Indian mathematics will appear from Princeton University Press in early 2009.

Address: Department of Mathematics, Union College, Schenectady NY, 12308, USA. plofkerk@union.edu

SREERAMULA RAJESWARA SARMA was formerly Professor of Sanskrit at Aligarh Muslim University. He earned his MA from Visva-Bharati, Santiniketan, and PhD from Philipps Universität, Marburg, for his dissertation on the *The Pūrvagaṇita of Āryabhaṭa's (II) Mahāsiddhānta*. The main areas of his interest are history of exact sciences in India, transmission of scientific ideas across cultures, especially between Sanskritic and Islamic traditions of learning and between Sanskrit and regional languages. Currently he is preparing a descriptive catalogue of about 450 Indian astronomical instruments preserved in India, Europe and northern America.

His recent publications include 'Rule of Three and its Variations in India' (*From China to Paris : 2000 Years Transmission of Mathematical Ideas*, Stuttgart 2002); 'Śūnya in Piṅgala's Chandaḥsūtra' (*The Concept of Śūnya*, New Delhi 2003); *Astronomical Instruments in the Rampur Raza Library* (Rampur 2003); 'Broken String – Scattered Pearls: A Motif in Sanskrit Poetry and Mathematics' (*Arion Roşu Festschrift*, Bucharest 2004); 'Mathematics and Iconography in Līlāvatī 263' (*Journal of the Asiatic Society of Mumbai*, 2005-2006); *The Archaic and the Exotic: Studies in the History of Indian Astronomical Instruments* (New Delhi 2008).

Address: Höhenstr. 28, 40227 Düsseldorf, Germany.
SR@Sarma.de

AMRIT GOMPERTS graduated in physics from the University of Amsterdam and studied Sanskrit at the India Instituut in Amsterdam. He did research in Indonesia where he learned Javanese and Modern Indonesian. His main interests are Sanskrit influences in Old Javanese technical literature and Hindu-Buddhist archaeology in medieval Java. His publications include papers on *jyotiṣa* elements, Indian mathematical astronomy and time reckoning in Old Javanese inscriptions, Indian music and musical instruments in Old Javanese texts and inscriptions, and texts on traditional Sanskrit grammar (*vyākaraṇa*) from Java, Bali and Lombok. Currently he is working on Javano-Sanskrit erotic texts from Balinese libraries, and on the identification of the location and archaeological reconstruction of the vanished royal palace and capital of Majapahit, the last major Hindu-Buddhist kingdom in the Indonesian archipelago, on the basis of the description of the Buddhist poet Prapañca in the Old Javanese text *Nāgarakṛtāgama* of AD 1365.

Address: Willemsparkweg 147-I, 1071 GX Amsterdam, The Netherlands. amritgo@planet.nl

MARTIN GANSTEN is a Sanskritist and historian of religion specializing in classical and contemporary Hinduism. Research interests include astrology and other divinatory practices as well as Vedānta (particularly the Viśiṣṭādvaita school) and related philosophical/theological teachings. He has published annotated Swedish translations of the *Bhagavadgītā* and (with Dr Måns Broo, Finland) the early Upaniṣads, and is currently working on an English translation of the Utpattiprakaraṇa of the *Mokṣopāya*. A volume on astrology and divination in South Asia is forthcoming (Cambridge University Press).

Address: Lund University/CTR, Allhelgona Kyrkogata 8, 223 62 Lund, Sweden. martin.gansten@teol.lu.se

VIJAYA JAYANT DESHPANDE, trained as a chemist, turned to history of science, technology and medicine. She studied Sino-

Indian scientific contacts through Buddhism and compared evolution of alchemy in the two cultures. After working on Sanskrit and Chinese primary sources, she published several research articles on the topic. She worked on Nāgārjuna's ophthalmic works in Chinese and examined the influence of ancient Indian medicine on Chinese medicine during the medieval period, with a focus on ophthalmology. Her recent publications include 'Ophthalmic Surgery - A Chapter in the History of Sino-Indian Medical Contacts' (*Bulletin of the School of Oriental and African Studies*, 2000); 'Ancient Indian Medicine and its Spread to China' (*Economic and Political Weekly*, 2001); 'Nāgārjuna and Chinese Medicine' (*Arion Roşu Festschrift*, Bucharest 2004); 'Glimpses of Ayurveda in medieval Chinese medicine' (*Indian Journal of History of Science*, 2008).

Address: 76/37A Shantishila Society, Erandavana, Pune 411 004, India. vijaya.deshpande@gmail.com

GYULA WOJTILLA is a graduate of the Eötvös Loránd University of Budapest. He did his MA in classical Indology and history. He has got his PhD in Sanskrit philology. Since 1992 he has been professor and head of the Department of Ancient History at the University of Szeged in Hungary. He was research fellow at Banaras Hindu University in 1973-74, lecturer at the University of Delhi in 1980-1983.

His main fields of interest are Sanskrit philology, ancient Indian history and culture, history of agriculture in early India, comparative history of religion. He has published several books and nearly two hundred papers on these subjects. His important publications in the last five years: 'What can the Ṛgveda tell us on agriculture?' (AOH 2003); 'Notes on pākaśāstra, sūdaśāstra and sūpaśāstra' (*Arion Roşu Festschrift*, Bucharest 2004); 'The Sītādhyakṣaprakaraṇa of the Arthaśāstra' (K. Mylius Felicitation Volume, 2005); *History of Kṛṣiśāstra* (Wiesbaden 2006); 'On some Natural Devices describing Female Beauty in Sanskrit poetry' (Pandanus '06, Prague 2006).

Address: 1205 Budapest, Pannonia U.3, Hungary.
wojtilla@antiq.u-szeged.hu

MAKOTO KITADA studied Indology and linguistics at Tokyo University and earned his PhD from Martin-Luther University, Halle-Wittenberg, Germany, with a dissertation 'The body of the musician: An annotated translation and study of the Piṇḍotpattiprakaraṇa of Sārṅgadeva's Saṅgītaratnākara'. He is currently research assistant at the Eastern Institute (Toho Kenkyukai, Japan) and teaches Hindi at Kyoto Sangyo University, Bengali at Osaka University and Sanskrit at Kyoto University.

Address: Shizuki Mansion 102, Nakayamatedori 6-6-5, Chuoku, Kobe 165-0004, Japan. makotokitada72@yahoo.co.jp

JAMES MCHUGH grew up in Yorkshire in England. While studying philosophy at Cambridge University he attended some classes on Buddhism given by Dr Eivind Kahrs and became interested in Sanskrit and Indian culture. He went on to do an MPhil at Oxford University where he worked on a translation of Chapter Nineteen of the *Netra-tantra* concerning exorcism and demonology. At Harvard University he completed a PhD thesis entitled "Sandalwood and Carrion: Smell in South Asian Culture and Religion" in 2008. He has also collaborated with the noted perfumer, Christophe Laudamiel, on recreating some of the smells of medieval India.

Aside from his interest in the topic of smell, he is interested in the material culture of medieval India. Publications: 'The Classification of Smells and the Order of the Senses in Indian Religious Traditions,' *Numen: International Review for the History of Religions* 54.4 (2007): 374-419; a review of Rudi Matthee, *The Pursuit of Pleasure: Drugs and Stimulants in Iranian History 1500-*

1900 (Princeton 2005) in *Bulletin of the History of Medicine*, 81.3 (2007): 664-665. He is now Assistant Professor of South Asian Religions at the University of Southern California.

Address: School of Religion, University of Southern California, ACB 130, Los Angeles, CA 90089-148, USA. jmchugh@usc.edu